Stephen Darden
1640-1680

...arden, Sr.
...0-1798

George Williamson

John Dandridge
1701-1756

...c]
...74

Anne Newson

...urgis
1790

Jacob Darden, Jr.

Elizabeth Dandridge

Col. Elias Hilliard, Rev. War

Capt. John Darden, Sr.,
Rev. War, F & I War
1710-1798

William Flanders, F & I War

John Darden, Jr., Rev. War
1734-1800

...ary Ann Hilliard
1765-1846

Nancy Chestnut

Sarah Newton
1736-1786

Jacob Durden, Rev. War
1755-1845

William Grissom

Francis R. Flanders, Rev. War

...ilphta Durden
1764-1850

Sally Grissom

Nancy Jordon

William Durden
1775-1850

John L. Dekle

John R. Flanders, Sr.
1796-1848

Joseph Sumner
1761-1827

...untree
3

Mary Dekle
1754-1855

Lucinda Durden
1818-1891

Nancy Sumner
1800-1858

Mary Knight

...ton George
...intree
...58-1929

John R. Flanders, Jr. CSA
1843-1915

William Black, Rev. War
1818

Robert Black
1774-

Zannie Flanders
1870-1954

Emma Black
1838-1909

Joshua Black

Amelia

Otis Rountree
1888-1920

Lavicy Bruton

Michel Wells

...tis
..., Jr.
...1
...ucille
...ree
...4

Janet Griffin

John Bruton, Rev. War
1750-1818

...Clyde
...ree

James Griffin, Rev. War

...Holmes
...ree
...0

Rich Beyond Price

Portrait of a Georgia Family

[signature]
5/7/07

To Kevin, Peggy and Peggy with Appreciation and God's love Dotty and Miles Murray 2007

Rich Beyond Price

Portrait of a Georgia Family

By Warren C. Budd, Jr.

About the cover:

The locket on the cover was presented to Clyde Holmes by Otis Rountree in 1914. My mother Dorthy Rountree Budd, has had the necklace since her mother's death. On page 178, Clyde is wearing the family heirloom.

Warren C. Budd, Jr.
P.O. Box 1723
Newnan, GA 30264

Printed in the United States of America

Book design by Natalie J. Bishop

This book is dedicated to three women who are supremely important to me.

Sarah Underwood

Sarah loves history and genealogy. She has a multitude
of family stories. She is tough-minded and very spiritual.
When we were going through our darkest times, Sarah
would write and say, "Turn it over to the Lord." Without
the help of Sarah Underwood this book could
not have been written.

Dorothy Budd

My mother is a brilliant musician with an expansive repertoire. She is a profound optimist and generous almost to a fault. She supported my father through thick and thin. What a wonderful legacy she is leaving to her children and grandchildren.

VIII

Courtenay Budd

She is smart and unbelievably creative. Every minute she comes up with a new idea. She is devoted to the cause of Christ and totally committed to her children. She is the finest person I have ever known. My wife is my best friend. When God gave me Courtenay He blessed me one thousand squared.

ACKNOWLEDGEMENTS

This book is not a genealogical treatise. If you want that, read the book of Numbers in the Old Testament. Instead, my goal is to show how certain members of my family interfaced with Georgia and American history. For instance, I have tried to give you a sense of John R. Flanders, Jr., and tell you how he fit into the momentous events of the Great War. I have endeavored to intersperse his experiences with interesting stories so that you may know him personally.

I am technologically challenged and do not use computers. My wife says that I am not a twenty-first-century or even a twentieth-century man, but a nineteenth-century man. In fact, I have only recently mastered the ballpoint pen. This book was written by hand. Frankly, I prefer it that way.

The letters of Otis and Clyde Rountree give the reader a glimpse of what life was like in early twentieth-century south Georgia. Their observations provide every element of a good story – tragedy, humor, love, and triumph over hardship.

I hope you enjoy this book. It has been a pleasure putting it together. A publication of this nature could not have been compiled without the help of some very fine people. Sarah Underwood and Frank Flanders were indispensable in helping me compile the story of John R. Flanders, Jr. I made countless trips to Swainsboro, Georgia, and to Virginia; however, these visits were nowhere near as helpful as my conversations with these two great people.

Jim Flanders supplied me with volumes of information. While the project was in progress, Jim died. He was a terrific cousin. I miss him.

Ann Dixon, my mother's first cousin, got me started with terrific pictures, her wonderful stories, and the Autograph Book. Like so many of my other cousins, Ann is a very giving person. My wonderful cousins Becky Waldron; Mary Anne Hale; Chrissy Williams; Jeanie, Earl, and Johnny Anderson; Ann Underhill, and Jim Rountree as well as my cousin's wife, Marilyn Grist, trusted me with countless pictures and letters. They were indispensable.

I also greatly appreciate the support I received from Joe Chandler and Natalie Bishop, and from my editors, Tom Daye and Pam Davis. Tom helped

ACKNOWLEDGEMENTS

me initiate the project and when he was hurt in an accident and unable to continue, Pam stepped in and did a great job. She took a personal interest in the project and treated it as if it were her own. Our life-long friend, Betsy Smith Braden, gave us a wealth of advice and spent hours helping us edit this book. Betsy is such a rare individual and faithful friend.

The support of my family and especially my wonderful wife Courtenay were absolutely essential. There are many others who have been helpful. Here is a list. If I have left anyone out, it was certainly not intentional.

Beth Benefield
Lamar Black
David Boyd
Candler Budd
Wesley Budd
Becky Caramico
Palmer Carr
Frank Cummings
Tommy Dekle
Ann Dixon
Keith Dunnavant
Tad Evans
Christopher Fecteau
Jim Flanders
David Gambrell
Georgia Archives
Michael W. Hoff
Fred Holmes
Kyle James
Bob Krick
Ladson Library

Leroy Lewis
Kay Messink
Sandy Morrison
The Nature Conservancy
Steve Nelson
New-Tech Photo
Joe Nodvin
Caroline Rountree Price
Dorothy Rich
Gordon Rogers
Ann Ross
Bill Rountree
Don Rountree
Bill Scaife
Colonel and Mrs. Fred Smith
Bill Strother
Ann Underhill
VMI Alumni College
Bob Wilkes
Billy Wilson
John Zwemer

FOREWORD

"The men and women who came to this unchartered wilderness country 125 years ago or more, left kindred and friends and home-ties far behind to brave the wilds and dangers of a new country, to make for themselves and their children a new home. They braved dangers untold, endured hardships and suffered deprivations without end. Lived under the most primitive conditions; made a way where there was no way; learned by the hard way the great lessons of life of hard work, thrift, frugality, self-reliance, resourcefulness, courage, independence, and faith in God. Their experiences worked in them great permanence of character. Among the graces these lessons in life inculcated, were those of hospitality, kindness, patience and neighborliness. They were, for the most part, poor but a more honorable generation the world has never known. Measured by present day ideas, they were crude and illiterate, but they knew more about the essentials of life than this generation will ever learn. They were too plain in both speech and dress to be counted cultured and refined as we count such things today. We would not say they were perfect, but they were all honest, God-fearing, brave and hardworking. And they had no use for those who were not. Drones and dudes they despised, and undesirables found it healthier to seek other climes. To be a descendant of these hardy, God-fearing men and women is indeed an honor, and to share in their ideals is a privilege."

JUDGE FOLKS HUXFORD
Homerville, Georgia, June 1, 1951

Rich Beyond Price

Portrait of a Georgia Family

INTRODUCTION

My brother-in-law, Buddy Darden, is a former U.S. Congressman. One of his campaign slogans was that he was "pure Georgia." I also am proud to say that I am pure Georgia. For about two hundred years, most of my family has lived in this state. If you take a map and stick a pin in Swainsboro, Georgia, all six of my direct ancestor Confederate veterans lived within sixty miles of that spot. The last of my family came to Georgia in 1880 when James Wesley Budd, my father's grandfather, a Confederate veteran and Methodist pastor, moved to McCrae, Georgia.

Since 1972, our family has lived in Coweta County, Georgia, near Newnan. Coweta County is a great community, populated by wonderful, caring, people. Our county used to be a very beautiful spot, with some of the prettiest land anywhere, but now, since becoming part of the Atlanta exurbs, bulldozers, pizza parlors, "Wally Worlds," asphalt, tract housing, and strip malls have invaded it. Georgia natives refer to North Atlanta Metro as the "occupied city," and sadly, our county has also been attacked by this giant hydra. There are those who seek to pave over our entire state from Tybee Light to Rabun Gap, all in the name of progress and capital. The real Georgia is rapidly disappearing.

I am one of those eccentrics who is in love with Georgia, its geography, and history. No state has a more fascinating story than the Peach State. There is the tale of the Indian tribes who first populated the various regions of our state; the first settlement of whites along the coast; the no-holds-barred struggle during the American Revolution; the migration of the Revolutionary War veterans, mostly Scots-Irish, who came down the trading path from North Carolina and Virginia; the move into the interior; the Indian wars and subsequent Trail of Tears; the titanic clash in the War for Southern Independence; the invasion of Sherman and his pillage; reconstruction and economic hard times that followed; slavery, Jim Crow, and the struggle of Georgia's black citizens; and finally, World War II and the modern era. I hope to illustrate how my family has interacted with Georgia history, with its conflicts, its trials, and yes, its triumphs.

In order to find the real Georgia, one must leave the Atlanta exurbs and travel south. There have always been two Georgias. There is Atlanta

2

with its preoccupation with money and its denial of its own history – a rather plastic place. The best illustration of this was during the 1996 Olympics, when Atlanta, in its continual quest for blandness, used as its symbol IZZY, a faceless, raceless, genderless, and ageless dummy. There is also the rest of the state with which I more closely identify. Even though I grew up in Atlanta, which was then a much more likeable city, the rich stories and fascinating people of the other Georgia have always grabbed my attention.

To tell the story of my family is to tell the story of the other Georgia – South Georgia. Until after World War II, both sides of my family were from that region. We must also go there, because to go there is to find the other Georgia.

The best way to drive to South Georgia from Newnan is to take Georgia Highway 16 west to Griffin and then take I-75 south to Macon. We then take I-16 east. Right as we get on I-16 we cross the Ocmulgee River. My father's family settled the Big Bend of the Ocmulgee near Jacksonville, Georgia. My great-great-great-great-grandfather, John Willcox I, was a veteran of the Revolutionary War and a member of the Regulators. He and his four Regulator companions were arrested by the Tories and sentenced to hang. The night before his sentence was to be carried out, he escaped, but his four companions were hung. During the War of 1812, his son, John Willcox II, made boats for the U.S. Government and participated in one of Georgia's last Indian battles, the Battle of Breakfast Branch. Wilcox County is named for John Willcox II. Another of my father's direct ancestors, Mark Pridgen, was abducted and killed by Indians.

If we continue on I-16 – right after crossing the Ocmulgee River – off to our left is Jones County, where my direct ancestor, D.Q. Morrison, fought the Yankees at the Battle of Griswoldville. Continuing east on I-16, we pass Dublin, which was the home of my grandfather's brother, George Rountree, by all accounts a kind, caring individual.

We exit I-16 onto Georgia Highway 19 and go south about thirty miles to the little town of Glenwood. Glenwood is where my great aunt Emma Rountree Curry lived. It is also the home of Ann and Charles Dixon. Ann is my cousin; she and her husband Charles were a super couple, always fun to visit. Charles died in December 2005. We miss him.

Just south of Glenwood is a giant live oak planted in 1862. This huge tree measures thirty feet in circumference. Eight or more branches are the size of a typical oak tree. The tree takes up over one half acre. Under the tree is a gravestone, which reads, "Sacred to the memory of Milly Troup

who departed this life on the eighth day of October 1863. Age 22 years."
Robert Troup, brother of Georgia Governor George Troup, had this stone
placed on that spot and the tree planted. Robert Troup obviously had a
close relationship with Milly, a slave. What that relationship was would
make a fascinating book.

After leaving Glenwood, we cross the Oconee River, then go east on
Highway 280 and pass through Mount Vernon, home of Brewton Parker
College, where my grandmother, Clyde Rountree, served as librarian. We
then go near the little community of Higgston, where, on Wilson Cemetery
Road, are buried four generations of my Wilson-Holmes ancestors. The
cemetery is on property that was once owned by my great-great-great-
grandfather, D.Q. Morrison.

Higgston abuts the Montgomery-Toombs county line. After crossing
into Toombs, we enter Vidalia. My mother likes to boast that she lived
there before the onion, but the onion has created long-term economic
prosperity, not to mention worldwide notoriety.

It is in Vidalia that a large part of our story takes place. This is where
my mother, grandmother, and their siblings spent their childhood. We
then travel north on Highway 297 to Emanuel County and its county
seat, Swainsboro. Emanuel County is the home of some good friends and
great people like Bill Rountree, Frank Flanders, and Sarah Underwood
– all cousins. Those of my family who went before settled hamlets such
as Kemp, Twin City, Norristown, Rountree, and the Cow Ford. It is here
that my great-great-grandfather, John R. Flanders, Jr., lived, along with
his brothers Joe and Ches. The three Flanders brothers were Confederate
heroes. Theirs is an amazing story.

There are people from Emanuel who, like my friend Smokey Hicks,
left and moved to Atlanta seeking their fortune. But it is also amazing how,
for more than two hundred years, so many families have remained. When
I ride around Emanuel, I think of my grandfather, Otis Rountree, as well
as that great line of Baxley, Georgia, author Janisse Ray's, "I was born from
people who were born from people who were born from people who were
born here" (Ray, p. 4). I asked Bill Rountree why Emanuel County natives
love the place to such an extent. He said, "Because it is the best place in
the world to stay."

South Georgian and former President Jimmy Carter put his finger on
one reason. "Like most Georgians, I am deeply attached to the land. I made
my living as a farmer. The soil has always been an important part of my life
and the lives of my family, friends, and neighbors. Through our love of the

Drawing by R. David Boyd

land we share a common bond and become a community" (Gillis, p. 6). The land has had a hold on Emanuel Countians. You can look at pre-War Between the States maps of Emanuel and see numerous land tracts that are still owned by the same families.

When those of us from north of the fall line visit South Georgia, many do not understand its attraction. The difference is cultural and it goes back to who settled South Georgia. We will delve into the fact that South Georgia was primarily settled by Celts, and those of English or other extractions adopted the Celtic ways.

INTRODUCTION

South Georgians love "suppers" given on a weeknight. The menu at suppers is usually fried fish, but it also can be wild game, barbeque, shad roe and eggs, or on cold winter nights, chittlins. These events are usually all male, and most of the time the libations and tall tales flow freely. A joke told at these events is not referred to as a joke, but as a story.

Such traditions as taking off Wednesday afternoon to go fishing or hunting, as well as closing the store to do so, are unique to rural Georgia. South Georgians also traditionally come home for "dinner" in the middle of the day. They are known to have a cabin in the country or on the river. As a boy, I remember many evenings spent on the front porch after supper, just rocking and talking. Many South Georgians still have a tradition of "meeting the boys" in the middle of the morning for coffee, or the women gathering at the ladies' sewing circle, in which not much sewing goes on.

Even children's games are different – from playing "Ain't No Boogers Out Tonight" to catching lightening bugs at night and having our mother punch holes in the jar top so we can keep them.

South Georgians have a strong sense of family, of their faith, their history, and most definitely of place. The Geechee, Hoopee, Altamaha, Satilla, and Canoochee are rivers whose unique beauty is unequaled. Let's face it – the place kind of grows on you.

But of course there is the South Georgia sand gnat. Most North Georgians hate the sand gnat. Personally, I kind of like them. Maybe it's because I agree with a T-shirt I recently saw in Cobbtown. It had a drawing of a sand gnat and under the depiction was the following inscription: "Protect the Georgia Sand Gnat lest we be ass-deep in Yankees!"

WILLIAM FLANDERS

FRENCH AND INDIAN WAR SOLDIER

William Flanders is my great-great-great-great-great-grandfather. The Flanders family migrated from Yelling-Hunts, England, and has been in America since the 1600's (Drake, p. 153). William was raised near Petersburg, Virginia, on land that straddled the North Carolina-Virginia border.

As William neared his majority, he joined the state militia. The French and Indian War (1754-60) placed his militia unit in the thick of the conflict. This war was a contest between the French and their Algonquin Nation allies on one side and the British and their Colonial settlers on the other. Each party had an agenda. The latter were attempting to secure their Western lands in Virginia, Pennsylvania, and New York. The French and the British were vying for control of the Ohio River basin as well as eastern Canada. The Indians, encouraged by the French, were attempting to drive the whites out of what they considered their ancient hunting grounds.

The French had taken a strategic British fort near present-day Pittsburgh and changed its name from Fort Prince George to Fort Duquesne. Governor Robert Dinwiddie of Virginia sent twenty-one-year-old George Washington to Fort Le Boeuf near present-day Waterford, Pennsylvania. There, Washington requested that the French give this area back to the British on the grounds that the British Army had first occupied it. Washington was politely turned down. Governor Dinwiddie then raised a small army of three hundred fifty men under the command of Washington and a Colonel Fry. The modest fortification they built near Fort Duquesne was dubbed Fort Necessity. The French, with nine hundred men, proceeded to wrest the fort from its occupants. Washington, Fry, and their troops returned to Virginia.

The British, realizing that it would take more than a small force to dislodge the French, sent General Braddock with two thousand, five hundred trained British regulars and Virginia militia to attack Fort Duquesne. William Flanders marched with them. The journey itself was difficult enough. The soldiers had to hack out a road in order to transport their equipment and artillery to the fort's vicinity. The French knew that they could not withstand a sustained attack so they came up with a plan to ambush Braddock about three miles from Fort Duquesne. The attack was successful. The Indians, camouflaged, fighting from behind trees and with very accurate fire, overwhelmed the British in their colorful red coats and their full frontal European marching mode of engaging the enemy. Braddock lost a majority of his force and was himself killed.

The surviving militiamen and British regulars then formed up on Chestnut Ridge with a young George Washington as their leader. Also in attendance were Daniel Boone and Daniel Morgan. The Indians, flush from their victory, began to lay waste to the surrounding area, killing settlers and destroying their property. These events prompted the settlers to move east, ending up in the Shenandoah Valley.

George Washington wrote to Governor Dinwiddie of Virginia that "I tremble at the consequences that this defeat may have upon our back settlers, who I suppose will all leave their habitations, unless there are proper measures taken for their security" (Freeman, Vol. 2, p. 84).

One of the residents of Chestnut Ridge was John Chestnut. Chestnut was of Scots-Irish descent. Some members of his family were Quakers. When the Scots-Irish immigrated to Philadelphia, the Pennsylvania establishment sent them west to form a buffer against Indian encroachment. The Scots-Irish were tough-minded people who were used to hardship.

Chestnut had a young daughter, Nancy, who accompanied him on the long journey to Virginia. En route, she met our Virginia militiaman William Flanders. Together they walked the six hundred mile trail back to Virginia. Shortly thereafter, William Flanders and the Chestnut girl were married. Three years later, William Flanders again served the Virginia militia and was given a land grant in Ohio. Apparently, he never took advantage of the grant.

Mrs. Johnny Flanders Sherrod tells of the Flanders-Chestnut romance in a paper written about 1940:

> "With William Flanders, we have a story of love and tenderness that should sustain many generations. William Flanders, as part of the Colonial Army under General Edward Braddock, cut a road from Virginia to within six mile of Ft. Duquesne. Ft. Duquesne was located at Three Rivers which is now Pittsburgh, Pennsylvania. This distance by the old Braddock Road exceeded 1,000 miles through passes and up

and down mountains. General Braddock was defeated in a rout and was himself killed and buried in the middle of the Braddock Road. George Washington had previously been defeated in a quickly built fortification called Ft. Necessity. The place of burial of General Braddock and Ft. Necessity are on Chestnut Ridge. Chestnut Hill overlooks Ft. Necessity. The Colonial Army rescued many settlers, among whom was the family of John Chestnut, the senior. This group, a rag-tag defeated Colonial Army and families of settlers walked back to Virginia. In the first few hundred miles of that walk, they were harassed by Indians. Among those who walked was a young couple, William Flanders and a daughter of John Chestnut. Subsequently, they were man and wife and lived in North Hampton County, North Carolina. It is the walk of romance through the mountains that we like to remember. Walking at night, close in together for defense in the daytime, no shelter from rain or cold, the only food was as provided by the hunters of the Militia. The journey was long and hard and not all were to survive. If it had not been for the determination to survive and bring the little lady to safety, you and I would not be here. It was along this same route that the first Federal highway was built. And today paved highways travel the route. We sincerely hope that members of the family will travel from Pittsburgh, Pennsylvania to Harpers Ferry, Virginia along what is mostly Highway 40. It may not be our highway, Chestnut Ridge does not belong to us, but to us, there's a special meaning, and if your eyes remain dry throughout the journey, then you are different from me" (Sherrod).

The Flanders couple produced several soldiers for the revolutionary cause. One of these patriots was Francis Richard Flanders.

William Flanders may have been, but probably was not, a Quaker. It is believed that the Chestnuts were of the Quaker faith and that William most likely was not. However, Quakers encouraged marriage within their denomination, and William's son, Francis Richard, married a Quaker, Nancy Jordan. The family, therefore, must have been approved by the Virginia Quakers. You will see that the Flanders were not a pacifistic people. To quote Dr. Robert Drake, "William Flanders could have been a Quaker all along just proving that the Flemish family of Flanders with part Norman ancestry has never lost their inherent bellicosity" (Drake, p. 50). Land grants show that William Flanders moved from near Petersburg, Virginia, to near Williamsburg. This may have been because of the conflict between the Tories and Patriots or because of the inherent prejudice against

Quakers displayed by Anglicans. By 1775, he was in Lunenburg County, Virginia. It was in Lunenburg County that William's son, Francis Richard, married Nancy Jordan Flanders (Drake, p. 57).

FRANCIS RICHARD FLANDERS
AND NANCY JORDAN FLANDERS

Francis Richard Flanders and Nancy Jordan were married about 1779, most likely in Lunenburg County, Virginia. Revolutionary War records show the couple living in Halifax District, Northampton County, North Carolina, near the Virginia border. North Carolina records indicate that Francis Richard fought in the Revolution with a unit from that area. I have not been able to find any specifics on his service.

Nancy was from a family with a fascinating history. Her Quaker ancestry goes back to the House of Jordans in Leicestershire, England. It is near the House of Jordans that William Penn, the Quaker founder of Pennsylvania, is buried.

The Society of Friends (established about 1650) is nicknamed "Quakers" after founder George Fox's admonition to "Quake before the Lord."

Nancy's ancestry goes back to Samuel Jordan of Virginia, a member of the first legislative session ever held in America. Mr. Jordan achieved considerable fame during the Indian massacre of 1622. The governor of Virginia had ordered the settlers to leave their homes, which would have allowed the Indians to pillage their farms. Instead, Samuel prepared his house for attack and, with his family and some neighbors, fought off the Indians without loss of life.

One of Nancy's two brothers who accompanied them to Georgia was also named Samuel. The three were descended from Thomas Jordan, son of Samuel Jordan. Mrs. Sherwood's article reported that, up to World War II, many in the Georgia Flanders family dressed similar to Quakers. They referred to themselves as "Quaker Methodists."

An interesting aside is that my roommate at Virginia Military Institute in Lexington, Virginia, Samuel Peele Jordan, Jr., was from near Smithville, Virginia, and is also descended from Sam Jordan.

Like James Park, Francis Richard Flanders was one of many of Revolutionary General Nathanael Greene's veterans who migrated to Georgia. After the war, the veterans returned home, gathered their families and belongings, and moved to what they saw as more fertile land, as well as new opportunity. These were tough people, conditioned by the hardships of war. One only has to read the story of the American Revolution in Georgia and North and South Carolina to see what these people endured.

In his book *The Descendants of Exum Drake, Volume V* on the Flanders family, Dr. Drake puts it quite well:

"That rag tagged armed force known as the Southern Continental Line, reinforced by men from the Continental Line, populated the state of Georgia... When Francis Richard Flanders returned to Northampton County, North Carolina following his tour of duty, he found a people impoverished from seven years of war. Morale was low, homes burned, stock decimated, and a land worn out by usage and a lack of agricultural technology. New land, a new life, and a future for his family existed for the asking and moving to Georgia. When we examined written records of other moves from Virginia and North Carolina, we find that the usual expected time of the move was two years with a stopover to plant and raise crops on two separate springs and summers. These moves were complicated with the usual format consisting of the men going ahead by ten or twelve miles to find a pasture for the cattle. The cattle were then moved to a new location. Next were farm tools, seed, furniture, and stable goods. Chicken and swine loaded on wagons were the last things to be moved before returning for women and children. These complicated moves were usually done by larger groups working together. Individual family movements were almost impossible. Some of the items carried on these journeys of up to a thousand miles seemed to one who did not make such a trip to be amazing. Such items as iron stoves, chicken coops, split rails for pigpens or cow lots; hog troughs and feeding bins. However, it seemed that all were needed at the next ten-mile stop and was easier carried than made anew. Such moves in non-planting season and good weather were done two or three times a week.

"When one realizes that the men were ones with experience in the armed forces, one is quick to realize that this migration was probably similar to movements of large bodies of armed forces of that particular era. It was a move where the necessities were present at all times.

"With an estimate of two years or less as the period of time necessary for the move to Georgia, it is now possible to know about when the family left North Carolina and Virginia" (Drake, p. 126).

The family left North Carolina about 1786.

FRANCIS RICHARD FLANDERS AND NANCY JORDAN FLANDERS

Francis Richard and Nancy Jordan Flanders moved to Georgia with their children as well as her two brothers, Samuel and William Jordan. Francis Richard's brother Thomas also accompanied them, as did their married sister and her family. They arrived about 1788 (Drake, p. 126).

Francis and Nancy had seven children. My ancestor was their third child, John R. Flanders, Sr., born 1796. Nancy and Francis Richard Flanders were leaders in their new frontier community. They are credited with starting the first Methodist congregation located in Emanuel County. Their son Jordan was a prominent Methodist pastor.

Tragedy struck in 1802, when Creek Indians killed Francis Richard and his brother, Thomas. Family legend says that Francis Richard and Thomas were working their fields when the attack came. Their bodies were mutilated. This calamity left Nancy as the sole supporter of seven children: Barnabas (16), William (12), Jordan (9), John R. (6), Nancy (7), and Catherine (2). It is amazing that Nancy endured and produced such prominent children. She must have leaned heavily on her brothers, Samuel and William. The 1805 census shows her living near them.

The family left North Carolina about 1786.

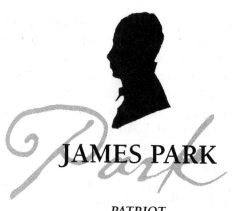

JAMES PARK

PATRIOT

When you drive east on I-20 toward Augusta, the first overpass in Greene County has the name "Park's Mill Road." My great-great-great-great-grandfather, James Park, and his two brothers, Joseph and Ezekiel, founded that mill.

James, whose family originally called themselves Parks, was born and raised in Prince Edward County, Virginia. In 1776, at the age of twenty, he signed the Petition for Religious Liberty. He was instrumental in the formation of the local militia company and that same year he was listed as a private in the 11th Virginia Regiment. In May of the following year he was promoted to second lieutenant. From 1776 to the end of the war, he also served with the 13th, 9th, and 7th Virginia regiments.

James Parks' family members were fervent supporters of the Revolution. James' uncle was killed by Tories in his front yard and his house was burned. Another Parks uncle was killed at the Battle of Cowpens. He was said to have sustained thirty "saber cuts." Another Parks uncle was captured and spent nine months in a British dungeon in Saint Augustine, Florida (Pressly, 1984).

James, Joseph, and Ezekiel took part in General Nathanael Greene's strategic retreat through North Carolina. Greene's goal on this difficult mission was to wear out British General Charles Cornwallis, and he succeeded. This episode culminated in the Battle of Guilford Court House, located near present-day Greensboro, North Carolina.

A skirmish occurred a few days before Guilford Court House in which the Colonists, under Otho Williams, attempted to cross Reedy Fork Creek. They were attacked by the British and a sharp engagement ensued. The

Colonists withdrew across the creek and were supported by cavalry under Lieutenant Colonel "Light Horse" Harry Lee, the father of Robert E. Lee. Both Joseph and Ezekiel were wounded. Ezekiel was wounded again at Guilford Court House and carried off the field by a friend, Hugh Haralson. Ezekiel and Joseph were also with American pioneer Daniel Morgan at the battles of Kings Mountain and Cowpens in the Carolinas.

James Parks took part in the Battle of Guilford Court House and was a witness to Cornwallis' surrender at Yorktown. (For more on Guilford Court House and events leading up to it, read *The Road to Guilford Court House* by James Buchanan, a great read).

After the war, the three brothers resumed their involvement in civic affairs. Joseph Parks became a founding trustee of Hampton-Sidney College in Virginia, whose other trustees included James Madison, Patrick Henry, and Reverend Richard Sanky. In 1787, James married Mary Sanky, the daughter of Reverend Sanky. They had two children. Later that year, James and Mary moved to what is now Greene County, Georgia. It was at this time that the three Parks brothers changed their last name to Park.

Many Revolutionary War soldiers were moving to Georgia because the new Georgia government was giving them land at favorable prices. The area along the Oconee River was frontier country. A year before James arrived, what would become the county seat town of Greensboro had been burned by Indians. The Parks settled on the eastern bank of the Oconee River. The opposite shore was Indian territory. In 1804, the Indians moved west of the Ocmulgee River.

Shortly after James and Mary arrived in Georgia, Mary died. In 1793, James married Phoebe Hogue, eighteen years his junior. They had twelve children. Our ancestor is their eleventh child, Phoebe Park Wilson. She had a twin brother, Wallace.

Phoebe Hogue's family was of French Huguenot decent, her father Jonathan Hogue, having come to Georgia in 1781 by way of Ireland.

About 1572, after enduring persecution and the St. Bartholomew's Day Massacre, which many have referred to as the French Holocaust, the Hogue family abandoned France for a friendlier, Protestant Holland. Thousands of surviving Huguenots left France. This exodus of middle-class Protestant artisans, craftsmen, and professionals severely damaged France for years to follow and infused the British Isles as well as America with hard working, frugal, disciplined, God-fearing people. Among them are the DuPont family of Delaware and Georgia's own Governor Sonny Perdue.

After the Hogues arrived in the Netherlands, Jonathan's grandfather hooked up with William of Orange who was recruiting soldiers to defend English Protestants against James II. The Catholic James II had been deposed by English Protestant leaders. Since William of Orange was the grandson of Charles I, he had been installed in James' place. James II was supported by France and had raised an army in Ireland.

Because a large part of William's army was in France, he recruited Protestants from Holland, Germany, and Denmark to aid him against James II. One of these was Jonathan Hogue's grandfather.

James had been embarrassed by a large group of Irish Protestants who had withstood a long siege at Londonderry. Even though they were starving and constantly bombarded, the defenders had written in their own blood, "No surrender." This 1688 siege in Northern Ireland was an inspiration to future generations. James and his Irish Catholic allies were later defeated at the Battle of the Boyne. Like the Scots-Irish Rountrees, the Hogues remained in Northern Ireland. They intermarried with the Celtic community and in mid-1700 joined the great Scots-Irish migration to America.

James and his brothers established Park's Mill at the fork of the Oconee and Apalachee rivers. The settlement was located on Three Chop Road, which became the main road linking Georgia with Philadelphia, Richmond, and New Orleans. Three Chop was one of the first roads surveyed in the southeast.

The Park's Mill community contained a tavern, a gristmill, and later, a fine home that still stands today. The Park family also operated a toll bridge and later a ferry.

During the War Between the States, James Park's grandchildren operated the mill. When Sherman's troops came through, an old slave, Cyrus, was credited with saving the house. A younger grandchild, Neal Park, was ten years in 1865. Years later he describes the events:

> "When the Yankees appeared, my mother sent for an officer and told him she was alone with several small children, her husband was away and he was a mason, and she would appreciate his kindness to see that she and the children were protected from the Federal Soldiers. The officer stationed a guard at the front and back doors of the house for three days as the soldiers passed by, and the family was not molested.
>
> "On November 20, Sunday morning, they burned the three-story mill on the river. They stole all the mules, horses, dogs, cows, and provisions. During the three days the mill burned, sparks fell on the roof

War Department, Washington, D. C.

WAR DEPARTMENT,   ESB/EVC
                    ORD
THE ADJUTANT GENERAL'S OFFICE

WASHINGTON
                              Mar. 19, 1927.

Respectfully returned to

    Mr. Harry A. Davis,
    316 Shepherd St., N.W.
    Washington, D. C.

        The records of this office show that one James Parks (surname
    also borne as Park and Parkes) served in the Revolutionary War as
    a private in Capt. George Rice's Company, 11 Virginia Regiment, also
    designated 11th and 15th Virginia Regiment and 7th Virginia Regiment
    commanded by Col. Daniel Morgan. He enlisted in December, 1776, for
    three years; was transferred in December, 1778, to Capt. Philip
    Slaughter's Company, also designated Lieut. James Wright's Company,
    same regiment, and his name last appears on the muster roll for No-
    vember, 1779, dated Camp near Morristown, December 9, 1779.

                    (Signed)   Robert C. Davis
                               Major General,
                        The Adjutant General,
                               by E.W.M.

    ****
    ****

    Copied from photostatic copy of typed letter, on which the under-
    lined part is printed.

of the house. Mother got wet blankets up to the roof, where old Cyrus, the slave, smothered out every spark that caught. The home still stands today. For years after, we had little to eat but cornbread, fish, and a few vegetables, which we grew, and some times meat from a more fortunate neighbor, and syrup. The only salt we had was filtered out of the dirt of the smokehouse floor. The mill was owned by my father, James B. Park (a son of James Park, Jr.) and he also operated the ferry. The tolls were put in Uncle Dickie's strong hickory wood chest, which had only one slot in the top, and was not opened until his death, when inside the box was found $100,000.

"Tradition says that Jefferson Davis slept at the Inn House, two days before he was arrested. Mrs. Park delayed the ferry so the Federal troops could not get across soon enough to catch him."

James and Phoebe Park are buried in Baldwin County, Georgia, near Lake Oconee. His grave marker reads:

Jas. Park
Lt. VA. Militia
Rev. War
1823

THE TRAIL OF
JOHN R. FLANDERS

Ches Flanders, Joe Flanders and John R. Flanders, Jr.

CHAPTER

One

INTRODUCTION

As a young lad growing up on Clifton Road in Atlanta, in the home of Dorothy and Candler Budd, I was fascinated by the War Between the States. At about age eight, my friends and I would build forts out of firewood and old lumber. We would imagine ourselves as Confederate heroes, defending the state against the "Yanks." The only problem was that nobody wanted to play a Yankee. Finally, Bill Fort moved to town from somewhere up north. For a while he played the enemy but later even he got tired of constantly losing.

During the summer, our family would visit Vidalia, my mother's childhood home. To me it was like going to the Promised Land. Besides fishing and swimming in the Ohoopee River, I would quiz Great-Grandmother Holmes, mother's grandmother, about what it was like when Yankee General William T. Sherman came through Washington and Montgomery counties.

Grandmother Holmes was born three years after the war ended. Her father, Wallace R. Wilson, and her grandfather, D.Q. Morrison, both fought for the Confederacy. We would sit on her front porch every evening and she would relate stories of that sad time. Sophie Holmes' memories about the devastation caused by the invading Yankees are tales I will never forget. She related how the Yankees used fences for firewood, killed all the livestock, and took what was left of the families' food from the pantry. She never minced words as to her strong dislike for the Union soldiers.

Grandmother Clyde Rountree, my mother's mother, told me that John R. Flanders, Jr., her husband Otis' grandfather, was a Confederate hero. Clyde was a member of the DAR (Daughters of the American Revolution) and always interested in genealogy. She told me about her great-great-grandfather, James Park, who fought in the Revolution with Nathanael Greene, but the person who interested me the most was John R. Clyde knew a few details about the Flanders brothers, John R., Ches, and Joe, but

I was never able to put the complete story together until, as an adult, I met my cousin and now good friend, Sarah Flanders Underwood.

Sarah is a first cousin of Otis Rountree and granddaughter of John R. Flanders, Jr. She is also a consummate family historian. At age 94 she remembers John R. from her childhood. She related how Mr. Flanders would show her and her siblings the scars from his five wounds. Since getting to know Sarah and checking other sources, I have pieced together much of John R.'s war experiences as well as those of his brothers Ches and Joe. I have been to every major battlefield on which John R. fought. I have stood at the spots where the 38th Georgia and the 48th Georgia rendered such admirable service. The more I have learned about John R. the more my admiration for him has grown and the prouder I am to say that I share his lineage.

John R. Flanders, Jr., grew up in Emanuel County near the Bethel Church community off of what is now Georgia Highway 57, which runs between Swainsboro and Kite. His family's farm was located near the Little Ohoopee River. Not far from the farm was the spot where his grandfather, Francis Richard Flanders, was killed by Indians while working his crops. John R.'s great-uncle, Thomas Flanders, was also killed. The family worshipped at Bethel Church, which had been founded by Francis Richard and his wife Nancy Jordan Flanders. Services started as early as the 1790's, with congregants worshipping under a brush arbor. John R.'s uncle, Jordan Flanders, and his brother, Alexander Chesnut Flanders (Ches), later pastored at Bethel. The members of the Flanders family were very devout people and were credited with being the founders of Methodism in Emanuel County.

John R. had either four or five brothers. We are unsure because Jesse could have been either a brother or a nephew – in the 1850 census he was shown as living with the John R. Flanders, Sr., family, and in the 1860 census he was living with his sister (or mother) Martha. Either way, he and John R. grew up together. The Flanders monument committee considered Jesse as a probable nephew but for purposes of this article I will refer to him as John R.'s brother. John R. also had four sisters, Jemina, Nancy, Delilah, and Martha.

Like most Confederate soldiers, the Flanders boys were reared on a farm that they worked themselves. They were blessed with some education. The Flanders boys were strong, intelligent young men who never backed off from a fight – certainly not an opportunity to defend Georgia against the Yankees.

21

CHAPTER

Two

JOHN R. JOINS THE BEN HILL GUARDS

Emanuel County was not a hotbed of secessionist feeling. The citizens favored a "go-slow" approach. On 19 January 1861, Georgia held a secession convention in Milledgeville, then the state capital. Two of Emanuel County's most prominent citizens, Abraham Lot Kirkland, a farmer from Canoochee, and John Overstreet, a farmer-legislator, were selected to serve as representatives. Both men voted against the Ordinance of Secession. Later, though, in a demonstration of unity, they signed the formal draft. In November 1864, Sherman's soldiers showed the Yankee government's appreciation for Overstreet's vote by burning his home (Rogers, p. 29).

When John R. was seventeen, Lincoln pushed the issue, and South Carolina troops fired on Fort Sumter. John R., along with his five brothers, joined the Confederate Army. Like most young southern soldiers, their motives appeared to have been to defend home and hearth as well as to stand for the state of Georgia. They also wanted to see the "big show." John R. joined the Ben Hill Guards on 1 October 1861. This was a volunteer militia composed of men from Emanuel and Bulloch counties. The unit was formed by a local merchant-planter, Neill McLeod, whose son, William McLeod, was its company commander.

William McLeod, one year older than John R, had attended Oglethorpe College, then located in Milledgeville. After two years there, William, like every other student at Oglethorpe, left school in order to join the Army. By mid-July 1861, he had joined the Ben Hill Guards forming in Swainsboro.

It is a mystery why John R. joined the Ben Hill Guards rather than the 48th Georgia Regiment. Ches and Joe Flanders would become members of the 48th and Ches would become an officer. Since John R. and William were about the same age and joined at about the same time, perhaps they were friends and William persuaded John R. to join with him. After William was killed at Gettysburg, John R. joined his brothers as third sergeant of Company H, 48th Georgia.

The Ben Hill Guards were initially assigned to be a part of Wright's Legion, and plans were to make it an artillery unit. It later became a part of the 38th Georgia Regiment of the famous Georgia Brigade, which was also referred to as Lawton's Brigade and Gordon's Brigade.

There were two famous brigades from Georgia, the Doles-Cook Brigade, which performed so magnificently for Stonewall Jackson in the 1862 Valley Campaign and helped hold the line at Spotsylvania, and the Georgia Brigade, which was often cited by the Confederate leadership for meritorious service.

Wiregrass Georgia was populated primarily by Scots and Scots-Irish citizens who did not make a habit of giving in. Its Confederate units were filled with McLeods, McNatts, Morrisons, McClains, Moxleys, Wilkeses, and Curles. In his book *The Georgia Brigade,* William Scaife tells about their formation:

"The concept of an elite Georgia Brigade originated with Brigadier General Alexander Robert Lawton at Savannah, Georgia, in the spring of 1862. Lawton at the time held the highest military office in the state, Commander of the Military District of Georgia, and since the autumn of 1861 had been assembling in and around Savannah, the finest volunteer regiments from throughout the state.

"The greatest threat facing Lawton was thought to be from a sea borne invasion of Georgia under the protection of superior federal naval power and he therefore concentrated the military forces of the state to resist such an attack. By the spring of 1862, it became apparent the federals felt such an all-out invasion would be too costly. They instead elected to only blockade the coast. At that time General Lawton prevailed upon General Robert E. Lee, then President Jefferson Davis' chief military advisor in Richmond, to allow him to select an elite brigade of Georgians for the action everyone felt was impending in Virginia. When General Lee accepted the proposal Lawton assembled the Georgia Brigade from the 13th, 26th, 31st, 38th, 60th and 61st Georgia Regiments, six of the finest in his command and in May of 1862 left Savannah for Virginia. When the brigade entered its maiden battle at Gaines Mill on June 27, 1862, with 3,500 men, it was the largest brigade in the Army of Northern Virginia. From that day until it surrendered 42 officers and 622 men with General Lee at Appomattox, almost three years later, its record of accomplishment was unsurpassed by any brigade in the Confederate service" (Scaife, I).

John R. joined the Ben Hill Guards about the time it arrived in Savannah. The 38th Georgia was stationed at three camps, Lawton, Barlow, and Mercer, all located around Savannah. The troops spent most of their time on Skidaway Island building fortifications, drilling, and obtaining food. The troops of the 38th in 1861 did not wear t-shirts, flip-flops, and cotton shorts. Their attire was primarily cotton long-sleeved shirts, thin wool pants, and brogans. The bugs and the heat must have been quite an ordeal.

CHAPTER

Three

GAINES MILL

Events in Virginia in the spring of 1862 were not going well. On the bright side, General Stonewall Jackson, who was, before the war, a little known professor at the Virginia Military Institute, had whipped three Yankee armies in the Shenandoah Valley and was threatening Washington, D.C. The Yankees were in a state of trepidation, fearful that their beloved capital would be invaded. But General Lee had used Jackson to divert Federal troops away from Union General George McClellan and take pressure off of the Confederates defending Richmond.

Gaines Mill at Cold Harbor battlefield. L to R - Tom Sanders, Anna Sanders, Warren Budd, and Bob Krick, noted author and War Between the States historian.

On the negative side, McClellan was marching up the Virginia Peninsula towards Richmond and was within sight of the Confederate capital.

John R. Flanders' unit was ordered to Virginia to form part of the famous General Jackson's corps. In late May, in Savannah, he boarded a train that would take him on his life's greatest adventure. He passed through Charleston and Florence, South Carolina; Goldsboro, North Carolina; and Petersburg, Virginia, and arrived in Richmond on 5 June 1862. Bill Scaife reports that "most of the men rode in open rail cars and suffered severely from the elements during the nine-day journey that involved frequent stops to refuel the wood-burning locomotive" (Scaife, p. 19). You can imagine the soot and wood smoke while riding packed in an open car.

Upon their arrival, the Georgia Brigade moved again by rail, this time across the Blue Ridge Mountains to Rockfish Gap to join General Jackson in the beautiful Shenandoah. This was a diversionary move designed to give the Yankees the impression that Lee was reinforcing Jackson in the valley. In actual fact, Jackson was preparing to march to the outskirts of Richmond in order to aid Lee. John R.'s Company C of the 38th Georgia fell in with Jackson's "foot cavalry."

Company C, 38th Georgia, joined Jackson's "foot cavalry" on its march to Richmond. This was the first time the young man from Emanuel County had seen such a great spectacle. John R. must have been awed by the huge army marching as far as the eye could see, kicking up voluminous clouds of dust – Jackson was famous for marching his troops at a pace the likes of which no one had ever seen. I am sure John R.'s first exposure to such a tactic was quite a shock as well as physically demanding. Nevertheless, he and his comrades knew they must reach Richmond quickly. Stonewall's men marched through Charlottesville and Gordonsville, reaching Ashland on 25 June, then moved to Gaines Mill east of Richmond. The Georgia Brigade found itself near the right flank of General McClelland's opposing force. The next day John R. would see his first combat.

John R. and his comrades had left their baggage under guard at Hanover Station, where they assumed that they would reclaim it later. Afterward, however, the unit moved at such a rapid pace that, after John R. was wounded, his belongings were never recovered.

Before Jackson arrived, the Confederates had attacked the Union troops at Beaver Dam Creek. Once on the scene, Jackson's corps was late getting into position and by the time it did, northern General Porter had moved his troops to a secure position behind Boatswain's Swamp. In order to get at the Yankees, the Georgia Brigade would have to cross an open field adjacent to a wooded area known as the Watt House Hill. The next day began with more confusion. Jackson again had difficulty getting his forces to their assigned spot. But by five o'clock in the evening, the three thousand, five hundred men of the Georgia Brigade were in position to support General Ewell on the Confederate left. The arrival of Jackson's troops had an electric effect on the other Confederates. When

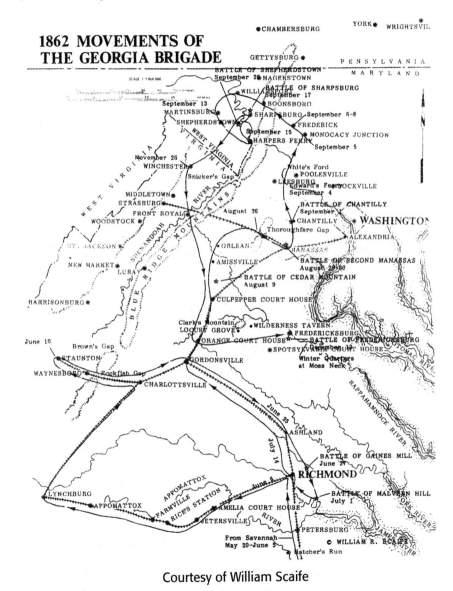

Courtesy of William Scaife

seeing this line of Georgians, General Ewell held up his hat and shouted, "Hoorah for Georgia!" (Scaife, p. 25).

The Georgia Brigade faced the best that the Yankee Army could offer – General Sykes' crack division of regular U. S. troops. When the attack was imminent, the Georgia Brigade was ordered to double time into position. They formed up in the woods, then began moving across the open field towards Sykes' division.

Jackson had ordered the Georgians not to fire until they overran the first Yankee line and then to "sweep them with the bayonet." One soldier described how they did so, all the while screaming the famous Rebel Yell. The determined Georgia Brigade captured the Hoboken Battery at a very critical moment and later was personally complimented by General Jackson. It was during this fight across the open field, which is still preserved, that John R. received his first wound. He was among four hundred ninety-two members of the brigade who were either killed or wounded (Scaife, p. 26).

It is interesting to note that the 38th Georgia received more killed and wounded than any of the other regiments in the brigade. They must have been in a very hot spot as well as key to the victory.

My VMI roommate Sam Jordan and I are standing on the Gaines Mill battlefield. The woods in the background were a focal point in the Georgia Brigade's first engagement. John R. Flanders, Jr., was wounded in this battle. On May 24, 2006, Sam died following a five-month battle with cancer. He was a faithful friend, a terrific roommate, and a loyal VMI alumnus.

CHAPTER

Four

FREDRICKSBURG
John Is Wounded A Second Time
Marries Emma Black

Private Henry Bellflower of Company F, 31st Georgia Regiment, was killed in the charge that saw John R. Flanders wounded. Private Bellflower, from Hawkinsville, Georgia, would experience only one day of battle. Bill Scaife's book *The Georgia Brigade* quotes a letter from Private Bellflower's father, signed with an "X," requesting Henry's back pay (Scaife, p. 27). It is quite sobering to reflect that if Private Flanders had been killed instead of wounded, many productive descendents would not be here.

According to his pay records, John R. was sent home on 27 July 1862 to recuperate. While at home, he married Emma Black, 12 November 1862. Emma was from a large and prominent family (see article on Joshua Black). John R. returned to duty later that month. He missed the battles of Second Manassas and Sharpsburg (Antietam), engagements that saw the Georgia Brigade suffer four hundred sixty-five out of two thousand killed or wounded at Second Manassas, and at Sharpsburg a staggering five hundred sixty-five killed, wounded, or missing, out of one thousand, one hundred fifty (forty-nine percent).

When John R. returned, the brigade was a different unit. It was definitely seasoned as well as decimated. But the men's spirits were high. They had defeated the Yankees at Second Manassas and fought them to a draw at Sharpsburg. This was the case even though Lee's army was greatly outnumbered in both men and material.

Upon his arrival, John R. rejoined the 38th Georgia at a camp in the Shenandoah Valley. Food and clothing were becoming a big problem. Many of the men had no shoes or winter clothing, and the march they were about to undertake would prove to be very difficult.

Colonel Edwin Warren stated:

"The worst part of it is that we have in the Brigade under my command not less than 175 men in their bare feet, a large number are without overcoats, and many are deficient in blankets. My heart used to bleed as I would read the account of the sufferings of the Patriot Army at Valley Forge, and little did I then think that the time would come when I would command men in like destitute condition" (Robertson, p. 634).

Jackson's forces now numbered thirty-eight thousand, five hundred thirty-two soldiers. It had also changed its name from the Army of the Valley to Second Corps of the Army of Northern Virginia (Robertson, p. 634).

Jackson had taken his men one hundred seventy-five miles in just twelve days. An anonymous Confederate soldier once said, "If Stonewall Jackson had led the children of Israel through the wilderness, it would not have taken him 40 years, for he would have made the march in three days on one-half rations" (Scaife). There were reports of bloodstains on the snow from the barefoot soldiers.

Local citizen Cornelia McDonald reported that the soldiers marching

L to R – Courtenay, Wesley, and Warren Budd, standing at the spot where the Georgia Brigade broke the Yankee charge and ran them across the railroad, thus saving the Confederate Artillery. The railroad track can be seen in the background.

through Winchester, Virginia, looked destitute. "Many were without shoes and all without overcoats or gloves although the weather was freezing. Their poor hands looked so red and cold holding their muskets in the biting winds... they did not, however, look dejected, but went their way right joyfully" (Robertson, p. 643).

When the Union army made a move toward Fredericksburg, General Jackson moved his troops from the Shenandoah Valley to Orange County Courthouse, thirty miles west of Fredericksburg. After about eleven days rest, Jackson marched them to Fredericksburg, arriving on 1 December. Jackson's troops then took a position southeast of Fredericksburg, near Skinner's Neck. There were really two battles of Fredericksburg fought on the same day – one on the southeast, led by General Jackson and the other at Marye's Heights, commanded by General James Longstreet. The Confederates won both battles, but we shall concern ourselves with the battle on Lee's right fought by General Jackson's troops.

Once they arrived on what would become the Fredericksburg battlefield, the Georgia Brigade was positioned in a reserve area behind the Confederate lines. December 13, 1862, would be a day on which the Georgia Brigade would give its most noble effort and cover itself with glory.

On the morning of 13 December, John R. and Company C waded through a swampy ground and positioned themselves in a thickly wooded area near the base of Prospect Hill. The men lay down and attempted to get some rest.

In front and to the left of the Georgia Brigade, the division commander, General A.P. Hill, had allowed a six hundred yard wide gap in the line between Lane and Archer's Brigades. Hill deployed General Maxie Gregg's South Carolina Brigade into the gap as a precaution. The gap was heavily wooded and General Hill, even after the objections of Lane and Archer, thought the Union Army would not or could not break through. General Gregg, an ardent South Carolina firebrand, assured Lane and Archer that they need not worry. Events would prove otherwise.

At about ten o'clock in the morning, as the fog burned off, Union General George Meade moved his troops directly toward the Southern lines. It was said by the Confederates that the ordered mass of Union soldiers, with their shining bayonets flashing in the sun, presented a most impressive military display. One South Carolina soldier said, "I would see fully half of the whole Yankee army, reserves and all. It was a good sight seeing them come into position ... but it seemed that that host would eat us up." One Tennessean wrote, "I feel sorry for those Yankees as they marched into the very jaws of death" (O'Reilly, p. 52).

Suddenly, the gallant Major John Pelham, General Jeb Stuart's twenty-four-year-old artillery chief, opened up on the Yankees and completely held up the Union Army with his aggressive artillery tactics. It was like a mosquito fighting an elephant. Finally, Northern artillery got the best of Pelham and he had to withdraw. His battery had held up nearly six thousand Yankees and prevented one entire division from joining Meade (O'Reilly, p. 45).

At about one p.m., after an awesome artillery barrage, Meade directed his attack at the gap between Lane and Archer. Maxie Gregg and his South Carolinians were taking it easy, not thinking that anyone could get through the thick brush that filled the gap. Suddenly, Gregg's pickets started firing at the approaching Yankees. Gregg, unaware of the approaching storm, admonished his men to hold their fire. The Union troops were pouring through the thick woods. Gregg, partially deaf, never heard the approaching Pennsylvanians. Men began to drop abruptly, and Gregg was knocked off his horse with a mortal wound to his hip. The Federals completely overran the South Carolinians and opened a huge hole in General Jackson's line. They then turned on Lane and Archer, and it looked as if they might roll up the entire Confederate line.

The 19th Georgia tried desperately to hold its position on Gregg's right, but it was soon overrun. General Archer's division, also located on Gregg's right, was in danger of being completely overrun. The 19th Georgia had collapsed and Archer's Tennessee Brigade was in trouble. Archer sent a plea to Colonel Edmond Atkinson, commander of the Georgia Brigade, that his aid was urgently needed and time was of the essence. The fighting was hand-to-hand and Archer's men could barely hold on. It looked as if Stonewall's artillery batteries could very well be captured. The Tennessee "hog drivers" were on the edge of annihilation.

John R. and the men of the 38th Georgia could hear the sounds of battle and see the defeated men from Gregg's brigade filtering through the woods. Archer's soldiers could also be seen trying to regroup. John R. must have known that he was about to be involved in one fierce fight.

Confederate General Jubal Early ordered Atkinson's Georgia Brigade to attack in the gap. Normally, one brigade would not have been enough to stem this tide, but the Georgia Brigade moved through the thick brush determined to meet the challenge.

Immediately, the 13th and 26th Georgia became disoriented and was lost to the brigade. After marching about two hundred fifty yards, the remaining

Georgia Brigade regiments slammed into the attacking Yankees.

It was with only four regiments, including the 38th, that Atkinson hit the Union troops. In his book Stonewall at Fredericksburg, Frank O'Reilly reports:

> "Within a few minutes of leaving the 26th Georgia, the rest of the Georgia Brigade struck the Federal line. Atkinson's brigade poured a volley into the northerners and charged screaming the notorious Rebel Yell at the top of their lungs. The Georgians cut a swath through the Federals where the woods sloped down the hill and drove them across the railroad tracks.
>
> "Daunted by the Rebel Yells and Rebel lead, the overextended Unionists quickly folded and fell back. Along the way, small pockets of Federals fought defiant holding actions trading ground for time and hoping reinforcements would arrive soon and shift the balance back in their favor again. ...Atkinson's arrival stabilized the Confederates' sorely tested line. The tide was slowly turning" (O'Reilly, p. 115).

Atkinson then led the Georgia Brigade in a valiant charge to dislodge the Yankees from across the railroad. O'Reilly further reports:

> "The Southerners raced down the hill or through the woods and slammed into the Bluecoats. Both brigades howled into the bottoms, mixing the wildish yells and gruff hoorays. The Unionists waited for the gray onslaught and then thundered fire into their closing ranks. A Georgian remembered that his regiment was 'met with a terrific and murderous fire'" (O'Reilly, p. 130).

An artillery shell wounded Captain William McLeod, commander of the 38th, but the valiant Georgians continued without a leader. The 38th charged over the railroad embankment and it was every man for himself as the men of the 38th fell upon a ditch filled with Pennsylvanians. Fierce hand-to-hand fighting ensued, using knives, guns, gun butts, and fists. John R. was a big man, as his pictures in later life show. I am sure he gave as much as he got. The Pennsylvanians finally broke away from the fight. The Georgia Brigade and Hoke's North Carolina troops had re-taken the railroad.

The 38th captured a huge number of prisoners. After the battle, the Georgians claimed that they had captured more prisoners than any other unit in the Army of Northern Virginia. One member of the 38th Georgia,

Jasper Horben, captured a lieutenant and three privates. The proud teenager quickly took them to the rear and, in his excitement, showed them to his division commander, General Early. However, the fight was not over yet, and as O'Reilly says, "The Georgia Brigade had an even greater surprise in store ... as they prepared to follow their success" (O'Reilly, p. 130).

The Georgia Brigade then became involved in an intense contest with the 38th New York, the Mozart Regiment. Its commander, General Ward, estimated that he lost three hundred of his eight hundred troops in a five-minute fire fight across the railroad. The boys from Emanuel, Bulloch, and Montgomery counties were doing themselves proud.

The 38th New York broke away but not until their color bearer was killed and their leader, Colonel Nelson Gesner, was severely wounded. Colonel Atkinson then saw elements of General Ward's Union brigade entering the woods on his left. He led the Georgia Brigade in driving the Yankees back fairly easily.

O'Reilly writes:

> "Many of Atkinson's enthusiastic soldiers dashed after the fleeing Bluecoats, driven by their officers' spirited calls of 'forward boys.' Atkinson's assistant adjunct general, Captain Edward P. Lawton, seized a brigade standard and rode along the lines shouting encouragement to the men. Colonel Clement A. Evans of the 31st Georgia thought Captain Lawton to be 'the bravest among the brave.' The soldiers' élan rewarded their commander's efforts. The butternuts chased after the broken Federal ranks, 'yelling as they advanced like savages. Edmond N. Atkinson intended to drive the Yankees out of the copse of woods and secure the timberline against any further attacks.'
>
> "Colonel Evans obtained his 'bravest of the brave' from Napoleon's description of Marshall Ney. Later, General Clement A. Evans named his son Lawton in memory of Captain Lawton. Evans County Georgia is named for Evans" (O'Reilly, p. 134).

The Georgia Brigade chased Ward's New Yorkers to the edge of the timber and then into the open field (shown in picture), which made the men easy targets for Union artillery. The Yanks pounded the Southerners with it as soon as they were exposed. The Georgians then realized an even greater potential prize and turned in an attempt to capture the Federal artillery. Atkinson's men valiantly charged from less than two hundred yards away, endeavoring to obtain the coveted brass guns. The Federals, however, released a horrendous barrage, inflicting tremendous damage. It was here that Captain Edward P. Lawton's horse was shot and he was pinned under the steed. Lawton injured his leg but continued to fight with the brigade. This is also where John R. likely was wounded for the second time, receiving wounds on his back, shoulder, and neck from a bursting artillery shell.

The 57th Pennsylvania found itself between the Georgia Brigade and the Union artillery. The Georgians rolled right over the Pennsylvanians as well as what was left of Ward's New York troops. A 57th Pennsylvania veteran later described its struggle with the Georgians as the "hottest fight our regiment had ever been in."

Captain Lawton urged the Georgians to follow him as he charged towards the 5th Michigan, which was guarding its artillery. Lawton's men followed through a hail of bullets but accurate Southern fire soon found Union Lieutenant Gully and he fell from his horse. He died immediately. The 5th Michigan historian described the moment as decidedly "the most severe action in which the regiment had ever participated." The Yankees then threw the 3rd Michigan into the fight, trying to stop the heroic Georgians. In the hail of artillery and rifle fire, the Georgians set up such a Rebel Yell that one Michigan's soldier described it as "hideous yelling" (O'Reilly, p. 150).

The Pennsylvania and Michigan units then turned and ran, but the Union artillery was becoming too hard too handle. The Yankees tried to move their big guns, but the Georgians shot their horses. The cannoneers cut away the dead horses and beat the surviving animals prod them to move the cannons. As the Georgians got within seventy-five yards of the one remaining Union cannon, fire from other artillery decimated the Southerners. One Union soldier said it blew gaping holes in the Georgia Brigade and that they fell in wind rows.

Captain Lawton urged the brave Confederates to follow him as he was closest to the Yankee guns, but the fire was too intense and the intrepid captain died on this field of honor. As the Southerners retreated from the withering fire, a Federal officer later described the scene: "The dead and the dying, heads off. Legs off and arms ... if that was not a slaughter, I give up" (O'Reilly, p. 151).

During the engagement, Colonel William Stiles of the 60th Georgia saw his son go down in a hail of artillery fire. Even though the fire was intense, Colonel Stiles rushed to aid his badly wounded son. His father's namesake, Captain Stiles urged his daddy to leave the field of danger. Colonel Stiles replied, "I will not be killed, but if I should be, there is no better spot to fall than by the side of my gallant son" (O'Reilly, p. 151). Other men of the Georgia Brigade hustled Captain Stiles off the field. Colonel Stiles continued to lead the 60th Georgia. Can you imagine the colonel's pain as he directed his regiment? The four Georgia Brigade regiments had suffered terrific losses and were now faced with their right being flanked by the 17th Maine. The Confederates turned on the 17th Maine in what was again a fierce firefight.

The Georgians tried to reform their line by using a ditch as cover. Edmond Atkinson, the fourth leader of the Georgia Brigade in three battles, was wounded, and Colonel Clement Evans took command. It became apparent to Evans that the brigade was in serious trouble. The wounded and dead Georgians littered the ground on what would be known as the Slaughter Pen. The Yankees threw in another regiment of brightly uniformed Zouaves. The Georgians were forced back to the railroad in a hail of bullets in less than good order. O'Reilly states:

> "Despite their small numbers and their loosely knit formations, the Rebels (the Georgia Brigade) had almost broken completely through the Union lines. If they had, not only could they have captured the Northern guns but they could have driven the broken remains of two Union divisions into the Rappahannock [River] and possibly severed the Federal left from the pontoon bridges" (O'Reilly, p. 157).

General David Bell Birney believed that he had "dodged a bullet and was simply content to re-establish the original Union line." General Early met the Georgia Brigade at the railroad tracks. He praised the Georgians for their bravery, but later chewed out the officers for taking on the whole Yankee army alone.

In describing the scene after the battle, O'Reilly states:

> "Lieutenant Phillip H. Powers of Jeb Stuart's cavalry gasped at the awful scenes of carnage in the Slaughter Pen. The dead lay in heaps. Standing at his command post with binoculars in hand, General Robert E. Lee also watched the lines recede from one another. Looking over the wreckage, the dead, and the wounded, the General whispered with emotion 'it is well that war is so terrible -- we should grow too fond of it.' The pageant of the morning was over" (O'Reilly, p. 157).

General John Gibbon made one last attempt to break the Confederate line but was driven back. Lee's ninety thousand troops had soundly defeated one hundred twenty thousand Federal soldiers. Four regiments of the Georgia Brigade had played an integral part.

But John R. was again wounded in his second battle, in which his brigade lost seven hundred nineteen killed and wounded out of two thousand troops. This time, he was sent to a hospital in Richmond. He returned to duty on 29 December 1862.

The Georgia Brigade, as part of the Second Corps, was under the command of what many feel was the greatest tactical general this country ever produced. James Robertson, in his terrific biography *Stonewall Jackson,* gives us some personal insight:

"The great General Jackson had been a part of another triumph. Who was this icon of the Second Corps? His men adored him even though many thought of him as somewhat eccentric.

"Like most of us, he had many sides to his character. Congressman Boteler reports that the night after the Battle of Fredericksburg, he spent the night in Jackson's tent. 'The Congressman awoke as Jackson entered the tent and watched his friend through almost closed eyes. Jackson lit a candle and laid aside coat, sword, and other accoutrements. He opened the door of the little stove that warmed his Sibley tent to get more light. After taking a seat at his table, Jackson brought out a well-worn Bible and read for a while. He followed this by kneeling in prayer. Then he removed his boots, lay down beside Boteler, and fell instantly asleep.'

"Around 2 a.m., Jackson awakened as if by signal; he arose carefully, trying not to disturb his guest. The light-sleeping Boteler was now aroused but said nothing. Lighting a candle, Jackson began reading at his table. He looked up at one point and saw that the candlelight was shining in Boteler's face. Quietly Jackson secured a book and adjusted it so that it would shield the light from his friend's direction. 'It was a little thing for him to do,' Boteler stated, 'but it was sufficient to indicate to me the thoughtful goodness of that great heart of his, which was as bold as a lion's and as gentle as a lamb's.'

"After visiting the dying Maxie Gregg and urging him to make his soul right with God, Jackson rode pensively with Hunter McGuire and other members of his staff. He then said, 'How horrible is war!' 'Horrible, yes,' McGuire replied, 'but we have been invaded. What can we do?' 'Kill them, sir!' Jackson said in savage tones, 'Kill every man'" (Robertson, p. 663).

I am sure John R. as well as so many other men in the Corps was proud throughout the remainder of his life for having served under the great Stonewall Jackson. An example of the love that was constantly shown Jackson was that, later in the afternoon, Jackson rode down the ranks of his troops. The constant adulation shown him was almost embarrassing as he frequently tipped his hat to the men. In the words of James Robertson:

> "The soldiers in the ranks knew that those who were blessed to survive the war would harbor memories that would impart warmth to old age and inspiration to their children. So they lined the road for miles that icy afternoon and they voiced their love for old Jack. Thousands of soldiers made him uncomfortable with their open displays of affection. That, too, was part of Jackson's mystique" (Robertson, p. 665).

CHAPTER

Five

CHANCELLORSVILLE

John R. Flanders and the other men of General Jubal Early's division spent the late winter and early spring of 1863 obtaining food and trying to make life as comfortable as possible. They were camped at Moss Neck near Fredericksburg. Many of the boys from south Georgia had never seen snow. This gave rise to regimental snow battles on a very large scale.

One problem was that an unpopular reserve officer would appropriate food from the men. A Private Nichols of the Georgia Brigade tells what happened:

"The Georgia Brigade had a rear guard commanded by a bigoted lieutenant. He would take everything he could from the boys who were out foraging. He kept this up for some time until the boys grew to hate him. So three of the boys who were acquainted with him before the war determined to get ahead of him. They went out, caught and killed a real fat dog, dressed him nicely, cut off one of his hind quarters, cut off the foot, wrapped it up and came up in the rear of the guard in a real suspicious way, apparently trying to conceal it.

"The lieutenant saw that they had something...the men apparently gave it to him very reluctantly...the lieutenant took it and gave it to his Negro cook and told him to cook it for his supper.

"The Negro cooked some and the lieutenant sat down to eat it. He cursed the Negro and told him he had poisoned it, for he had never eated as strong mutton as that was. The lieutenant then cooked some himself, but it was no better. The next day, he asked the man he had taken it from what it was. He said in a low, drawling way, 'Why, Lieutenant, it was a piece of dog.' Such a laugh that was raised!

"It was such a good joke; it was all over the camps in a few hours. That night, men would holler out, 'Who eat the dog?', and you would

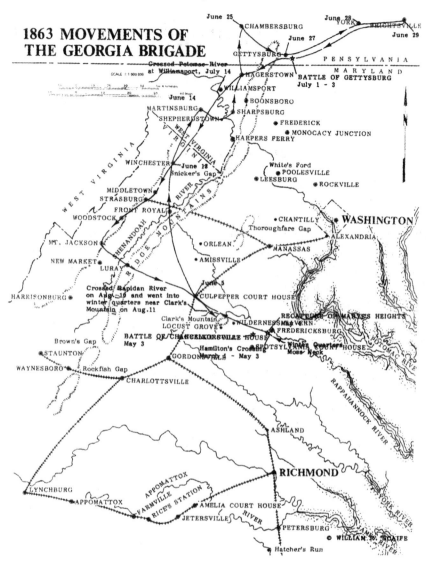

Courtesy of William Scaife

hear from all over the camps, 'The lieutenant.' Men would also imitate the sound of dogs. They ran that so far until the lieutenant ran away and quit the army" (Scaife, p. 62).

Late April saw General Stonewall Jackson move his corps back to the old Fredericksburg battlefield. It was at this time that the Georgia Brigade obtained a new commander, General John B. Gordon. Gordon, a Georgian, was a rising star in the Confederate Army and was instantly very popular.

In describing his brigade, General Gordon said, "On my return to the army, I was assigned to the command of perhaps the largest brigade in the Confederate Army, composed of six regiments from my own state, Georgia. No more superb material ever filled the ranks of any command in any army" (Scaife, p. 62). General Gordon had been shot four times at Sharpsburg. But for the fact that his wife was in attendance to nurse him, he probably would have died. He suffered one wound in his face and happened to fall on his hat. Had the hat not had a bullet hole in it, he would have drowned in his own blood.

On 29 April 1863, Yankee General Joe Hooker crossed the Rappahannock River. This action initiated the battle of Chancellorsville.

General Robert E. Lee had split his army into essentially three parts in an effort to flank Hooker's larger army. Early's division, including Gordon's Georgia Brigade, was assigned to hold the Confederate right. His ten thousand Confederates were to hold off thirty thousand Yankees under General John Sedgwick.

General Jackson had moved part of his corps from the Confederate right and behind his own lines in order to strike at the Union right.

The 2nd of May saw the great Jackson's famous flank march, which destroyed an entire Union corps. That same day, on the Confederate right, Sedgwick's troops stormed Marye's Heights and drove the outnumbered Confederates from their position. If Sedgwick continued his assault, he would drive into Lee's rear. General Early withdrew his division a few miles and planned on attacking Sedgwick the next morning. Early ordered General Gordon to seize Marye's Heights, the ground previously taken by Sedgwick. General Gordon describes this action:

"I was officially a comparative stranger to the men of the Georgia Brigade. I said a few sentences to them that we should know each better when the battle of the day was over: that I had trusted we should go together into that fort, and that if there was a man in the brigade who did not wish to go with us, I would excuse him if he would step to the front and make himself known. Of course, there was no man who desired to be excused, and I then announced that every man in that splendid Brigade of Georgian's had thus declared his purpose to go into the fortress. They answered this announcement by prolonged and thrilling shout, and moved briskly to the attack. When we were well under full headway and under fire from the heights, I received an order to halt, with the explanation that the other troops were to unite in the assault; but the order had come too late. My men were nearing the fort... were rushing upon it with tremendous impetuosity!...it was too late to halt them. General Early playfully but earnestly remarked, after the fort was taken, that success had saved me from being court marshaled for disobedience to orders" (Scaife, p. 60).

Late that same afternoon, the Georgia Brigade joined other units in attacking Sedgwick's left flank. The Georgians pushed the Federals back towards the river until darkness halted the action. During the night of 4 May, Sedgwick withdrew across the Rappahannock.

Chancellorsville was a great Confederate victory. It was considered Lee's and Jackson's masterpiece. But it would prove to have been won at a very high price. On the night of 3 May, Stonewall Jackson had been severely wounded, accidentally shot by some North Carolina troops who mistook him and his party for northern pickets. *Stonewall Jackson* by James Robertson contains a superb description of this tragedy.

After the battle, the men of the Georgia brigade were ordered to Guinea Station, where they were to escort two thousand Union prisoners to Richmond. Guinea Station is a small community with about ten buildings and a railroad track. General Jackson was being treated there at the Chandler house. John R. and the other members of the Confederate Army were praying hard for his recovery. After John R.'s unit left with the Yankee prisoners, General Jackson died.

Later in the war, the Georgia Brigade visited Jackson's grave. Private Pharris Johnson summarized the feelings of his fellow soldiers:

"As we filed around his grave, I felt that I was stepping on holy ground. The last resting place of a Christian hero. Tears came into the eyes of many as they remembered the splendid leadership of this wonderful man. Truly the hand of Divine Providence was with him. His name will be an inspiration to the South and the world as long as history is written. His name carries with it everything that is true and noble. He presented to the world the greatest military genius at the same time, the most devout Christian faith. All modern military critics consider him the greatest general of ancient or modern times" (Johnson, p. 177).

John R. walked with the prisoners all the way to Richmond. The journey was hot, dusty, and slow. The road on which they traveled ran parallel to the Rappahannock River. As they set out, the men of the 38th got word of a plot the prisoners had hatched to surprise their guards, kill them, and take their weapons. The Yanks then planned to dispatch the sleeping reserves and escape to the river where they would hail passing vessels. That first night, the men of the 38th camped with the prisoners near the small hamlet of Bowling Green. Captain John G. Rankin called the men to fall in and ordered them to double their guard and be extremely vigilant. The regimental commander, Captain W. L. McLeod, knew of the rumored plot but didn't buy it at all. In fact, McLeod went to town to seek some entertainment.

Rankin proceeded to march his reserves out of sight and ordered that they not start fires. "Boys, we will sleep with one eye open tonight," he told them. His actions of doubling the guard and marching the reserves out of sight completely buffaloed the prisoners. After a while, the guards could hear them talking amongst themselves, "Hello Johnny, where's your reserves?" No one responded. The prisoners repeated the question several times. Finally, the men of the 38th lost their patience and one Confederate yelled, "Your scheme to escape from us tonight has leaked out, and if you make the attempt, we are prepared for you, and there will be none of you left to tell the tale." Because of the swift action of Captain Rankin, not a peep was heard from the prisoners the rest of the night. Had the plot been successful, the 38th Georgia might have ceased to exist (Hudgins, 1908).

John R. and the other men of the 38th delivered the prisoners to Belle Isle Prison in Richmond. As their regiment was leaving the city, it met General Jackson's funeral procession entering. C.L. Hudgins of the 38th observed, "His horse was following the procession without the gallant Stonewall, who had led us to victory on so many hard fought battlefields" (Hudgins).

CHAPTER

Six

GETTYSBURG
John R. Loses His Good Friend

Chancellorsville was the first major battle John R. Flanders had survived without a wound, but I am sure he realized that there would be many more fights before this war was over.

General Lee knew that the South could not conquer the North. But Southern forces could make things so difficult that the Yankees would leave the Confederacy alone. The South needed food and supplies, but Virginia had been stripped bare. It was for these reasons that General Lee took his troops into Pennsylvania.

1 June 1863 saw General John B. Gordon's Georgia Brigade moving north under its new corps commander, Lieutenant General Dick Ewell. The brigade's division remained under the able command of General Jubal Early. The Georgia Brigade left Hamilton's Crossing, Virginia, marched through Culpepper, and proceeded down the Shenandoah Valley (north) to Winchester, Virginia. In his book *Under the Southern Cross*, Private Isaac Bradwell of the Georgia Brigade reports:

"We traveled only at night for some time, camping only a short time before day, lest our movements should be observed by the enemies, scouts and signal men. When we had gone several days and were entirely out of sight, we made rapid day marches by way of Culpepper Courthouse and Front Royal, where we crossed the Blue Ridge into the Valley. The weather was hot and the roads were dry and dusty. This dust worked up by the wagons, trains and artillery, settled on us until we were as brown as the dust itself. General Gordon, riding along by us, said in a loud voice: 'Boys, if your mothers could see you now, they wouldn't know you.' Some of us were limping along on blistered feet, and the General greatly endeared himself to us by his conduct on this occasion. Getting down from his horse he mounted a private soldier in the saddle, while he fell in ranks with a gun on his shoulder and trudged along with us" (Johnson, p. 115).

It was at Winchester that Ewell's Corps would face eight thousand troops under Union General Milroy, a very unpopular character. Bradwell reports:

> "From this secure place, Milroy exercised his authority over the defenseless Southern people in a manner so arbitrary as to secure for himself the ill will of everybody. But now the moment had arrived, and the ax was about to fall with a mighty stroke and break up this happy state of affairs, for General Lee had planned to invade Pennsylvania and Winchester was on his route" (Johnson, p. 115).

General Early ordered Gordon to form the Georgia Brigade outside Winchester in order to clear the Yankees from a ridge that was blocking their entrance. The Georgians drove the enemy from behind a stone wall and across an open field. The Yankees took refuge behind the main fortifications at Winchester and, during the night, stole away without a fight. About four thousand were captured on the road north of Winchester. Later that day, General Gordon came riding up on a huge black horse he dubbed "Old Milroy" as the horse was supposed to have belonged to the unpopular Yankee general.

The Georgia Brigade next marched into Pennsylvania, where the troops were greatly impressed by the tidy farms and beautiful landscape – untouched by the ravages of war. The Georgians were given strict orders by generals Gordon and Lee not to disturb private property. General Lee's orders were read to the troops, forbidding Confederate soldiers from "trespassing on private property under pain of death" (Johnson, p. 115). This was quite a contrast to Sherman in Georgia a year later.

Ewell's Corps then marched to Gettysburg and linked up with elements of Lee's army. While in Gettysburg, crowds of young people assembled, asking the Georgians when they were going to burn the town. They were told that "southern soldiers didn't burn towns" (Johnson, p. 123).

After a night at Gettysburg, John R. and the men of the 38th Georgia marched with Ewell's Corps and the Georgia Brigade northeast of Gettysburg toward York. They passed through York and proceeded toward Wrightsville in an effort to capture the bridge across the Susquehanna River. This would put them in a position to capture the state capital of Harrisburg. After marching at a rapid pace in very hot weather, Gordon's men reached the bridge – just as Union forces set it afire. The blaze rapidly spread to Wrightsville, where Gordon's men aided the local citizens in quenching the flames. The Georgians then marched back to York. They had gone further into Union territory than any other Confederate infantry unit. Late that evening – 28 June – Gordon received orders to march to

The spot where the Georgia Brigade defeated the Yankees on the first day at Gettysburg. Captain William McLeod died at the bottom of the hill. Shown with me is my good friend, Pete Scogin.

Cashtown and back to Gettysburg.

The next day, after three sleepless nights, the men of Gordon's Brigade arrived "much fatigued." As they approached Gettysburg from the northeast, they could see that A.P. Hill's Corps was already heavily engaged. The Georgians could hear the boom of cannons as well as the Yankees' "Hip, hip, hooray!" There were also the unmistakable shrieks of the famous Rebel Yell.

General Hill's Corps included Robert Rhodes' Division. Rhodes, a VMI graduate, was considered by many to have been the Confederate Army's best division commander. Rhodes' Division included the famous Doles-Cook Brigade, populated primarily by men from southwest Georgia as well as Milledgeville in central Georgia. On this day, however, Rhodes' Division was in danger of being overwhelmed. In order to take pressure off of him, General Early ordered Gordon to take a small hill, known locally as Blochers Knoll. This vantage point was occupied by the 153rd Pennsylvania and the 54th and 68th New York Regiments of Barlow's Division. Two of these regiments were filled with German immigrants.

The men of the 38th, under the command of Emanuel County's Captain William L. McLeod, moved forward in double quick time. They could see General Gordon on his great black horse, his eyes blazing, imploring the Georgians to move forward and keep their ranks tight. That day it was said of Gordon, "He's the most prettiest thing you ever did see on a field of fight. It 'ud put fight into a whipped chicken just to look at him" (Pfanz, p. 238).

The Yankee soldiers of Barlow's Division were formed atop Blochers Knoll with their bayonets glistening in the sun. General Gordon drew his sword and the 38th, along with the other brave men of the Georgia Brigade, attacked with a deafening Rebel Yell. The Georgia Brigade, with the 38th on its left, moved "through a field of yellow wheat, like a dark gray wave" (Pfanz, p. 229).

The Yankee pickets were pushed across a stream known as Rock Creek. As the boys from Emanuel, Bulloch, and Montgomery crossed the creek, their formation broke up as they looked for a ford and climbed the slippery creek bank. Captain McLeod was leading his men from the creek to a rail fence, where they became easy targets as they leapt over. It was at this point that the gallant McLeod was struck in the head by a minnie ball, mortally wounded at age twenty-one.

As the fight continued, the Georgia Brigade drove the Yankees off Blochers Knoll. Gordon's Brigade had sustained a great victory. The number of Yankees killed and wounded there exceeded the total number of men

Lieutenant Colonel William L. McLeod. Used by permission of Edith C. Smith, widow of the late Michael W. Hofe.

in the Georgia Brigade. Gordon wanted to press the attack, believing that Cemetery Ridge was obtainable. He was, however, prevented from doing so. General Gordon was later quoted as having said, "Oh, for Stonewall Jackson!" (Johnson, p. 125). If only General Ewell had listened to Gordon, Meade would probably have arrived that night facing the high ground, and two days later things might have been very different.

The death of William McLeod must have been a terrific blow to John R. They were the same age and had grown up in the same area of Emanuel County. Unlike his brothers Joe and Ches, John R. had joined the 38th instead of the 48th, most likely because of his friendship with McLeod. We will see that three months after Gettysburg, John R. transferred from the 38th to the 48th, primarily because his friend William was dead and because his brothers were members of Company H, 48th Georgia.

Back in Emanuel County, Georgia, William McLeod's mother Mary was sitting on her front porch with her husband Neil. She turned to him and said that she felt very sad, she had a feeling that something awful had happened to their son. About that time, a mourning dove landed in their front yard. She then told Neil, "I believe William is dead" (Hofe, p. 35).

The wounded men of the 38th Georgia were taken to the Kime Farm, where the brigade hospital had been set up. Captain McLeod's body servant, Moses, found the wounded officer and was with him in his final hours. After McLeod's death, Moses wrapped the body in a blanket and buried William near a peach tree on the Kime property. After the Confederate Army retreated into Virginia, Moses made the fifty-day journey back to Georgia to report the sad news to a distraught family. At the war's end, Moses returned to Gettysburg with William's brother-in-law John Prescott. The two men carried William's remains back to Emanuel County in a wagon.

The 38th spent the next two days at Gettysburg as a reserve unit, backing up Early's other brigades. But victory eluded the Confederate Army at Gettysburg. The 38th Georgia, along with the rest of the Southern army, began the long trek back to Virginia.

CHAPTER

Seven

JOHN R. JOINS HIS BROTHERS

On the afternoon of 4 July 1863, John R. Flanders and the other members of the 38th Georgia accompanied Lee's army on its sad retreat from Gettysburg, Pennsylvania, towards Virginia. The weather reflected their mood. Rain was coming down in sheets and the mud was knee deep. The men could hear screams from the seven-mile-long hospital wagon train – those wagons had no springs and each bump must have been hell for the wounded soldiers. Joe Flanders drove one of the ambulances, as before the battle he had been given the unenviable task of caring for his company's wounded.

During the retreat, the Georgia Brigade had the honor of serving as the rear guard of the Army of Northern Virginia. Several times the Georgians had to turn on the pursuing Yankees in order to keep them at a safe distance.

John R.'s first cousin (and Frank Flanders's great-grandfather), William A. Flanders, also took part in Lee's long march south from Gettysburg. As he lay on his deathbed many years later, with his family gathered at his side, William told them that he knew he was dying and that he had only one sin on his conscience that made him hate to have to meet his Maker. He proceeded to relate how, as a member of Company H, 48th Georgia, he had been assigned to Lee's rear guard scouting the Yankee movements. As he walked out of a patch of woods after having been involved in a firefight, he looked to his left and saw a Yankee soldier a few feet away frantically loading his rifle. Williams's rifle was also unloaded, but he immediately rushed the Yankee and assaulted him with its butt. He said the soldier begged for mercy but he felt so much anger that he clubbed the man to death. William related that he had lived a straight and honorable life but did not look forward to seeing the Almighty, for he was not sure how this incident would be treated. His obituary in the Swainsboro *Forest Blade* contained the following words:

"At Sharpsburg, at Chancellorsville, at Gettysburg, at a hundred other places where Greek met Greek on fields of carnage made immortal, he acted well and bravely his part, and it was the souls of such men as be that made Lee's army the most formidable the world has ever seen" (Anonymous, n.d.).

In the early hours of 14 July, the Georgia Brigade crossed into Virginia. The men then marched to a camp on the Rapidan River near Clark's Mountain.

On 15 September 1863, John R. transferred to Company H of the 48th Georgia, commanded by his brother Alexander Chesnut (Ches) Flanders. Ches had been elected lieutenant on 4 April 1862 and captain on 29 October 1862. He served with Company H throughout the war and was one of its few remaining men to surrender at Appomattox.

Another of John R.'s brothers, Joe, was also with Company H. He was wounded at Mechanicsville on 26 June 1862, one day before John R. had

William A. Flanders in his late 70's. He was 32 years old when he enlisted in 1862. He died in 1905 at the age of 83.

been wounded at Gaines' Mill. Joe would also be wounded at Myers Hill and Hatcher's Run. At the close of the war, he was hospitalized in Richmond.

A third brother, Richard Bird Flanders, was likewise a member of Company H. He died at home on 11 November 1863, apparently one of the countless Confederate soldiers who succumbed to disease. We will see that of the three Flanders boys who died in the war, two lost their lives due to illness.

The 48th Georgia had suffered mightily at Gettysburg. On 2 July, Wright's Brigade, of which the 48th was a part, attacked over the same ground that would see the famous Picket-Peddigrew charge of 3 July. Wright's Brigade actually reached its goal but, because it had no support on its flanks, had to retreat. It lost fifty-two percent killed and wounded. Every line officer, except Ches Flanders and one lieutenant, was killed or wounded.

After the war, Ches – named for his great-great-grandmother Chesnut – returned to Emanuel County and became a Methodist minister as well as a farmer and an officer of the Confederate veterans organization. In addition to being a respected leader, he was quite a character, known as a passionate individual with a fiery temper. One Sunday morning, Ches was leaving with his wife for church when he noticed that his hogs had gotten into his corn and were doing a good job of uprooting it. He chased the hogs back into their pen and, in doing so, used some very spicy language. After fixing the hog pen, he dropped to his knees and asked the good Lord for forgiveness. He got back on his wagon, turned around and went back to the house. When his wife asked him what he was doing, he told her that in his present state of mind it would not do for him to preach.

Ches also had the reputation of being a man who could give a prayer the likes of which no one had ever heard. Once, during a severe drought, a group of farmers implored Ches to pray for rain. Ches prayed hard for about three days and then it started raining. Cousin Alan Flanders said that his mother told him that it rained so much that the farmers returned and asked Ches to discontinue his prayers.

Reverend Billy Key, a prominent United Methodist minister and a great-grandson of Ches Flanders, remembers an incident when the Methodist church in Swainsboro, Georgia, was having a revival but it was not going well. The pastor called a meeting of the church stewards one morning to see what could be done. As the group was discussing various options, Ches came riding by on a wagon, dressed in overalls, taking his cotton to the local cotton gin. The pastor ran outside and talked Ches into leading the group in prayer for the revival. As Ches was praying, the stewards got up

Ches Flanders preaches from his bed. Drawing by Kyle James.

and gathered around and, according to Key, suddenly revival broke out.

In the last year of his life, Ches would preach from his bed. On Sunday afternoons, people would come from all over to hear him give anointed sermons while lying down. They would fill the house as well as the porch and the yard. Because of the example set by Ches, as well as his uncle, Jordan Flanders,* countless progeny of both men have served the church. Even today I know of several missionaries, youth directors, and pastors who trace their lineage back to these two devout men. Both Ches and his brother Joe were wounded in battle and it is quite remarkable when you think how close this great man came to death.

After Ches Flanders' first wife died he married Catherine Thompson Kitchen. She was the widow of James Smith Kitchen, a soldier in Company H who had been killed on the second day at Gettysburg. He was one of the seven color bearers who had led the 48th in the charge against Union lines. Ches Flanders' step-granddaughter, Cynthia Kitchen Overman, tells of her childhood experiences with Ches:

James S. Kitchen. Co. H. 48th Ga, Killed July 2, 1863 at Gettysburg. One of seven flag bearers killed or wounded. After the war, Kitchen's wife married Ches Flanders. Courtesy of Scott Thompson and John Zwemer.

"Chesnut Flanders holds a fond place in the hearts of his step grandchildren of which I am one. As a little girl I used to climb into his lap and plait his long snow white hair while he told stories about the war. There was an indenture in the top of his head where I used to put my finger while he recounted how he received the wound, while fighting, that left a hole there. He was a Captain of Company H, 48th Georgia regiment of the infantry division of Georgia, in which my real grandfather, James Smith Kitchen, was enlisted. James Smith Kitchen was killed in Gettysburg on July 2, 1863. His body was never returned to his family.

"After twenty years, when Chestnut Flanders became a widower, he married Catherine Thompson Kitchen, the widow of James Smith Kitchen. I became his step-granddaughter. Many are the days I spent in his home. This is where I received my earliest impressions of the Christian life. We knelt in prayer around the breakfast table each morning. In the evening, Grandfather read the scriptures, and he and Grandmother prayed while we all knelt by our chairs. On rising each morning, Grandfather would kneel by his bed and pray for several minutes, no matter how cold the floor or room was. This devotion to God made a deep impression on the minds and hearts of their grandchildren.

"So I wish to memorialize and give praise for this man whose religious life had such great influence, in the church of that day, and is still strong in the church today. This is written not only in remembrance of this man, but that all his descendants can know of their rich heritage of Christian people" (Scott, p. 75).

The 48th Georgia stayed in camp until the spring of 1864. Both armies had been decimated at Gettysburg and it took a while to refit. The Confederate Army had lost many good men, especially irreplaceable line officers. Supplies were very slim and finding food was a constant chore. On 4 May, the 48th Georgia broke camp and prepared to take part in the Battle of the Wilderness.

The Yankees had a new overall commander, General U.S. Grant. The battles of Wilderness, Spotsylvania, Myers Hill, North Anna, Cold Harbor, and Petersburg together made up the Overland Campaign. This was Grant's attempt to out-flank Lee in order to get to Richmond and occurred north,

Drawing by R. David Boyd

east, and south of the Confederate capital. At the battles of Wilderness, Spotsylvania, and Cold Harbor, Grant would lose more men than Lee had in his whole army. Persistence, however, was the name of the game, and Grant did not seem to mind how many casualties he took as long as the ultimate goal was achieved.

During the Battle of the Wilderness, the 48th Georgia was used as a reserve unit. After the Confederate victory there, the 48th was guarding the Confederate rear while the Army of Northern Virginia moved to Spotsylvania. Early one morning an enemy cavalry unit rushed across the Po River and tried to steal the brigade's wagon train. The 48th had a spirited exchange before driving off the Yankees, leaving several dead and wounded.

The Battle of Spotsylvania was a titanic struggle in which the Confederate Army narrowly averted disaster.

On 12 May 1864, the Confederate salient known as the Mule Shoe was overrun by a host of Yankees under the command of General Winfield Scott Hancock. A salient is a bulge in the line similar to that created by the Germans at the Battle of the Bulge in World War II, the Soviets at Kurst, and the Confederates at Spotsylvania. The problem brought about by a salient is that it leaves the occupants vulnerable to attack from three sides. But for the work of generals John B. Gordon, Robert Rodes, and Stephen Ramseur, the Confederate Army would have been cut in half and the war could have ended at Spotsylvania. The Southerners had moved their artillery and were caught completely by surprise. One whole Confederate division was destroyed and three thousand Southerners were captured. The famous Georgia unit, the Doles-Cook Brigade, was overrun. At this critical moment, John R.'s former brigade, the Georgia Brigade, helped plug a gap created by the Union breakthrough. They did so with great loss but helped save the day for Dixie. This contest was known as the Bloody Angle. For sheer audacity and intensity of fighting, nothing can equal the twenty hours that the two sides slugged it out here. To walk on this battlefield is to get a sense of the immense courage displayed by both armies. It is truly hallowed ground.

The fight at the Bloody Angle had taken place in the rain and this terrible weather continued for five days. One Confederate soldier wrote his family:

"You can hardly imagine how uncomfortable we are lying in the mud for nearly two weeks. Our men have been in the line of battle – exposed to all the inclemency of weather – first the insufferable heat and now the

Camp 48th Georgia Regiment
May 28th 1864

Dear Cousin,

I this morning seat myself to reply to your letter which I received a few days ago. I have no news of interest to write. There is a big fight going on here now which you have undoubtedly heard of. We have been very successful so far and I hope that we will be in the future.

Old Grant is down on the peninsula with his army where McLelan was. He could have got where he is without losing a man but he has lost about fifty or sixty thousand.

All the company are generally well so far as I know and all in good heart. In fact our whole army is in the best heart I ever saw it.

We have had three men wounded and one killed in this fight. Bill Cowart was slightly wounded in thigh; Stephen Boyt's legs taken off; P. Nunez killed; and Joe Flanders wounded slightly in left hand.

You wanted to know the mark of those sheep. My marks are crop and two splits in one ear and under bit in the other; and crop and two splits in one ear and over slope and under bit in the other; and under slope and over bit in one ear and crop and two splits in the other.

Mary Beasley's mark is crop and half crop in one ear and underslope and over bit in the other; and some has two over bits.

Nothing more to present. I remain as ever your affectionate cousin.

William A. Flanders

drenching rains – and yet they stand and fight ... I am worn out wearied in mind, with continual anxiety. Oh, if it could all end, and this terrible turmoil cease" (Furgurson).

But it was not to be. General Lee moved his troops to a new line and, on the night of 13 May, General Grant began moving his army to the left. This resulted in the fight for Myers Hill.

*The story is told that Jordan Flanders, a pioneer of Methodism in Emanuel County, was lying on his deathbed. He knew that he did not have long, so the night before he died, the noted Methodist pastor requested that his children, grandchildren, and their families join him in his room. He told the assembled household that he had spent his entire life serving the Lord. He felt that his family was called of God to continue his work. He then asked, as his last request, that his family members promise that they would encourage as many of their kin as possible to enter full-time Christian service. As his family members walked by his bed, he gave each a special blessing. Jordan Flanders' family heard his request and exceeded what I am sure were his fondest expectations.

CHAPTER

Eight

MYERS HILL
Ches and Joe Are Wounded

It was at the fight for Myers Hill, located north of Richmond, that both Joe and Ches Flanders were wounded – Joe in the left hand and Ches in the skull. Myers Hill occurred on 14 May 1864, just prior to the battle of North Anna.

Myers Hill was a strategic point on the Union left that allowed a view of both Confederate and Union positions. General Grant, in overall command, knew that if he wanted to attack the Confederates he could not do so unless he occupied the site.

The aggressive young Union general, Emory Upton, assured his superiors that he would take the hill and consequently was ordered to do so. Upton, along with Lieutenant Colonel Elwell S. Otis' 5th Corps, took the hill fairly quickly. The 9th Virginia Cavalry, greatly outnumbered, left the field to the Yankees. General Upton began fortifying the hill with rails from the Myers farm and was reinforced with troops of the 2nd and 10th New Jersey regiments, who came across the Ni River.

General Grant planned to attack General Lee from Myers Hill but General Lee, as usual, was about to put a big damper on Grant's plans. His initial step would be to retake Myers Hill and he turned to his tough corps commander, General Jubal Early, to do it. Early ordered General William Mahone (VMI Class of 1847) to use two of his brigades. General Ambrose Wright's brigade, of which the 48th was part, would lead the attack. It had not had a tough fight at Spotsylvania and was fairly fresh. General Nat Harris' Mississippi Brigade would be in reserve. It had seen the worst of the fighting at the Bloody Angle, and the twenty-hour ordeal had decimated one of the Confederate Army's best units. General John Chambliss' cavalry would screen these two brigades.

General Early led the Georgians and Mississippians close to Myers Hill, where they quietly formed a battle line. They could see the Yankee soldiers milling around the entrenchments, completely unaware of Early's presence. Union General Upton knew that he was in a vulnerable position, anticipated the worst, and continued to press his men to improve their breastworks. From his vantage point, he could see six hundred yards across the field to some thick woods. It was from these woods that Ches, John R., and Joe, with other troops of Wright's Brigade, would come.

General Upton ordered Lieutenant Colonel William H. Lessig to take his 96th Pennsylvania and investigate those distant woods. As the Pennsylvanians were approaching the trees, they ran into Wright's Brigade, led by Colonel Matthew Hall of the 48th.

The 3rd Georgia Regiment charged forward, confronting Lessig with a deafening Rebel Yell, firing as they ran. Confederate Captain D.B. Langston, leading the regiment, fell wounded, and Captain L.F. Luckie halted the men within sight of the Yankee guns. There was confusion in the ranks. Captain Luckie saw his mistake, realizing that it was much safer to attack, and he urged his men forward. Lieutenant H.G. Hyman grabbed the regimental colors and shouted, "Rally your colors, 3rd Georgia!" Hyman's show of bravery inspired the Georgians to rout Lessig's men and proceed toward Upton's entrenchments (Rhea, p. 85).

The 48th and 22nd Georgia then sprang tiger-like, attacking the enemy. Ches was leading Company H when he was wounded. Although blood was streaming down his face, he led his men over the breastworks. A witness to the battle says:

> "No nobler bearing on the field of battle could have been exhibited than they displayed. Their alignment was perfect. Their steps regular and unwavering. When cannon shots or bullets made gaps in their line, they promptly filled up and when a color barrier was shot down, another man at once seized the flag" (Rhea, p. 85).

General Early then pulled a move reminiscent of Old Jack (Stonewall Jackson). He had hidden Harris' Mississippians and Chambliss' dismounted cavalry in the woods on the Yankee flanks. When the Georgians attacked, the Mississippians cavalrymen caught Upton in a double envelopment.

The Yankees' only way out was across the Ni River. A soldier in the 5th Maine said, "It was really a ludicrous and laughable retreat. Some tall running was done to prevent capture." Many Yankees could not swim and were fished out of the river. One Union officer said a Confederate soldier was running behind him shouting, "Halt, you Yankee son-of-a-bitch!"

L to R – Doug Walker, Warren Budd, Park Historian Greg Murtz, and Courtenay Budd standing beside Upton's entrenchments at Myers Hill. Doug is a fellow VMI "Brother Rat" and was a terrific athlete. This picture was taken the day after friends and family gathered to celebrate the life of our beloved "Brother Rat" Sam Jordan.

(Rhea, p. 86).

This contest was appropriately named "Upton's Run." The debacle was particularly embarrassing to General Upton because he had asked General Meade, commanding general of the Army of the Potomac, to watch the engagement. When Nat Harris' Mississippians flanked Upton, Meade "bolted for the rear." A major in the 13th Virginia tried to grab the general, who was saved by members of his headquarters company. The brave major was, himself, captured. Meade lost his spectacles in the fracas (Rhea, p. 86).

The Georgians and Mississippians had saved the day. The 10th New Jersey regiment had been severely "cut up." The Georgians captured two hundred Federals as well as three stands of colors. Dead Yankees were robbed of their provisions by hungry southerners.

CHAPTER

Nine

NORTH ANNA

After the fight at Myers Hill on 15 May, Mahone's Division, of which the 48th was a part, moved to Hanover Station. They encamped east of the Brock Road between the Fredericksburg Road and the Massaponox Church Road. While there, one of the Georgia boys met an unlikely and mysterious death. Phillip A. Nunez, an Emanuel County schoolteacher and farmer, and a highly regarded member of Company H, was treating a wounded friend. When the injured man asked for water, Nunez picked up several canteens and, at about six p.m., set out for the Po River. Although the river was some two miles away, his trek was through Confederate-controlled territory. Late that night word got around that Nunez had not returned and a search party was sent out the following morning, only to discover his body lying next to the river. Nunez had been stabbed to death. No one ever discovered what had happened (Rogers, p. 36).

On 24 May, Mahone's Division and the 48th proceeded with the rest of General Lee's troops to Ox Ford on the North Anna River. As the Blue and Gray armies faced each other across the water, Lee developed a plan to deploy his troops in an inverted V with the tip of the V centered on the river. This would force Grant to divide his forces. Lee could then safely go on the offensive for the first time in many months by attacking a smaller section of Grant's army. Mahone's Division was selected to form the tip of the V at the river. The 48th Georgia was placed next to two brigades that had distinguished themselves at the Bloody Angle – Harris' Mississippians and Sanders' Alabamians.

Grant's goal was to fight the Confederates on an open battlefield and engage them before they could dig in. Thinking that Lee was marching to Richmond, he took the bait and split his forces into three parts. He had fallen into the trap but did not know it.

Grant sent a Massachusetts aristocrat and a drunkard, General James Ledlie, to crack Mahone's lines. Ledlie was inebriated, literally, as he ordered the 35th Massachusetts to attack Mahone. But Mahone's troops had learned that fortifications could save lives. In his book *To the North Anna River,* Gordon Rhea describes Mahone's entrenchment:

"Ledlie had reached the Western end of the inverted V, near where the apex rested on Ox Ford. The ridge made an impressive natural fortification that Mahone's men had strengthened by employing lessons learned at Spotsylvania Courthouse. Earthworks topped with head logs formed the face of the works. Traverses every 15 feet provided shelters from the enfilading fire of guns across the river. Ledges created elevated steps for shooting and shallow trenches in the rear afforded safe havens for loading. Artillery, well entrenched, stood at strategic intervals and ditches connected gun on placements with ammunition storage depots in the rear. The earthworks varied in detail from regiment to regiment. Some officers insisted on geometrically precise lines and angles. Others favored rounded corners, and a few permitted lopsided structures that looked like the work of children. Altogether, however, the rebel entrenchments across from Ledlie were among the most formidable construction during the war" (Rhea, p. 337).

The ambitious Ledlie realized that if he could dislodge the Confederates from Ox Ford, he would have a real feather in his cap. So, as rain fell, his troops threw themselves against the Georgians, Mississippians, and Alabamians. But Mahone's men held and the attack failed. Ledlie lost four hundred fifty men killed and wounded and one hundred fifty captured. The Confederates suffered seventy-five casualties.

The North Anna battle played out in such a way that General Lee could have destroyed a whole Yankee corps, but he was physically unable to follow up the stunning defense. He was in terrible shape, suffering from dysentery and so run down that he used a carriage rather than sit astride his beloved horse, Traveler. His doctor reported that he had not slept more than two hours any night in the past two weeks. Nor did Lee have an able second in command. General Stonewall Jackson was dead, General James Longstreet had been wounded, and General A.P. Hill was quite ill.

CHAPTER
Ten

COLD HARBOR

Grant dodged a real disaster at North Anna River and moved his troops further south, establishing a line near the small crossroad of Cold Harbor, Virginia. The Battle of Cold Harbor would take place over some of the same ground on which John R. Flanders had experienced his first taste of war at Gaines Mill. The Confederate entrenchments at Cold Harbor ran north and south. Mahone's Division was first placed to the north of the Confederate line, backing up Georgian General Alfred Colquitt. But on 2 June 1864, the night before the big fight, they were moved to the south, backing up General John C. Breckenridge and General Cadmus Wilcox's divisions. Grant hoped that the Confederates would not be able to adequately dig in. But, because they were greatly outnumbered and knew that good fortifications were their greatest defense, the Southerners had become "world class diggers...skillful, self-taught, military engineers" (Ferguson, p. 134).

If Southern soldiers were given as much as twelve hours, they could create elaborate earthworks. At Cold Harbor, they built entrenchments two or three rows deep with small holes for firing and cannon emplacements that were quite sophisticated. Roads were constructed for supplies and bridges were erected across creeks. Both sides knew that the Southerners were well dug in and the Yanks were aware that they faced a terrible ordeal. Many sewed their names on the backs of their uniforms so that they could be identified when killed.

Captain Ches Flanders had been back in action since North Anna. I am sure that John R. spent the night of 2 June wondering what the next day would bring. He remembered Fredericksburg and Gettysburg and must have known that this would be a heck of a fight.

Before daybreak, Union forces mounted a huge attack, overrunning part of Breckenridge's Division. Finegan's Floridians of Mahone's Division and the 2nd Maryland from Breckenridge's Division heroically plugged the gap. The 48th Georgia was in the line between Breckinridge and Wilcox. Confederate weapons grew hot as they continually fired, killing the charging Yankees. The Northerners would holler "Huzzah!" and charge forward as the Confederates poured artillery and musketry with "good effect" (Ferguson, p. 149). The Southerners kept up the fire until the Yankees realized it was no use. In commenting on this slaughter, Georgian General Evander Law said he could see "the terrible havoc made in the ranks of the assaulting column" (Ferguson, p. 149). In front of Colquitt, a southern reporter wrote, "Never have I seen as many dead in one place" (Ferguson, p. 149). He noted that the Yankees came up to the butchery "splendidly, and our men liked shooting them so well, that they say as long as they can get ammunition and something to eat, they will stand in the breast works and let Grant bring up the whole Yankee nation." General Law later wrote, "It was not war. It was murder" (Zwemer, p. 49).

Some Southerners, though, did feel sympathy for the imperiled Yankees. A Mississippian in Mahone's Division wrote in his diary, "We could do nothing. It is as if there is an impassable gulf between us. We mowed them down in good number. We felt sorry for them and wished they had sense enough to stay at home" (Rhea, p. 369).

That afternoon, soldiers on both sides could hear the cries of the wounded, piled high in front of the Confederate works. For some, the heart-rending sound became too much. Lieutenant Joe D. O'Hern of the 2nd Florida finally could stand it no more and began gathering canteens. "What are you going to do, Joe?" a companion asked. "I'm going to get some water for the boys," he replied. "Man, you can't do it," his friend warned. "A rat couldn't pass over that field unhurt." Undaunted, O'Hern slung the canteens over his shoulder and started running across an open space towards a small stream. "For the first one hundred yards, the balls from the Federals fell so thickly around him that it seemed he must fall every second," a witness recalled. Then the Northerners sensed the purpose of O'Hern's mission and stopped shooting. Reaching the water, O'Hern filled the canteens and started back across the field. As he neared the Confederate lines, the Federals gave him a cheer. "Good will, however, was short lived and the combatants returned to killing with a vengeance" (Rhea, p. 368).

Another such instance was related by a Mississippi surgeon. "I am thankful we have all escaped. The ground out there is nearly covered with their dead and wounded, and it is really distressing to hear those poor fellows out there crying for water and help." A wail rose from the battlefield "that chilled our blood and caused our hearts to stand still," LeGrand James Wilson, 42nd Mississippi surgeon, later wrote. Three soldiers insisted on going into no man's land to rescue a sufferer. While they slipped over the entrenchments, Wilson and Captain Nelson went along the line, warning soldiers not to shoot. After an anxious interval, the three men returned and lifted a wounded Federal over the works. Severely injured and parched from thirst, he thanked them for saving his life. "After supplying his wants," Wilson recollected, "I had him carried to the hospital, dressed his wounds and the next morning sent him into Richmond to the City Hospital" (Rhea, p. 394).

After three days, General Grant finally offered a flag of truce so as to gather his wounded. Many of the poor Northern soldiers had already experienced a torturous death. I asked a friend, Lieutenant Colonel William W. "Scurvy" Patton (VMI Class of 1952) why Grant was so callous in waiting three days to rescue his wounded. Lieutenant Colonel Patton put it quite succinctly, "He was just too damned proud to admit he had lost the battle." In the nineteenth century, a flag of truce requesting to retrieve your wounded was a sign of defeat.

One soldier who fought at Cold Harbor and other battles with the Flanders brothers would become their brother-in-law. Robert Bird Thompson, a cousin of William A. Flanders, was from the same part of Emanuel County as John R., Ches, and Joe. He was a well-known sharpshooter and had been credited with zapping several Yankee officers before his trigger finger had been shot off. In addition, while scouting, Thompson had single-handedly captured seven Union soldiers. He had pulled this off by slipping up on them and threatening the first one that got out of line. John C. Coleman, a fellow soldier in Company H, said that Thompson was the best all-around soldier he had ever seen.

At the Battle of Cold Harbor, after Grant's troops were repulsed, Thompson was sleeping in his trench. His rifle was at his side and he was using a block of wood for a pillow. The Yankees were periodically shelling the Confederate lines, and Thompson suddenly heard a shell hit about four feet from his head. The shell did not explode but he could hear the fuse burning inside the deadly weapon. He knew if he got up and ran it would be certain death, so he just lay there for several tense seconds. Finally, after what seemed like an eternity, the shell sputtered out. Upon examining the bomb, Thompson discovered that it had hit in the mud and the fuse had been extinguished by water. The much-despised rain did have its advantages.

The members of the Thompson family were famed as consummate horsemen, a family tradition that endures. After the war, Bird's brother Allen, also a Confederate veteran, had three of his horses stolen. This could not be allowed to stand, so Allen, Bird, and another brother went after the thieves. After about three days, the brothers returned with the horses. Knowing that the Thompsons were skilled horsemen, trackers, and marksmen, everyone clamored to know what had happened, but no one could find out. Years later, after his brothers had died, Allen Thompson was again quizzed about the incident. All he would say was that "there's plenty of fish bait in Brier Creek."

After the war, Robert Bird Thompson married Elizabeth Hall, the widowed sister of John R., Ches, and Joe Flanders. Her first husband, Tom Hall, had died of nephritis in a Richmond, Virginia, hospital on 4 September 1864. He had been a second corporal in Company H, 48th Georgia. Richard Bird and Elizabeth Thompson had ten children.

CHAPTER

Eleven

RIDDLE SHOP
John R. Returns to Swainsboro on a Stretcher

After his defeat at the Battle of Cold Harbor on 3 June 1864, General Grant realized that his troops could not prevail in a head-on attack. He was also beginning to understand that, as Union General George Meade had written in a letter to his wife, "Lee and his Army of Northern Virginia are not [General Braxton] Bragg and the Army of Tennessee."

Frank Flanders and Sarah Underwood standing by the cot that carried the wounded John R. Flanders home from Virginia. The original springs are still in place. Also notice that the cot folds up for storage. Frank and Sarah are standing in front of one of the oldest homes in Emanuel County. Sarah saved the building from destruction by having it moved to her property and restored.

Grant's assault on the morning of 3 June had cost him seven thousand casualties in half an hour. From 3-12 June there was constant sniping on both sides of the line. Grant, however, was a very determined man. He still wanted to get Lee in the open. But Marsh Robert – as many a Confederate soldier called their beloved General Lee, using the southern diminutive term for "master" – would not cooperate. Grant finally moved to disengage from Cold Harbor and on 12 June the Northern army marched south to cross the James River. Grant used General Gouverneur Warren's Corps as a shield to protect its flanks.

John R. Flanders woke up on the morning of 13 June with no enemy to face. Grant had adroitly moved his huge army. No one knew what the Union general had in mind. Georgian Robert Stiles writes:

> "When we woke on the morning of the 13th and found no enemy on our front, we realized that a new element had entered into this move – the element of uncertainty. Even Marsh Robert, who knew everything knowable, did not appear to know what his old enemy proposed to do or where he would be most likely to find him" (Ferguson, p. 249).

That day, John R. and the rest of Company H of the 48th Georgia moved across the Chickohominy River trying to find the Yankee Army. Late that afternoon, the 48th ran into a much larger force. The fight at Riddle Shop was a little-known engagement between Union troops belonging to Chapman's Brigade of Wilson's Cavalry and the 48th Georgia, plus other elements of Confederate General A.P. Hill's Corps. Chapman had traversed White Oak Swamp in an effort to block the Confederates from flanking the Union Army. The Federal cavalry threw up earthworks using their infantry and dismounted cavalry. The enemy was equipped with the new repeating rifles, which made it even more difficult for John R. and the men of the 48th to overcome a fixed position. The Confederates attacked and, after a sharp engagement, withdrew. During the night, the Yankees retreated across the James River and became Grant's rear guard.

Even though they did not overrun the Yankees, the 48th Georgia felt that they had bested their opponent. The 48th lost only four killed and thirteen wounded. One of the thirteen, however, was John R. Sarah Underwood, his granddaughter, remembers that when she was a child John R. showed her where he was shot in the calf. This had to have been one of his most serious wounds. I surmise this because he was not sent to a hospital in Richmond with the idea of returning to the front in a few months. Instead, he was put on a cot and shipped home. It took John R. about two weeks to reach Swainsboro. He was first transported by train from Virginia to Midville, Georgia, then by wagon to Swainsboro.

The cot on which John R. was carried survives in good shape and is in Sarah's possession. It was made with legs that folded under so that it could be easily stored. After the war, family members used it as a bed. On 30 April 1909, Emma Black Flanders, John R.'s wife, told her husband that she was not feeling well. She lay down on the cot and John R. went for the doctor. When they returned, Emma was dead. She was seventy years old.

Some forty-five years earlier, Emma had begun the long process of nursing her husband back to health. John R. returned home from the war around 1 July 1864, to an Emanuel County that was experiencing very difficult times. The War Between the States had created tremendous economic dislocation as well as personal hardship.

John R. had lost his brother, Richard Bird, who died at home on 11 November 1863. His brother Jessie was also dead, of wounds sustained at the battle of Second Manassas. John R. would lose a third brother, William Jordan, in April 1865. Of John R.'s four sisters, three had lost or would lose their husbands. Jemina lost John Woods. Frances Delilah lost Warren Kea on 2 August 1862. 4 September 1864, would see Martha lose Tom Hall to nephritis in a Richmond hospital.

During the summer of 1864, Union General William Tecumseh Sherman's army besieged and burned Atlanta and began its infamous trek to Savannah. Swainsboro, Georgia, lay directly in its path.

CHAPTER

Twelve

EMANUEL FACES SHERMAN'S ARMY

Rarely in the annals of western warfare has a government waged such total war on what it maintained were its own citizens. Wanton destruction and the senseless burning of homes and crops caused widespread hardship on the civilian population. Women and children were not spared as the Federal government exacted meaningless revenge on the southern people. This is particularly tragic when you see that most of the destruction served no military purpose.

The Macon *Telegraph* did not mince words in its condemnation of General George Stoneman's raids:

> "Perhaps there never was a more consummate band of plundering thieves...the officers themselves...joined in...pillage. They entered private homes and stripped ladies...of rings and pins; broke open drawers and trunks and stole silver and plate of every description. In many instances house girls were ravished...no savage dog ever committed more fiendish brutalities" (Bryan, p. 160).

Like most of Georgia, the people of Emanuel County were yeoman farmers and the war had made the production of food very difficult. One can only imagine what it must have been like to have twenty-five thousand Yankee troops traipse through such a small county.

Nancy Dekle Brown, a distant cousin, was typical of the many Emanuel County women who had to face the Yankees alone. She lived near Canoochee, about fifteen miles north of Swainsboro. Nancy had lost four young children to illness, her husband and son were off serving the Confederacy, and she was doing her best to maintain some semblance of normalcy for those at home. Mrs. Brown recounted that on the night of 29 November 1864, she stood in her house with her young children watching "the sky aglow with the reflection of neighboring homes being destroyed by fire and...with Yankee campfires, thousands of them." The next day, Nancy was leading the family horse into the woods when "the reins were jerked away and I looked into the face of a giant man in a blue uniform. He said, 'Hell, you ain't got no need of him!' And he rode off with the only animal the Yankees had not taken."

The Yankees took every bit of food the little family possessed and they killed most of what stock they did not take. Nancy reported going to bed hungry that night and many nights thereafter. There was no food in the house for her or her children. A few days later, Nancy's sixteen-year-old son Billy returned from the Battle of Atlanta, having followed the Yankees to Canoochee by hiding during the day and traveling at night. A half-eaten chicken on a fence post saved him from starvation – he said that even though he had had to brush away the maggots, that chicken saved his life. Billy later fulfilled his promise to God by becoming Reverend Billy Brown (Rogers, p. 42).

Cousin Sarah Underwood tells a story of her grandmother, Sarah Brinson Coleman, being shown some small bit of Yankee kindness. In 1864, Sarah Brinson was twenty years old and served as the postmistress of Canoochee. Ever since she was a little girl, Sarah had been in love with John Emmett Coleman. She and John Emmett were planning to get married and, in anticipation, John Emmett had built a log cabin that would be their home.

John Emmett had joined the 5th Georgia Calvary and was with them as they attempted to delay Sherman on his march through Georgia. The Confederate calvary was so outnumbered that they could not engage the enemy, but merely harass them. Just a few minutes before the Union cavalry rode into Canoochee, John Emmett arrived at the post office and warned Sarah of their presence. She rushed to her parents' farm, only to find it being trashed by the Union cavalrymen. Their animals were being loaded into wagons and what was not being loaded was being shot. One of the Yankees had even snatched the butter from the butter dish. Another intruder had stuck his bayonet in the family clock in an effort to disable the works (Sarah Underwood still has this clock). Sarah Brinson somehow remembered that her father, who had died in 1861, had been a Mason and she gave the Masonic distress signal. It was recognized by a young lieutenant, who immediately stopped the vandalism. He ordered all of the Brinsons' personal possessions returned and posted a guard to back up his command. He had dispatched another group of soldiers to burn the family barn and mill and he ordered this stopped, also – but the enlisted men, in

72

an act of defiance, left the mill running, which ground out the millstone. They also drained the mill pond. Before they could torch the barn, a free black man inside, who worked for the Brinsons, fired at them. Tragically, he was killed and the barn burned around him.

Sherman's plundering troops headed on to Savannah, with the Confederate cavalry – and John Emmett – still nipping at their heels. Savannah surrendered rather than risk being razed, and Sherman presented it to President Abraham Lincoln as a Christmas gift. After the Yankees finally abandoned the city, word got to John Emmett's mother that her son was there in the hospital and very ill. She hitched up a horse and drove the family wagon ninety miles over dirt roads to find him. When she arrived, hospital officials told her that John Emmett was near death and that she should return home, obtain a coffin and a burial suit and, by that time, he would be dead. Mrs. Coleman did as she was told and either made then, or already had made, an attractive linen suit for John Emmett. She also asked the distraught Sarah Brinson to accompany her back to Savannah. The long journey must have been mighty grim for the two women. One was mourning the loss of a son and the other of her first and only love. When Sarah and Mrs. Coleman arrived, they found, to their joy and surprise, John Emmett much improved, but still very weak. They promptly retraced their steps to Canoochee with John Emmett lying in the wagon.

The family needed Sarah to nurse John Emmett back to health. So, in order to make things proper, the couple was married and moved into the log cabin that John Emmett had built. On the day of their wedding, he wore the suit that his mother had originally brought to bury him in. Years later, after John Emmett died, two of his children were arguing over who would get the treasured pair of trousers, which was all that was left of the suit. Sarah Brinson Coleman took the pants, tore them in two, and gave half to each sibling. Sarah Underwood now has those pants, which are back in one piece.

Sarah Underwood grew up in what was John Emmett Coleman's home, which is still in good shape. Behind her home is a thick swampy wood. A path on which Sarah and her siblings used to walk to school traverses the swamp. In the middle of the wetland is an island with no vegetation and it was there that the Colemans took some of their cattle, hogs, and horses to wait out the Yankees. With this seed stock the family replenished their herd.

One clever Emanuel County resident, eight-year-old William Durden, also a distant cousin, convinced the Yankees that he was suffering from

William Durden faking scarlet fever. Drawing by Kyle James.

scarlet fever. They left him alone, thereby saving the family treasures, stuffed in the mattress on which he lay (Rogers, p. 42).

Frank Flanders tells a story that involved his sister Luck Flanders Gambrell's Cunningham Plantation:

"At the Cunningham Plantation, now owned and restored by my sister, located in Jefferson and Emanuel Counties, a wounded Yankee soldier crawled on the porch at the big house one night. He would have been of the 20th Army Corps [Sherman's]. No one was there but women and children. He begged them to open the door. Afraid of a trick, they refused. He died on the porch that night. They buried him and, after the war, notified his mother in New Jersey. They were able to obtain her address from a letter the soldier had on his person. The soldier's mother came to Wadley on the train and exhumed his remains for burial in New Jersey" (Flanders).

The following is a paper written by Ella Mae Garrett Curry on Sherman's march through Emanuel County. It describes Mrs. Curry's grandmother, Kitsie Hall Flanders. She was the wife of Bill Flanders, a grandfather of Frank Flanders and a member of Company H. Kitsie was a sister to Tom Hall – who was married to Martha Flanders, John R.'s sister – and to Winnie Hall, who was married to Jordan Flanders. He was a brother of John R., and died in the war. Kitsie was also a sister to Sally, who married Joe Flanders.

SHERMAN'S MARCH THROUGH EMANUEL COUNTY, GEORGIA
By Ella Mae Garrett Curry

"My great-grandfather, William Arnold Flanders, lived in the northwestern part of Emanuel County, Georgia. He was serving in the Army of Virginia in 1865 when Sherman captured Atlanta and began his march to Savannah. My great-grandmother, Kitsie Hall Flanders, lived in the home with four small children – John, Jim, Jane, and Mary. The youngest, Mary, was my grandmother. John, the oldest, remembered about the 'Yankees' coming through. This is the story he told.

"Great-Grandmother had heard that the Yankees were coming through the section of the state where her family lived. She tried to prepare so they would have food during the time the army was passing through. She and a lady friend butchered a hog she had in a pen. They hid the meat. She buried what money she had and hid the horses in the woods. She pinned land deeds and other important papers inside her clothes to save them.

"She and the friend were on their way to the grist mill with sacks of corn to have meal made for bread when they saw dust rising and the soldiers coming (the mill was near where Blundale is now). They hurried back to be with the children.

"The army was three days passing through. They killed every hog, cow, and chicken on the place except one hen. Uncle John had a little white hen that an aunt had given him. He begged the soldiers not to kill his hen. The officer said, 'Let that boy's chicken alone.' So they had one chicken left.

"Inside the house, the soldier ripped open mattresses and ransacked everything looking for money and legal papers, which they didn't find.

"Grandmother Kitsie had knitted socks and made butter to send to her soldier husband. The soldiers put on the socks and ate the butter. They ate or destroyed all the food she had in the house. Uncle John said, 'All we had to eat was one hoe-cake of cornbread for three days.' That was for two adults and four children.

"During the time the soldiers were passing through, some camped at Bell's Pond near Kite and some at Coleman's Lake and McKinney's Pond.

"One Federal soldier got sick. His brothers asked Grandmother Kitsie to care for him after they left. She put him to bed and cared for him until he died.

"Her father-in-law was too old to go to the army. He helped her and the children. One day when he was coming to see about them, he found another sick Union soldier in an old house in the woods. He brought him to Grandmother's. She cared for him until he died. She and her father-in-law buried both soldiers in the field on their plantation (this is the present Talmadge Peebles Place).

"After the war was over, the brothers of the first soldier that died came back and exhumed his body and took it back to their home to bury it. They were very nice to her and regretted what they were forced to do to the South. The second soldier that died is still buried somewhere in that field.

"After the war, they were looking for Great-Grandfather to come home. The children called him 'Pap'. Uncle Jim liked to play jokes. He would call his mother and say, 'Yonder comes Pap.' He did this so often until she stopped listening to him. When he did come, he surprised her (walked right in the house before she knew he was there).

"He came back to a devastated farm with nothing much to work with, but he had his home and family, which grew from four to ten children. They all grew up in the same house on the same farm. Grandmother Kitsie died before he did. 'Grandpa Bill' lived to a ripe old age."

John R. was lying in bed when the Yankees approached Emanuel. There were a few old men, young boys, and wounded Confederate soldiers who joined together in a band to give some semblance of resistance. Sarah Underwood told me that the family story was that John R. joined these brave fellows (probably led by John Clifton of the Georgia Militia) and became involved in a firefight. John R.'s pension application reports that he was wounded a fifth time in this engagement. He was captured and taken as a prisoner to Savannah, transported to Hilton Head Island, and then taken by boat to Point Lookout Maryland Prison Camp.

Meanwhile, in Virginia, after John R.'s medical evacuation, Ches Flanders led Company H of the 48th, part of Mahone's Division, to Petersburg. The most famous action at the siege of Petersburg was the fight at the crater. When it blew and the Yankees poured through, Mahone's Division was brought forward to plug the gap.

After Petersburg, Ches accompanied General Lee on his long fighting retreat to Appomattox and was present when the Army of Northern Virginia surrendered. Ches had been promoted to major and was to command the 48th Georgia. The Confederate Congress, however, did not have time to act on this before the end of the war.

The 48th Georgia was typical of many hard-fighting Confederate companies. My friend and cousin, Jim Flanders, compiled the following figures, which show the dedication and sacrifice of Company H:

Men served	129
Died from disease	35
Killed in action	24
Resigned due to disability	8
Discharged	4
Surrendered	18
Went AWOL	2
POW at Point Lookout	11
POW at Elmira, NY	1
POW at Old Capital	2
POW at Libby	1

Acts of depravity visited on Georgia's citizenry caused no small amount of bitterness. My friend, Rives Hardy, lives in Callao, Virginia. His great-grandfather, Charles Betts Hardy, was a second lieutenant in the 9th Virginia Cavalry. Lieutenant Hardy wrote a poem that expressed the sentiments of many southerners:

"O, I'm a Good Old Rebel"*
by Charles Betts Hardy

O, I'm a good old rebel, now, that's just what I am,
For this "Fair Land of Freedom" I do not care a damn;
I'm glad I fit against it, I only wish we'd won;
And I don't want no pardon for anything I've done.

THE TRAIL OF JOHN R. FLANDERS

I hates the Constitution, this Great Republic, too,
I hates the Freedman's Buro, in uniforms of blue;
I hates the nasty eagle, with all his brags and fuss,
The lyin', thievin' Yankees, I hates them wuss and wuss.

I hates the Yankee nation and everything they do,
I hates the Declaration of Independence, too;
I hates the glorious Union – 'tis dripping with our blood –
I hates their striped banner, I fit it all I could.

I followed old Mas' Robert for four year, near about,
Got wounded in three places and starved at Pint Lookout;
I cotch the moomatism a campin' in the snow,
But I killed a chance o' Yankees; I'd like to kill some mo'.

Three hundred thousand Yankees is stiff in Southern dust;
We got three hundred thousand before they conquered us;
They died of Southern fever and Southern steel and shot,
I wish they was three million instead of what we got.

I can't take up my musket and fight 'em now no more,
But I ain't a going to love 'em, now that is sarten sure;
And I don't want no pardon for what I was and am,
I won't be reconstructed and I don't give a damn.

*For those readers who cannot speak proper English (southern-style), I am defining the following words in Mr. Hardy's poem:

Fit=fight
Buro=bureau
Brags=conceited
Wuss=worse
Mas=marsh/master
Pint=point
Cotch=caught
Moomatism=rheumatism
Chance=crops sufficient for one year
Sarten=certain

CHAPTER

Thirteen

POINT LOOKOUT

Lest you think otherwise, Union prison camps were every bit as horrendous as Southern camps, and Point Lookout Prison was no exception. In fact, the percentage of southerners who died in Federal prison camps was higher than the percentage of Yankees who died in Confederate prisons.

Point Lookout is situated on the southern tip of coastal Maryland, where the Potomac River meets the Chesapeake Bay. It is a sandy place, cold in winter and hot in summer. In the warm months, it is infested with mosquitoes.

Point Lookout is located in Saint Mary's County, which during the War Between the States was not in sympathy with the Union cause. In Maryland, members of the state legislature who sided with the South had been thrown in prison without trial. At Point Lookout Prison, some two hundred fifty other civilians had also been locked up for southern sympathies.

Secretary of War Edwin Stanton, who was known to hate southerners with a passion, denied Confederate prisoners proper food and shelter as a way to get at the South. An example of Stanton's policies was that Camp Commandant William Hoffman recommended wooden barracks but, instead, Stanton ordered that sibley tents be used. Sibley tents were bell shaped and had a hole at the top (Douglas, p. 28). Twelve men slept in each sibley tent with their feet towards the center. Each man tried to prevent lice and fleas, but the close quarters made this almost impossible. These tents, of course, gave the prisoners very little protection against cold winters. Elmira, New York, on the shores of Lake Erie, would see the temperature drop to 40 degrees below zero. It had the highest percentage of death rates in the entire war. Point Lookout, though, was close behind. This camp saw more than four thousand Confederates die from malnutrition, scurvy, dysentery, and a host of other illnesses (Bietzel, p. 40).

From the middle of 1863 until the end of the war, Point Lookout swelled to more than twenty thousand prisoners. The northern Provost Marshall was said to have made more than one million dollars skimming food money from the unfortunate prisoners. On Christmas Day 1864, a Confederate prisoner wrote, "I only got a piece of bread and a cup of coffee for breakfast and a small slice of meat and a cup of soup and five crackers for dinner and supper, I had none" (Bietzel).

One very unfortunate aspect of the prison was the fact that discipline had been greatly eroded by the use of former slaves as guards. These men had not been given proper training and were often brutal in their treatment of prisoners. There were numerous reports of guards firing at random into groups of prisoners. When word arrived of the assassination of President Lincoln, the guards fired all night, killing fourteen men and wounding twenty-eight.

It was into this hellhole that John R. Flanders came in November 1864. After having been wounded five times and in poor physical condition, it is amazing that John R. survived. Upon his arrival, his clothes were taken from him and thrown into the bay. He was then given some used clothing and one blanket, and assigned to the sibley tent that was to be his quarters for the next seven months.

The medical situation was also quite desperate. One Confederate captive, a doctor who worked in the camp hospital, chronicles:

> "Present signs prognosticate nothing but unrelenting war. It is no longer a war for the union, but one of conquest and revenge. My opinion of the Yankee character has always been anything else than exalted. But I've seen so much meanness among them since my capture, that I wish I could never see one again… indeed, had it not been for my profession, which entitles me to the position which I occupy, I believe that I should not be numbered with the living, for I could never stand the hardships to which the prisoners of camp are exposed. Many of the prisoners die of scurvy, a most horrible disease. I believe Dr. Thompson, U.S. surgeon in charge of camp, does all in his power to alleviate their sufferings, but he is furnished with neither proper diet nor a sufficiency of medicine to correct the malady" (Bietzel, p. 41).

Chances of survival were lessened even further when one entered Point Lookout while wounded. One Emanuel Countian, David Douglas, was captured at Gettysburg, nursing a gunshot wound. (Because soldiers from the same unit were grouped together, it is very likely that David and John R. lived in the same tent.) David's wound got progressively worse, and on 12 January 1864 he was admitted to the camp hospital. Even though he had his leg treated, he was given little hope. David finally breathed his last on 10 March 1864. His cause of death was listed as "gun shot fracture of the right leg" (Douglas, p. 29). The tragedy of his and other deaths at Point Lookout was that, had the prisoners been given better care, they very well may have survived (Douglas, p. 29).

John R. was in prison at Point Lookout until June 1865, even though General Lee had surrendered in April. This delay can probably be attributed either to the sluggish pace at which governments operate or the fact that, in his poor physical condition, John R. could not make the difficult trip home. On the day of his release, John R. was required to take an oath to the Yankee government. That must have been a bitter pill.

CHAPTER

Fourteen

JOHN R. RETURNS HOME

It is not recorded how John R. Flanders made his way back to Swainsboro, Georgia, from Virginia, but I can make an educated guess based on how other Georgia prisoners got home.
He walked.

In his classic book *Longpondium,* Sid Johnson describes how his grandfather, Peter Johnson, of the Georgia Brigade, returned home to Long Pond, Montgomery County, Georgia. Peter was released from Point Lookout 6 June 1865, and, after taking the Federal Loyalty oath, walked outside of the prison and met other friends from Montgomery County. Joe McAllister was reported to have said, "C'mon, Peter, we've been waiting for you. Let's see if these old shoes'll get us to Long Pond" (Johnson, p. 119).

Frank Flanders' great-grandfather, John C. Coleman, also walked. After General Robert E. Lee's surrender, John was transported from Elmira, New York, to Point Lookout, Maryland, and released, to begin his long trek with a friend. Family lore has it that while he and his friend were walking, tired and fatigued, John fell into an open well. After trudging on for a few minutes, his friend realized John was not behind him and he started hollering for him. A voice finally replied, "I'm down here, you son-of-a-bitch, come get me out!" John C. went on to become one of Emanuel County's most prosperous citizens. He died owning thirty-two thousand acres in Jefferson and Emanuel counties.

My cousin Billy Wilson had a great-great-grandfather, T.J. Coursey, who was a member of the 61st Georgia, part of the Georgia Brigade. T.J. was captured on Lee's retreat from Petersburg to Appomattox and sent to one of the infamous New York state prison camps. During this process, camp officials began spelling Coursey's name "Causey." T.J. became a victim of the bureaucratic shuffle.

John C. Coleman

T.J.'s parents already had lost two of their four sons to the war. Both had died from disease while convalescing at home. They had gotten word that T.J. was in prison but no details had been forthcoming. After the war's conclusion, they were anxious to hear of T.J.'s whereabouts but, again, no word came. After about a year, the elder Courseys concluded that T.J. had died either in prison or on the way home. They held their third funeral service for a departed son. Some time passed, and one Sunday afternoon, after worshipping at Higgston Methodist Church, the family was eating Sunday dinner under the shade of some big oak trees. Suddenly, one of the children spotted a gaunt man walking up the dirt road with a small pack under his arm. His clothes were in rags. As the man got closer someone commented that he sure did look like T.J. Realizing that it was, the entire family rushed to greet their long lost loved one. T.J. had finally returned.

T.J. never talked about what had happened to him after his release from prison. He said only that he had been very sick and had almost died.

T.J. returns. Drawing by Kyle James.

To the family his return was, indeed, a miracle.

Like John R., Reverend Malachi Bowden of Greenville, Georgia, was paroled from Point Lookout, June 1864. The Yankees carried him by boat to Richmond, Virginia, and dropped him and his companions at the dock. From there they walked to Georgia, first to Washington, Georgia, about fifty miles west of Augusta, then to Covington, then by way of Atlanta to Grantville, and finally to Greenville. Bowden recapped his homecoming:

> "I shall never forget when I first came upon my father. He was in the field at work, directing a number of hands. Among them was a poor widow woman, who was struggling to make bread for her family. Seeing who it was, father ran to meet me, and caught me up in his arms. As the poor woman witnessed this, she screamed in a fit of hysterics, 'Where is my boy! Oh, where is my boy!' He had been killed in one of the fights about Richmond" (Bietzell, p. 99).

There is a family story about William Arnold Flanders, who readers have met before. William was in Company H, 48th Georgia, and is the great-grandfather of former U.S. Senator Gambrell's wife, Luck, as well as her brother, Frank Flanders. William had seen the war's most intense fighting, having served – with distinction – as a scout for General Lee. William was also involved in the previously mentioned incident in which, after the Battle of Gettysburg, he bludgeoned a Yankee soldier to death.

William had a farm near Kite, Georgia, and was blessed with several children. In November 1864, the Yankees came through Kite and took every morsel of food the Flanders family possessed. This left his wife, Kitsie

Hall Flanders, and their children in danger of starvation (see Chapter 12). Word of their plight reached William in Virginia. He immediately made a request to his commanding officer, Captain Ches Flanders, for leave. His application was granted and William struck out for Emanuel County. It was the dead of winter and he walked most of the way, riding the rails when he could. He was emaciated and his clothes were in tatters. When William saw the outline of his house, he picked up the pace. About that time his son, John, was looking out of the window (you remember John, the boy who saved his chicken from the Yankees). It was a cold January morning and John did not expect to see a solitary figure walking toward his house. He watched as the unexpected visitor came closer and closer. Suddenly, John was filled with excitement. He ran into the kitchen, shouting to his mother, "Mama, Mama, yonder comes Pap!" Because John had previously played tricks on his mother, Kitsie did not believe him. But just then the back door opened and in walked their husband and father. The family

John R. and Emma Black Flanders in front of their home. L to R – Samuel Joshua Flanders, Vinnie Flanders Curl, John R. Flanders, Jr., Emma Black Flanders, and Joseph. Eugene Flanders (father of Sarah Underwood).

John R. Flanders
2 Timothy 4:7 "I have fought the good fight, I have finished the race,
I have kept the faith."

circle remained unbroken. Unfortunately, John R. lost his brother on his own journey home. William Jordan Flanders died of pneumonia in April 1865 while walking from Bentonville, North Carolina.

John R.'s trip home had to have been similar to these men's and just as taxing.

Large groups of Confederate soldiers were making their way home. The civilian population, though sympathetic to their soldiers' plight, had very little food to share. My sense is that John R. and his companions lived off the land. In June, they could have picked berries and plums, but I would guess that the trip took a minimum of two months, possibly four.

I imagine that John R.'s homecoming was similar to that of Reverend Bowden. His wife Emma must have been overjoyed to see him. No more

86

Emma Black Flanders

Proverbs 31:10-15a, 16b, 20-21, 23, 25-30 "A good wife who can find? She is far more precious than jewels. The heart of her husband trusts in her, and he will have no lack of gain. She does him good, and not harm, all the days of her life. She seeks wool and flax, and works with willing hands. She is like the ships of the merchant, she brings her food from afar. She rises while it is yet night and provides food for her household...with the fruit of her hands she plants a vineyard. She opens her hand to the poor, and reaches out her hands to the needy. She is not afraid of snow for her household, for all her household are clothed in scarlet. Her husband is known in the gates, when he sits among the elders of the land. Strength and dignity are her clothing, and she laughs at the time to come. She opens her mouth with wisdom, and the teaching of kindness is on her tongue. She looks well to the ways of her household, and does not eat the bread of idleness. Her children rise up and call her blessed; her husband also, and he praises her; 'Many women have done excellently, but you surpass them all.' Charm is deceitful, and beauty is vain, but a woman who fears the Lord is to be praised."

would she watch John R. leave and wonder whether or not he would come back alive. Ches and Joe had already returned and were making new lives for themselves. But the family had paid a heavy price. They had lost three brothers and three brothers-in-law.

Southerners, however, had to deal with not only economic travails but also the humiliation of Reconstruction. Northern soldiers were not only the government, they were also the law. One family story deals with John R.'s cousins, who obtained a bit of revenge.

After the war, money was almost non-existent and southerners were looking for any means possible to obtain funds. The two Emanuel County brothers, both Confederate veterans, decided to go into the moonshine business to maximize the slim profits obtained from corn crops. One night, the brothers were operating their still when three Yankee soldiers found them and attempted to make an arrest. Their elderly father, who was sitting at the base of a tree, shot and killed the intruders. In an attempt to conceal the bodies, the brothers buried the corpses and set the woods on fire – a common practice at the time to encourage the growth of wiregrass and yellow pine. Later, telling the story to confidants, the father said, "I

OBO FOREST-BLADE, SWAINSBORO, GEORGIA.

OFFICIAL RETURNS OF THE DEMOCRATIC PRIMARY.

	49th District	50th District	53rd District	57th District	58th District	59th District	395th N. District	395th A. District	1206th District	1833rd District	1429th District	1462nd District	1502nd District	1560th District	TOTALS	MAJORITY
ORDINARY—																
JNO. R. FLANDERS	68	44	430	111	109	90	75	155	65	79	118	122	37	294	1797	1018
JNO. J. MOORE	4	69	212	39	103	21	70	26	37	3	19	32	109	35	779	
CLERK SUPERIOR COURT—																
H. G. JOHNSON	70	113	646	149	215	107	148	183	102	82	137	154	141	328	2575	2575
SHERIFF—																
RUFUS W. COURSEY	47	52	348	32	127	67	55	102	29	32	64	98	78	109	1235	421
JOHN D. KIGHT	1	36	21	11	36	25	67	51	9	31	51	20	19	154	526	
JAMES M. MOORE	23	24	274	107	52	19	24	30	68	15	21	38	54	65	814	
TREASURER—																
JAMES R. BROWN	58	54	242	82	101	71	66	42	29	59	118	28	40	273	1263	
JNO. T. SMITH	13	55	399	68	113	40	80	138	71	23	16	124	108	66	1298	35
TAX COLLECTOR—																
W. C. KEA	25	10	323	85	26	16	17	94	31	34	32	51	13	139	896	
STEELY MOORE	46	103	315	64	190	94	128	86	71	46	103	100	138	181	1660	764
TAX RECEIVER—																
J. W. EDENFIELD		18	86	24	134	10	28	9	1	1	7	2	43	12	375	
JNO. A. MOXLEY	5	7	105	20	3	1	5	15	71	1	7	42	44	8	304	
Wm. D. STEPHENS	63	25	266	49	66	42	65	71	23	65	109	48	56	234	1182	466
JOHN W. THOMPSON	2	60	191	57	13	58	48	86	6	15	11	62	32	75	716	
SOLICITOR CITY COURT—																
A. S. BRADLEY	48	65	370	91	91	44	57	73	37	65	75	71	75	223	1385	208
THOS. N. BROWN	23	48	265	58	124	67	91	106	63	15	62	83	69	103	1177	
SURVEYOR—																
E. WARREN	70	114	632	145	212	100	138	18	1	102	73	137	150	145	315	2514	2514
RONER—																
H. DURDEN	61	114	614	141	212	111	138	18	1	102	81	136	145	123	327	2486	248

Sarah Underwood and Wesley Budd standing beside the memorial to John R. and Nancy Sumner Flanders, parents of John R. Flanders, Jr.

do believe that if I hadn't been sitting there the boys would have let those Yankees take them in." The Yanks' bodies were never discovered.

John R. and Emma, like so many young southern families, started with literally nothing. John R. took up farming in the Gary community, about five miles south of Swainsboro. On 17 August 1866, they had their first child, William Ridgeway (Ridge), who would die at age twenty-five. Their marriage was also blessed with Richard Alexander, Zannie (mother of Otis Rountree, my grandfather), Samuel Joshua, Lavinia (Vinnie), and Joseph Eugene (father of Sarah Underwood).

Due to hard times and the war, there were numerous orphans. Both John R. and Ches kept orphans and homeless adults in their home. John R. and Emma housed fourteen orphans over a period of years.

John R. was known as a man of deep faith. A few years after the war, the family came home from church and discovered that their home had burned and all of their belongings destroyed. Rather than lament how unfortunate they were, John R. had the entire family drop to their knees and thank God that no one had been hurt. I imagine that what John R.

89

had witnessed during the war helped put things in proper perspective. A Sunday school class at Swainsboro First United Methodist Church was named for John R. and is still active. John R., as well as Ches, was a man who had a powerful influence for good.

Emma Black Flanders was a redhead with a reputation of being a no-nonsense, get-things-done individual. When Arlis Rountree (Otis' brother) was young, he lived with his grandparents so that he could attend the Swainsboro schools. One day, Otis and their first cousin, Ivy Rountree (father of Bill Rountree) were visiting the Flanders near dinnertime. Food had to be cooked from scratch for almost every meal, a constant chore. Because Emma had to go help a sick friend, she asked Arlis to fix the rice. Along with instructions, Emma gave Arlis a rather large pot. She said that she would return shortly to finish the mid-day meal. Arlis, Otis, and Ivy filled the pot to the brim with rice and some water and started cooking. The contents, of course, began to swell, and when Emma returned, every container in the house was full of rice.

Emma died 30 April 1904. Her obituary stated, "The writer will always remember the hospitality of her home on many occasions. It was there that we learned to appreciate her real warmth and her unbounded kindness and love" (Anonymous, 1909).

As well as farming, John R. served the county as tax receiver. He was also the tax equalizer and jury reviser. In 1907, John R. was overwhelmingly elected Emanuel County Ordinary, a position similar to today's probate judge. He served two terms.

John R. died 2 June 1915. His obituary included, "He was a kind husband, a loving father, a true brother, a Christian gentleman, a patriot of high order, a man who stood for the best things in religious and personal life, having a heart of charity toward all mankind" (Anonymous, 1915).

In announcing his death, a front page article in the Swainsboro *Forest Blade* eulogized,

"His life remains an open book, a model for emulation. He was a most consistent man in all things, his life work was noble, dutiful, earnest and Christian-like ... the *Forest Blade* drops a tear here and mourns with the bereaved" (Anonymous, 1915).

D.Q. MORRISON AND MARY WILKES MORRISON

QUINTESSENTIAL SCOTS-IRISH

D.Q. Morrison was born in Montgomery County, Georgia, on June 17, 1818. He was the son of Daniel Morrison and Catherine McCrimmon Morrison, early Montgomery County pioneers.

D.Q.'s wife, Mary Wilkes Morrison, was born November 20, 1820, in Robeson County, North Carolina. While still a young girl, Mary moved with her family to Montgomery County, Georgia. Her great-great-grandfather, Isaac Wilkes, fought in the American Revolution. Her maternal grandfather, Duncan Hughes, migrated from Kinggoldrum, Angus, Scotland, to Robeson County, North Carolina. Mr. Hughes later moved with his family to Montgomery County, Georgia, where he died in 1837.

Mary had four siblings who later moved from Montgomery County to Berrien County, Georgia. After Mary's father, Solomon Wilkes, died in 1839, Mary's mother, Margaret, married William M. Walker. The marriage did not work out so Margaret also moved to Berrien County to be with her other children. Even today there are many Berrien County Wilkes.

Mary's great-grandmother, Christian Gillis Morrison, and her husband, Norman, also migrated from Scotland to Robeson County, North Carolina, and then to Montgomery County, Georgia. As you can see, Mary also had Morrison in her line.

The Morrisons, Wilkes, McCrimmons, and Rountrees were all prime examples of the Scots-Irish and Scottish migration.

The year 1783 saw the treaty of New York, in which the Creek Indians ceded lands east of the Oconee River. The Creeks later moved west of the Ocmulgee and, as a result, large numbers of whites migrated to Georgia from North Carolina and Virginia. Bounty grants were given to Revolutionary War veterans and head rights were awarded to heads of households. There was also a series of land lotteries.

The slaveholders, mostly English Anglicans, came down the Philadelphia

91

Wagon Road through Augusta, Georgia, and settled in the Piedmont section of the state. The Scots and Scots-Irish, who were independent minded stockmen, crossed the Savannah River near Augusta and moved south into the wiregrass and longleaf pine country. The wiregrass provided abundant forage for their cattle and sheep. The longleaf pine gave them timber and naval stores. These settlers worked their stock themselves and had little need for slaves.

Manning Rountree, my great-great-grandfather, is a perfect example. His ancestors immigrated to Emanuel County from Northern Ireland by way of Tar River, North Carolina. Like other Scots-Irish, they came as a family from Northern Ireland, having moved there from England before the Battle of the Boyne. After the Battle of the Boyne, the Rountrees remained in Northern Ireland for about sixty years. Two generations after his family arrived in Georgia, Manning owned a thousand acres and no slaves.

Groups of Scots-Irish came from such places as Robeson County, North Carolina, and Tar River, North Carolina. These people brought with them their Calvinist faith and their strong sense of family.

After working on this book a short time, it became apparent to me that my mother's family, to a large degree, is Scots-Irish, with a smattering of English and Highland-Scots. Who were these people that had such a tremendous influence on American history? The Scots and the Scots-Irish were Celtic people. After the Celts arrived in America, their culture tended to dominate in places where they settled. English settlers in those areas adopted the Scots-Irish ways.

In his book *Main Currents in American Thought,* Vernon Louis Parrington states:

> "Of the different racial strains that mingled their blood with the earlier English-Irish, Huguenot-French, German, Scots-Irish – the last was by far the most important...they were desperately poor: the available lands near the coast were already preempted; so armed with axes, their seed potatoes, and their newly invented rifle, they plunged into the backwoods to become our great pioneering race. Scattered thinly through a long frontier, they constituted the outposts and buffer settlements of civilization. A vigorous breed, hardy, assertive, individualistic, thrifty, trained in the democracy of the Scottish Kirk, they were the material out of which later Jacksonian democracy was to be fashioned; the creators of that western type within politics and industry became ultimately the American type" (Parrington).

The Celtic people who moved to Emanuel and Montgomery counties were examples of the pioneer creed: "The cowards never started. The weak died along the way. Only the strong survived" (Webb, p. 7).

In his terrific book *Born Fighting, How the Scots-Irish Shaped America,* James Webb worries that stories of the Scots-Irish will be lost in an avalanche of political correctness and historic revisionism. He writes that these people were:

"...imbued with a unique and unforgiving code of personal honor. Less ritualized but every bit as powerful as the Samurai code. This legacy is broad, in many ways defining the attitudes and values of the military, of working class America and even of the peculiarly popular form of American democracy itself, and yet his story has been lost under the weight of more recent immigrations, revisionist historicals and common ignorance..." (Webb, p. 8).

In *Albion's Seed,* David Hackett Fischer maintains that, though the Scots-Irish were not well-off financially, they retained their pride:

"The Scots-Irish who came to America in the eighteenth century were not poor in any of these senses. Their pride was a source of irritation to their English neighbors, who could not understand what they had to feel proud about. It was said of one Scots-Irish-man that 'his looks spoke out that he would not fear the devil, should he meet him face to face...'" (Fischer, p. 615).

In talking about these Celtic people, who came primarily from northern England and southern Scotland by way of Northern Ireland, Webb states:

"Their bloodline was stained by centuries of continuous warfare along the border between England and Scotland, and then in the bitter settlements of England's Ulster plantation in Northern Ireland. Their religion was a harsh and demanding Calvinism that sowed the seeds of America's bible belt. It is on your feet independence instead of on your knees rituality, offending Anglicans and Irish Catholics alike.... They settled not in the plantations along the southern coast or in the bustling towns of New England, but in the raw and unforgiving wilderness. It was not unusual to find that their first task beyond building a cabin was to defend themselves against the blood curdling attack of Indian war parties.

They fought the Indians and then they fought the British, comprising forty percent of the Revolutionary Army. They were the great pioneers – Daniel Boone, Lewis and Clark, and Davy Crockett" (Webb, p. 9).

Webb also points out that many of America's great military leaders were of Scots-Irish ancestry, men such as Andrew Jackson, Ulysses S. Grant, Theodore Roosevelt, Stonewall Jackson, Sam Houston, Nathan Bedford Forrest, George S. Patton, Sergeant Alvin York, and Audie Murphy (Webb, p. 10).

"The Scots-Irish had nothing in common with either the English aristocracy in Virginia or the New England WASP settlements, nor for that matter did the typical English who made their way...to join them. Some of the English in these communities had come from Ulster with the Scots-Irish. Some came from the border areas between England and Scotland and were in contrast to the New England English, heavily Celtic in their origins" (Webb, p. 15).

Their bellicose nature could be traced to centuries of warfare. Webb points out that in the War Between the States, the Scots-Irish suffered an astounding seventy percent killed or wounded fighting for the Confederacy, and stood with General Lee when he surrendered at Appomattox. Webb further states:

"They are a culture founded on guns, which considers the Second Amendment sacrosanct, while literary and academic America considers such views not only archaic but also threatening, and yet it is not hyperbole to say that Al Gore lost the 2000 election by going against them on this issue, causing Tennessee and West Virginia to vote for George W. Bush" (Webb, p. 18).

Scots-Irish can also be credited with the invention of Jacksonian democracy. Webb states that "the Jacksonians are distinctly 'democratic and populist.'" Further, they believe that "the government should do everything in its power to promote the well being -- political, moral, economic – of the whole community. Any means are permissible...so long as they do not violate the moral feelings or infringe on the freedoms that Jacksonians believe are essential to their daily lives." Webb asserts that, "this political movement takes its views from the Scots-Irish definition of personal honor, equality and individualism" (Webb, p. 19).

Webb points out that to understand the Scots-Irish independence is to follow a "historically consistent cycle of, among other things, a values-based combativeness, and insistent egalitarianism, and a refusal to be dominated from above, no matter the cost" (Webb, p. 20).

"The prejudice exemplified by eighteenth century Anglicans against Scotch Presbyterians has passed down through the generations. Anglican Clergyman Charles Woodsmason described the Scots-Irish as 'ignorant, mean, worthless, beggarly Irish Presbyterians, the scum of the earth, and refuse of mankind.' Such invective was not unheard of in modern days. If a sensitive ear could substitute redneck for Irish Presbyterians, you might have an accurate picture of how modern day New Englanders and European elite still characterize rural southerners" (Webb, p. 157).

As the Scots-Irish came from the Old World to the New, most dropped Calvinist Presbyterianism and became Calvinist Baptists. Others, under the preaching of Francis Asbury, became Methodists. The reason so many became Baptists were the denomination's emphasis on scripture, and a congregational form of church government. One driving force of today's U.S. evangelical movement is the Calvinist fundamentalists who are primarily an outgrowth of Scots-Irish Calvinism.

Otis Rountree grew up in the Primitive Baptist faith, a Calvinist denomination. Although he attended the Methodist church with Clyde, he never joined. He did not want to upset Wash and Zannie, devout Primitive Baptists. Ivy Rountree also grew up in the Old Canoochee Primitive Baptist Church. He joined the Methodist church but is reported to have said, "This will improve both denominations."

The Scots-Irish trait of defiance to hierarchy was clearly illustrated in the War Between the States. The Scots-Irish were the backbone of the Southern Army. Webb says:

"It might seem odd in these modern times, but the Confederate soldier fought because, on the one hand, in his view he was provoked, intimidated and ultimately invaded, and on the other, his leaders had convinced him that this was a war of independence in the same sense as the Revolutionary War. For those who can remove themselves from the slavery issue and examine the traits that characterize the Scots-Irish culture, the unbending ferocity of the Confederate soldier is little more than a continuum. This was not so much a learned response to historical events as it was a cultural approach that had been refined by centuries of similar experience. The tendency to resist outside aggression was bred deeply into every heart – and still is today. The Jacobite Irish and the French laid siege to Derry and tried to starve a people into submission, but as the death toll mounted, these same people, men, women and children alike, wrote their vow in blood: 'No surrender'...During the American Revolution, the British sent an expedition into the Appalachian mountains to punish and lay waste to whole communities for not supporting the crown, and their predictable reward was to be starved, surrounded and slaughtered, (Kings Mountain), and now, (during the War Between the States) a federal government, whose leadership and economic systems were dominated by English-American businessmen and intellectuals, was sending armies into the sovereign territory of the southern states in order to compel them to remain inside a political system that their leaders had told them they had every right to reject" (Webb, p. 226).

Webb further points out:

"[The] South lasted for four horrific years, with far fewer men, far less equipment, far inferior weapons in a countryside which was persistently devastated as the Leviathan army worked its way like a steamroller across its landscape. It is fair to say that the Confederate army endured as long as it did against such enormous odds because it was so wildly and recklessly Celtic, that it did not know when to stop fighting" (Webb, p. 233).

I believe Webb has hit the nail on the head. The Morrisons, McCrimmons, Rountrees, and Wilkes fit the Scots-Irish bill to a "T".
In *History of Montgomery County Georgia to 1918*, Robert Scott Davis, Jr., describes part of the Highland Scot and Scots-Irish immigration to Montgomery County.

"The most significant and most lasting settlement of old Montgomery County was the Highland Scott-Irish. They arrived in significant numbers in Montgomery County during the war of 1812 and continued to come for at least another twenty years. No credible research has been done on these families as a group. They had almost all arrived from Scotland (and Ireland) within only one generation. Such a family typically moved to

Robeson County or Cumberland County, North Carolina in the 1780s from places like Isle of Skye, Argyll, and Inverness, Scotland...

"Harris Folsom wrote that during the War Between the States, 'it is doubtful if any of Georgia's contingents went to the front with as much Scotch blood as the gallants from Montgomery.' These families kept their ethnic roots longer than most communities in America. As late as the eighteen eighties, Gaelic was a second language in Montgomery County. Even their church services were given in Gaelic. A symbol of family pride was ownership of a Gaelic Bible.

"'Montgomery County was settled by a hearty Scotch colonist, and their descendants form about two thirds of the present population. They are a frugal, hardworking and honest people...They retained many traits and peculiarities of character so common in the old country- some have never abandoned their mother tongue, but have taught their children and even their servants, to speak their peculiar language'" (Davis, p.138).

If you doubt Folsom's assertion that no Georgia Confederate units came with as much Scottish blood as those from Montgomery County, check out the 38th Georgia, part of the Georgia Brigade. Company C of the 38th was an Emanuel County unit, and Company E was a Montgomery County unit. John R. Flanders, Jr. was a member of Company C. A partial roster of names from Company E shows the amount of Scottish and Scots-Irish blood present. Also note that the names represent some of Montgomery County's most prominent families.

John McArthur	A.H. McCrimmons
Thomas McRae	W.R. McKay
Wilson Conner	J.M. McQuaig
Peter Johnson	John McSwain
Joseph McAlister	Malcolm Peterson
Peter McBryde	Daniel and Thomas Currie

The D.Q. Morrison family exhibits many of the traits common to American Scots and Scots-Irish. The first is that they are a Celtic people, originally coming from either Scotland or the border region between England and Scotland. The second is that many came to America from Northern Ireland, having migrated there from the border region. The third is that they came in large family groups, both in the very difficult trip across the Atlantic and in the journey from North Carolina to Georgia. The fourth is that they exhibited a resiliency bred in them over the centuries. This toughness was a characteristic they had to adopt. They had suffered from rack-renting, border wars, and domination by the English lords, but they had survived. In America, they would ultimately prosper.

While in his late forties, D.Q. Morrison fought in the War Between the States. The age at which he fought was considered very old at the time, but I am sure that Morrison, like others of his race, was committed to defending home and hearth. In fighting to protect the Southland, Morrison exhibited the same traits as the Scots-Irish "over-the-mountain" men of Revolutionary War fame. Major Andrew Ferguson of the British Army had threatened to enter the North Carolina mountain country, burn the Scots-Irish homes, and hang their leaders. Instead, the over-the-mountain men attacked Ferguson at King's Mountain and completely annihilated his force.

This is typical of numerous instances throughout American history in which the Scots-Irish have shown that they were not to be pushed around. The greatest American General, Robert Edward Lee, was once asked what race makes the best soldiers, to which the general replied, "The Scots who came to this country by way of Ireland – because they have all of the dash of the Irish in taking a position, and all of the stubbornness of the Scots in holding it" (Kennedy, p. 14).

Morrison also revealed his roots through his membership in the Georgia Militia. Its engagement in the Battle of Griswoldville was a case of David taking on Goliath, except that Goliath won. Men too old or too young to serve in the Confederate army (some boys fought at thirteen and fourteen) charged a well-trained, well-equipped and more numerous Union army. The result was predictable. One interesting aside is that my great-great-grandfather on my father's side, Woodson Wilcox, commanded Morrison's company at Griswoldville.

After the war, Morrison continued farming on land located near the present-day Wilson Cemetery between Higgston and Vidalia. He was credited with donating the right-of-way for the railroad that passied through his property as well as providing the property for Higgston, Georgia. Mary and D.Q. Morrison had one child, Kathryn.

Like his son-in-law, W.R. Wilson, Morrison's life was fraught with tragedy. On July 8, 1872, his grandson, William Louis Wilson, died. Two years later, his daughter, Kathryn, succumbed a week after giving birth to D.Q. Wilson. Fifteen months after that, Morrison lost his wife, Mary.

Morrison married Georgia Palmer, thirty-seven years his junior, on February 13, 1879, when Georgia was twenty-four and Morrison was sixty-

Unidentified men in wagon picking up corn to take to the mill that is located in Higgston. Foreground, L to R - Georgia Palmer Morrison, Unidentified, Agnes Powell.

one – and definitely alpha male. Georgia was a faithful wife who took care of her husband during his later years. She and his first wife, Mary Wilkes Morrison, are buried on each side of D.Q. at the Wilson Cemetery.

My great-great-great-grandfather must have been a great man because a lot of people were named for him. Two are Tommy Q. Vann and D.Q. Wilson. No one has ever been able to tell what the Q. stood for in D.Q. Morrison's name. A family story told to me by Frank Cummings is that D.Q. was walking down the street in Higgston one day, and a friendly gentleman came up and said, "Tell me, Mr. Morrison, what does the Q. in your name stand for?" Morrison turned to him and said, "Q., dammit!"

From the Montgomery County *Monitor* on the death of D.Q. Morrison:

> "Daniel Q. Morrison, of Higgston, familiarly known throughout this county as 'Uncle Q.,' died rather suddenly Monday night. He was very old,

and had been in feeble health for quite a while. He was one of the oldest settlers of the county, and in his day a useful and public-spirited citizen.

'Uncle Q' was one of the best friends the Monitor ever had, never having missed a number since its establishment more than twelve years ago. Between him and its editor, the warmest friendship has existed for that time. He was an excellent man. Peace to his ashes and a tear to his memory" (Anonymous, 1898).

WALLACE R. WILSON AND
KATHRYN MORRISON WILSON

D.Q. and Mary Morrison had one child, Kathryn. She was born in Montgomery County, Georgia, on January 5, 1849. Kathryn's husband, Wallace R. Wilson, was born in Hancock County, Georgia, on March 13, 1830. He was the son of William Louis Wilson and Phoebe Park Wilson. William Wilson was a successful Hancock County planter. Phoebe Wilson was the daughter of James Park, a Revolutionary War veteran and

Wallace Wilson traveled Washington and Montgomery counties pulling teeth. His transportation was a wagon with "Extractions" painted on the back. Drawing by Kyle James.

prominent resident of Greene County, Georgia.

Wallace Wilson spent his early years in Hancock County. On 7 May 1862, he joined Company I, 59th Regiment, Georgia Volunteer Infantry, known as Turners Guards. It was during his service in the Confederate army that Wallace began pulling teeth, an occupation he practiced for the rest of his life. He was elected sergeant, and two days before the battle of Gettysburg, he was sent to a hospital in Staunton, Virginia, where he remained for several months. After August 1863, he was reported as "absent sick."

About seven months after the war ended, on November 5, 1865, the thirty-five-year-old Wallace married sixteen-year-old Kathryn Morrison. They set up housekeeping in Montgomery County. The couple had Mary (Cummings) on August 7, 1866, and Sophie (Holmes) on January 23, 1868. They were then blessed with twins, William Wallace and William Louis, born June 30, 1870. Tragically, William Louis died eight days later, on July 8, 1870. A third son, Daniel Q. Wilson, was born July 22, 1872. Seven days after the birth of this son, Kathryn Morrison Wilson died at age twenty-three. She left four very young children and a grieving husband.

Two years later, on February 8, 1875, Wallace married Margaret F. McQueen. She gave birth to Kathryn Julia Wilson (Vann) on February 1, 1876. Tragedy again struck Wallace's household when Margaret died on September 18, 1887. Wallace later married Mary Berryhill, but they had no children.

Wallace Wilson was an astute businessman. The Federal census of 1870 shows him with forty acres of improved land, and in 1880 with two hundred acres of improved land. The 1882 survey by the *Georgia State Gazetteer* shows Wallace to be one of Montgomery County's most prosperous farmers (Davis, p. 162).

Wallace was not only a successful farmer but also a prominent dentist. He would take his wagon with the word "Extractions" painted on the back and travel throughout Montgomery and Washington counties. He also had a practice in Higgston.

Later in life, Wallace moved to Chalker, Georgia, a now defunct town located in the northeast quadrant of Washington County. Chalker was a timber community, spawned by the large timber companies that were engaged in harvesting the virgin yellow pine and hardwood from the adjacent Ogeechee River swamp. Wallace's son, D.Q. Wilson, had a store in Chalker.

Wallace Wilson died on September 7, 1909, leaving his children substantial pieces of land. He also left an acre in Chalker to be used as the

Mary Cummings – sister to Sophie Wilson Holmes – shown with her family and husband Dave Cummings, about 1905.

Front row, L to R – Helen Wilson, Sophie Wilson Holmes, Georgia Palmer Morrison (D.Q. Morrison's second wife), Sophie Carr. Back row, L to R – Ruth Wilson, Pierce Holmes, W.L. Wilson (Uncle Willie, Grandmother Holmes' brother), Nell Wilson, Sophie Cumming, and Richard C. Wilson.

site of a future Methodist church. Wallace was buried in Chalker but family members later had his body moved to the Wilson Cemetery in Higgston.

The life of Wallace R. Wilson illustrates the extent to which quality medical care separates the lifestyles of twenty-first-century and nineteenth-century Georgians. Wallace lost a young son and two wives, most likely from complications associated with childbirth. In Wilson's day, death was not far away. You can see by the letters that these people wrote that health was a constant worry. Many would begin with the sentence, "I hope this letter finds you in good health."

WILL OF W.R. WILSON
State of Georgia, Washington County

I, W.R. Wilson, of said state and county, being of sound and disposing memory do make this my last will and testament, hereby revoking all wills heretofore made by me.

Item 1st...I wish my executors as soon as possible after my death to pay my debts. If a sale of property shall be necessary, I wish them to select for sale that which can be most advantageously used for that purpose and I authorize them to sell the same at public or private sale as they may see fit.

Item 2nd...I give to my beloved wife Mary deed to half the tract of land below the Ball Road being about sixty acres which is to go to D.Q. Wilson at her death, and by agreement between us I give to her one hundred and fifty dollars for a year's support.

Item 3rd...I have deeded my land to my children as I wished them to have it except about three hundred acres.

Item 4th...My son William Q. Wilson owes me fifteen hundred dollars ($1500.00) after paying him for all the services and all taxes paid for me.

Item 5th...My daughter Sophie D. Holmes owes me two hundred and seventy five dollars ($275.00).

Item 6th...My daughter Mary P. Cummings owes me three hundred dollars ($300.00).

Q. Wilson, brother of Sophie Holmes. Q. Operated a store in Chalker, Georgia.

Item 7th...My son D.Q. Wilson owes me eight hundred dollars ($800.00).

Item 8th...My daughter Kathryn J. Vann owes me eight hundred dollars ($800.00).

Item 9th...All the land I have in Toombs County I want sold at public

Pedolingham

712 BROAD STREET,
AUGUSTA, GA.

Sophie Holmes (right) with her father, W.R. Wilson and her half sister, Kate Wilson (Vann).

[auction] and the proceeds with all my notes and accounts then collected to go to equalizing my heirs and if there is any remaining after they have been made equal then the remainder to be divided among them equally.

Item 10th...I wish all my cows divided in lots and drawn for by my heirs as nearly equally as possible.

Item 11th...The horses and colts are to be sold and the proceeds to go in equal to the heirs that may be in arrears.

Item 12th...All other property that I may have at the time of my death I wish to be sold and to go as the other proceeds have been directed.

Item 13th...I do hereby appoint D.Q. Wilson and Jim Bob Carr executors of this my will.

In testimony whereof I hereto set my hand this 29th day of January, 1909.

Front row, L to R - Uncle Willie Wilson and Sophie Wilson Holmes. Back row, L to R - Kate Wilson Vann (Sophie's half-sister) and Uncle Q. Wilson.

WALLACE R. WILSON AND KATHRYN MORRISON WILSON

Witness:

Dock May
J.Q. Cobb
Wm. A. Gibson
W.R. Wilson

This is a transcription by Palmer Carr of the Will of W.R. Wilson as recorded in the Office of the Probate Judge of Washington County, Georgia, in "Will Book 1903-1925" on page 86.

108

JOSHUA BLACK

FATHER OF EMMA BLACK FLANDERS

Emma Black Flanders was the sixth child of Joshua Black and Michel Wells. The family would be blessed with eleven children, seven of whom lived to maturity.

Joshua Black was a prosperous farmer who lived in the small community of Bethany, located near Wadley, Georgia. He owned one slave. He was listed as literate in the 1870 census (Black, p. 1). Two of Joshua's grandfathers and a great-grandfather served in the American Revolution. Joshua Black's mother was Lavicy Bruton Black. Her grandfather was James Griffin, a Revolutionary War veteran.

John Bruton, Joshua's maternal grandfather, spied for the Patriot cause, possibly at the Battle of Brier Creek. It was customary after the American Revolution to award land to veterans and a grateful government gave Bruton both land and money. James Park and his brother also benefited in this way.

William Black, paternal grandfather of Joshua Black, was born in Mecklinburg County, North Carolina. He moved to Georgia before the Revolution, during which he served under Elijah Clarke. William's farm was shown on a British Army map as located on the north side of Black Creek in what is now Screven County, Georgia.

Emma Black Flanders' brother, Joseph Black, was a member of Company E, 48th Georgia, Jefferson Volunteers. February 1863 saw Joseph elected to the post of first sergeant, the highest-ranking noncommissioned officer in the company. He replaced John Wesley Cheatham, great-great-grandfather of my friend and next-door neighbor, Dr. Steve Umberger. Cheatham would later command Company E.

Joseph's army career was similar to that of John R. Flanders, Jr., in that both men ended up as prisoners of war. Joseph was one of three hundred thirty-three men of Wrights Brigade captured on the second day at Gettysburg. He was held at Ft. Delaware, Maryland, until exchanged on 17 March 1865. After the war, Joseph returned to farming and became a Methodist preacher. He was one of the founding pastors of St. Johns Methodist Church in Jefferson County, Georgia.

Rountree

THE ROUNTREES AND OLD CANOOCHEE CHURCH

Like other Scots-Irish families who came to America, the Rountrees can trace their origin to England. Joshua Rountree of Springfield, Missouri, wrote in 1867:

> "A good many years ago, there was a male child in Yorkshire, England, found by a rich landlord on his estate, laid under the Rowan tree (otherwise called the Mountain Ash), dressed in very rich clothing. He took compassion on the child and took it home with him. He raised it as if it had been his own child. Not knowing its origin, he called it Rowantree, after the tree under which it was found. The boy grew up and was educated by his foster father, and in time he married and raised a family. They became very numerous.
>
> William III, King of England, dethroned his father-in-law, King James II. James then went to Ireland and raised a large army of Irish, thinking to get himself reinstated on the throne of England. William also raised a large army in England at the same time and went over to Ireland. Two brothers of the Rowantrees went over in his army after the Battle of Boynewater (Boyne) when William's forces conquered James' forces. William then disbanded a part of his army" (Rountree).

The two Rowantree brothers then separated and lived in Northern Ireland. Our ancestor remained there until immigrating to America. Rountree continues:

"When there was a great immigration from Ireland to North America, one old man named Rowantree took passes for himself and [his] family for Virginia. Before the ship was ready to sail, his youngest son took the small pox and was not admitted aboard the ship. The father had paid his passage, so he and six of his sons sailed for North America... The seventh son was left in the care of his mother. He recovered from the attack of small pox. From that son, our family sprang. He remained in Ireland and married, raised a large family, and became very numerous. When my father was nineteen years old, he took passage for America. He stopped in the province of Pennsylvania and worked at the ship's carpenter's business some two or three years and then went back to Ireland. After staying there a few more years, he married Eva Sturgis, daughter of Andrew and Rachel Sturgis. After his marriage, he took passage for America again. He stopped in Pennsylvania and remained there, I think, until three of his children were born. Then he immigrated to North Carolina where the balance of their children were born, and there they died. Their earthly remains lie buried in the graveyard of Little River Meeting House" (Rountree).

Charles was the young Rowantree who was left in Northern Ireland. He was the son of Frances I, who went to Virginia with his six sons. Don Rountree points out in *Temerity and Adversity: A History of the Rountree*

Old Canoochee Primitive Baptist Church - circa 1910. Used with permission by the Georgia Archives.

Family 1550-1993 that the most likely reason the mother stayed in Northern Ireland with her son was to nurse him back to health. Years later, Charles married Lydia McMan, fathered a son, Thomas, and died in Northern Ireland in 1759. Thomas came to America and followed the course that is outlined in Joshua Rountree's account. Don Rountree further states that, "Thomas was nineteen years old when he booked passage to America. The year was 1752. He worked for two years as a ship's carpenter, probably in Philadelphia, then returned to Ireland to marry his sweetheart, Eva Sturgis, about 1754. Eva was seventeen; Thomas was twenty-two" (Rountree).

Like other Scots-Irish families in Pennsylvania, the Rountrees needed to move to more hospitable and fertile country. At that time, the governor of North Carolina, himself a Scotsman, was encouraging Scots and Scots-Irish to move to his state. The family, therefore, ended up in Tar River, North Carolina.

Don Rountree further reports:

"Travel was difficult and dangerous with few roads and fewer bridges. There was one real road about 435 miles long leading from Philadelphia to North Carolina. This great road led out of Philadelphia in a westerly direction by Lancaster, Pennsylvania and York, Pennsylvania, and then southwest to Winchester, Virginia, through the Shenandoah Valley to Staunton, Virginia. At Roanoke, it changed toward the southeast, crossing the Staunton River and the Blue Ridge Mountains north of Danville, Virginia. It then divided, with one branch leading to Winston-Salem, North Carolina, and connecting with the trading path just north of the Yadkin River at Trading Ford. The other branch leaving the fork at North Danville led southeast, crossing the Dan River, continuing in a southerly direction through Mebane, connecting with the trading path at Swetsonville, just above the Haw River. As early as 1720, there were records on what was known as the trading path mentioned above... Thomas Rountree and his family made this journey from Philadelphia to the Hillsborough area of North Carolina about 1760 and settled in the rich Piedmont farming area near the Tar and Little Rivers. About the time Thomas arrived in the area, a group of Scots-Irish settlers organized a Presbyterian church. In 1761, they built the Little River Meeting House. It stands between the north and south forks of the Little River in Orange County" (Rountree, p. 11).

Orange County was named for William of Orange, who in England had led the Protestants against James II and had established Northern Ireland as a Protestant enclave (Rountree, p. 13). Don Rountree points out that the community was led by Joseph Allison, a Scots-Irishman who also had come from Northern Ireland by way of Philadelphia. It is highly likely that he and Thomas Rountree had known each other "back home." Thomas purchased a farm of about two hundred acres and he and Eva raised six sons and two daughters. It was while there that the Rowantree family changed its name to Rountree.

John Rountree, son of Thomas and Eva Rountree, was born in 1760 in Pennsylvania and accompanied his parents to Tar River. When John was about forty years old, he and his wife, Nancy Manning Rountree,

W.E. (Bill) Rountree – a consummate fisherman, a southern gentleman, and Emanuel County's most respected citizen. Bill is shown standing in front of Old Chanoochee Primitive Baptist Church. Mr. Rountree is the son of Ivey Rountree, a first cousin to Otis Rountree. During the tense days of integration, Bill was credited with "keeping the lid on." Bill represented the Emanuel County School Board, and, even though he did not agree with the speed of integration, he urged the Emanuel County citizens to obey the law and support those trying to peacefully integrate. Because of his stand, Bill endured no little amount of harassment from a small element of the community; but he stood firm, and history has shown that Bill did Emanuel a great service.

Manning Rountree (1818-1893), shown with six of his seven sons. Front row, L to R - Manning R., Great-Great-Grandfather Manning, Ebenezer D., and Andrew J. Back row, L to R - Isaac W., Great-Grandfather Washington G., and Joseph B.

moved to Georgia, taking the trading route to Augusta. They later lived in Greene County for a short time before moving to Emanuel County where they purchased two hundred fifty acres from Moses Scarborough on May 9, 1801. John served as the first clerk of the Old Canoochee Primitive Baptist Church.

John and Nancy Rountree had two sons, George and Joshua. There is disagreement as to whether or not they were twins. For a more complete discussion, consult Don Rountree's book. Joshua became a prominent citizen and both he and his wife, Zilphia Durden Rountree, were active members of the Old Canoochee Church. They had ten children, one of whom, Manning, was the father of Wash Rountree. Wash, in turn, was the father of Otis Rountree.

The Rountree and Durden families played a prominent part in the Old Canoochee Primitive Baptist Church. I can claim direct ancestors who served in the church leadership from its founding until the turn of the twentieth century. John Rountree was clerk of the church from 1818 to 1820; Joshua Rountree from 1827 to 1832; John's brother, George Rountree, 1832 to 1852; and Manning Rountree from 1857 to 1874.

Another relative, William Durden, was clerk from 1825 to 1827.

Since its founding in 1818, the Old Canoochee has been a fixture in Emanuel County. In 1867, the edifice was moved to its present location on the highway between Twin City and Swainsboro. The graveyard where Manning Rountree and his wife, Lucinda, are buried lies across the road.

Like every Christian denomination I have studied, the theology of the Old Canoochee Church determines its mission and how its members react to the faith. Old Canoochee Church is a Primitive Baptist congregation and is strictly Calvinist. Not only is it Primitive Baptist, but it is Old Line Primitive Baptist.

Calvinism is an outgrowth of the theology of St. Augustine, developed by John Calvin after the Reformation. The essential doctrines are an emphasis on scripture and the sovereignty of God. Calvinism can be summarized by using the acronym, TULIP:

1. Total Depravity – Each person is trapped in sin and lost without God.
2. Unconditional Election – No one deserves salvation. Persons are elected unconditionally.
3. Limited Atonement – Christ died only for the elect. Since no one deserves salvation, God foreordains whom He chooses.
4. Irresistible Grace – If God foreordains that a person is to be saved, he or she cannot resist His wooing.
5. Perseverance of the Saints – Because God selects those who are to be saved, someone receiving salvation cannot become unsaved.

Although Calvinism may seem harsh, it is logical. During the mid-nineteenth century, the Baptist church in Georgia split and two denominations were formed – Primitive Baptists and Missionary Baptists. The Missionary Baptists believed in the importance of missions and Sunday school. The Primitive Baptists believed that, because persons were already preordained to be saved or unsaved, it was not necessary to spend energy on missions. The result is that the Missionary Baptists have grown into the largest U.S. Protestant denomination, while the Primitive Baptists are still a relatively small group. If, however, you look at the logic of the Primitive Baptist view of salvation, starting first with the sovereignty of God, you'll see that it makes a lot more sense than does Missionary Baptist theology. The Missionary Baptists generally adopt theology point number one, above (total depravity) and number five (perseverance of the saints). This leaves out the mid-doctrines and makes for what, I believe, is a rather shaky theology.

Like many nineteenth-century churches, the Old Canoochee Primitive Baptist Church practiced discipline. The November 1867 minutes show that:

"Brother Swain M. Anderson was charged with non-attendance and saying in the presence of Phoebe Durden and Eli Durden that Martha Marsh was a liar and would tell lies and Martha Marsh had been to see him and he denied it. On January the fourth, 1868, the case of Swain Anderson was taken up and disposed of by executing him from the church."

On September 2, 1876, in a reversal of fortune, Brother Anderson was

Martha Rountree

117

authorized to exercise his gift in the ministry. As you can see, he was not only redeemed but made a pastor.

Brother William Durden was said to have come forward on August 2, 1822, and make a complaint against Brother John Casey, indicating "fiddling, dancing, and fighting." Brothers William Durden and Joshua Rountree were appointed to look into the matter.

Ever since Old Canoochee Church was constituted July 10, 1818, it has served Emanuel County well. The minutes state:

> "Others have come into the church through the years and there has been a spirit of love and good fellowship manifested, which causes us to feel that the Lord has been, and is still, blessing us more than we deserve. We do not count progress through – or by – the number of members we have but through the steady, heart-warming love and fellowship that exists among the members and their devotion to the cause of Christ."

ELDER R.H. BARWICK

In his book *Memories,* written in the late nineteenth century, Elder R.H. Barwick traces the history of the Emanuel County Rountree family:

"From North Carolina two brothers, Joshua and George, who were twins, their father John and their sister Nancy came to Emanuel County about 1800. They settled first in Greene County and soon moved on to Emanuel, which was then almost a wilderness. They were earnestly seeking a new country where they might locate and build their homes and their fortunes. What must have been their feelings, their hopes and aspirations as they passed through the different sections of North Carolina and then Georgia – across rivers and freshets doubtless seeing much wild game and some Indians with only here and there settlers. It was all new to them and people of less courage would have turned back long before they came to this wilderness but they had the courage and strength that it takes to build in the wilderness. When they reached Emanuel County they felt that they would find nothing better. Like the patriarchs of old they struck camp and said – 'here we stay.'

"It is said that these brothers were so much alike that if they dressed alike it was difficult for their wives to tell them apart. They loved each other very dearly and the first one up in the morning would go out and holler, the other would hear and answer him. They were members of Old Canoochee Church, which stood then near the crossroad just north of Bartley Sconyer's place. It was moved to the present site in 1866. Their names often appear in the old church book as clerk, deacon, or messenger to the Association.

"Joshua married Zilphia Durden and George married Lavinia Neal. They reared families of 10 children each.

"My mother was a granddaughter of Joshua and my father was a grandson of George.

"These two old men and their wives and all their children are all gone. They filled their places with honor and credit in their day and generations and helped their fellows to lay the foundation of our present progress and development. They were a prolific people and most of them reared large families. The stock is here yet but it is not fashionable to

119

rear large families anymore. Short families came in fashion with short hair and short frocks, and some of them are going to come up short on judgment day, according to the Book. These two old pioneers wrestled with the problems of life as we do today. They had their financial worries and the responsibilities of rearing a family and giving their children the best advantages to be had in that day, and evidently they wrought well" (Barwick, 1890).

WASH AND ZANNIE FLANDERS ROUNTREE

Washington George Rountree   Zannie Flanders Rountree

Washington George Rountree was the eighth of nine children born to Manning and Lucinda Durden Rountree. He was raised in the Old Canoochee Primitive Baptist Church, where his great-grandfather, John, his grandfather, Joshua, and his father, Manning, were leaders.

Manning Rountree was clerk and deacon of the Old Canoochee Church. He also served as tax collector for Emanuel County from January 15, 1850, until January 16, 1851. Manning owned more than one thousand acres of land. Property records do not show him owning any slaves (Rountree, p. 38).

Redheaded Wash married dark-eyed, dark-haired Zannie Flanders on October 1, 1884, in a service conducted by Reverend Daniel Tyson. She was also from an outstanding Emanuel County family. Her father, John R.

121

Three happy Rountree siblings – George (left), Josh (center), and Mary Lou (right). This picture was taken in Cobbtown.

Front row, L to R - Aunt Hattie Flanders, Aunt Vinnie Flanders Curl, and Uncle L. Flanders. Back row, L to R - Great-Grandmother Zannie Flanders Rountree, Uncle Jot Flanders, and Aunt Letta Flanders (Uncle Jot's wife). This picture was taken at Emma Rountree Currie's home in Glenwood, GA.

Flanders, Jr., was a Confederate hero as well as a community leader. Wash and Zannie set up housekeeping near Swainsboro and later purchased a farm near Cobbtown in Tattnall County. Their son (my grandfather), Otis, never lived in Cobbtown.

Wash, a prosperous farmer, was also an active member of the Tattnall County School Board. As a Primitive Baptist, his devotion to the faith was a prime example of his Rountree Scots-Irish roots. My mother's first cousin,

Carrie (left) and Mary Lou Rountree, sisters of Otis. Carrie died as a child.

Taking the Hoopee Ferry, about 1880. Seated on the front row, second from the left is my great grandfather, Washington George (Wash) Rountree. My grandmother, Clyde Rountree, used to say, "If you ever get Ohoopee sand in your shoes, you'll never get it out," meaning that a love for the Hoopee will never leave. She was correct. I consider the Ohoopee to be the most beautiful Georgia river. Nothing compares with its sandy bottom, its copper colored water, and the moss covered oaks on its shore.

Rountree descendants still enjoy the Hoopee. L to R – Paul Anderson, a prominent Atlanta attorney; Walker Anderson, a senior at the University of Virginia and a star shot-putter; Wesley Budd, a senior at Emory University; and the author, Warren Budd. Paul and Walker are direct descendants of America Rountree. America is the daughter of John and Nancy Manning Rountree.

Ridge Rountree   Arlis Rountree

Anne Dixon, told me that when her mother, Emma Rountree Currie, wanted to attend Brewton Parker Institute, a Missionary Baptist college in Mount Vernon, Georgia, Wash would not stand for it because it was not a Primitive Baptist institution.

Around Christmas time, Wash was known to enjoy his adult beverages. The story is that when he would imbibe, he would later be "churched" by the other church members, and would return to the straight and narrow. However, the following December, he was prone to get into his cups again.

Wash and Zannie were very loving, caring, and generous people. After Otis died, they worried constantly about their widowed daughter-in-law, Clyde, and her children. When Clyde's automobile gave out, and she had no way to go to work, they gave her their only automobile.

When I called Anne Dixon and asked her about Zannie, she said that her grandmother was "the best in the world." She said that she never knew a better person – ever.

After I had sent my manuscript to be edited, my generous cousin, Mary Ann Crawford Hale, granddaughter of Aunt Mary Lou Rountree Crawford, called and told me that she had come across some letters to Otis from Wash, Zannie, and Mary Lou. Most of them had been written during 1912 and 1913. At that time, Otis had undergone an operation for his stomach ulcer. Zannie wrote to her son that she was "worried to death" about him.

Crops were terrible and later that year their son Ridge would be in the hospitalized at the cost of one hundred fourteen dollars, a huge sum in that day. Sam was at South Georgia College and Wash and Zannie were having a very tough time making ends meet.

On April 29, 1913, Mary Lou wrote her brother, Otis:

> "Mr. W.H. Cowert has just come in and said that the train ran over eleven pigs of Papa's. The old sow was with them but don't think she got hurt. Papa wouldn't have taken $100 for them right now. They were the prettiest hogs in this country. Our meat for another year has been ruined. I guess we will do without."

Like every family, the Rountrees had to deal with some very serious challenges. They were plagued with more than their share of health problems and were constantly fighting economic demands that were typical of small, early-twentieth-century Georgia farmers. Wash and Zannie were

Cobbtown School, around 1915. Emma Currie is in this photo. Wash Rountree was an active member of the school board. Photograph by C.T. Brinckley, travelling photographer.

126

This picture of George Rountree and his mother, Zannie, was taken shortly after World War II. Of the six Rountree sons only George lived past his forties. George died at age 59. George was so good to his widowed mother. After the war he taught school in Tarrytown and later worked for the U.S.D.A. George Rountree was loved by all who knew him.

trying to educate their children but it was a constant battle. Nevertheless, what comes through in these letters is the love that they had for each other. This is more important than riches, for it spans the generations. It is certainly an example of being *Rich Beyond Price.*

Anne Dixon remembers that Zannie would work from sun up until sun down. She had a big garden and grew loads of flowers. Anne says that she was very bright and well read, absorbing the *Savannah Morning News* from cover to cover every morning. My mother, Dorothy Rountree Budd, echoes Anne's sentiments, but adds that Zannie was quite "plain spoken." Several others in our family could fit that description, including this author.

Zannie knew what it was like to go through the valley of the shadow. Her life was marred by constant tragedy. She lost six of her nine children at relatively young ages. Carrie, a beautiful young girl, died when she was a child. Ridge died October 29, 1915, an apparent suicide. Arliss died July 24, 1932, from a liver disorder. Otis died November 1, 1920, at age

L to R - Sam, Ridge, Arlis, and Otis Rountree.

thirty-two, and Joshua died February 8, 1939, at age twenty-five. Another son, Sam, also died in his thirties, and her husband, Wash, died March 8, 1929. Wash, Josh, and Ridge, as well as Zannie, are buried at the Sunlight Primitive Baptist Church cemetery in Cobbtown.

Zannie, like her father, John R. Flanders, Jr., was said to be a person of great faith. I imagine that the only way she could keep going in the face of such tragedies was to draw constantly on that faith.

THE AUTOGRAPH BOOK

Wash Rountree

The most important find in my search for Rountree-Holmes family records is the autograph book. Ann Dixon found this treasure in her mother's belongings.

This book was the property of Wash Rountree and was written mostly in the early 1880's. Notes are written to Wash by his good friends and relatives. They show the love, moral compass, and Christian commitment of the Wash and Manning Rountree families.

The first two letters are written to Wash by his parents, Manning Rountree (1818-1893) and Lucinda Durden Rountree (1818-1891) to their son.

My Dear Son,

I desire you to remember that I have abiding confidence in your veracity: -- may you ever be enabled to follow the path of virtue

129

while in this world; and when done with time, my heart's desire and prayer to God is that you may share a rich portion of that free and reigning grace which belongs to the people of God.

Your Loving Father
December 29, 1882

The next letter is written by Lucinda Durden Rountree, June 6, 1884:

My Son,

May thy years be many and thy sorrows few, may thou life be like a long and cloudless summer day; and when at last, the summons comes from which there is no escaping – when thou art wanted and must go – mayst thou fall into the grave as softly as the leaves of the sweet roses on an autumn eve beneath the small sighs of a western wind as it drops to the earth.

Your Loving Mother
June 16, 1884

SIBLINGS

The following letters are written by Wash's siblings – Joseph B., Isaac W. (Ike), Andrew J., Mary, Ebenezer Durden, Janie, Manning R., and Sarah. The first note is written by Wash as an introduction to the book.

To all my friends:

My album is a garden spot where all of my friends may sew.
Where thorns and thistles flourish not, but flowers alone may grow.

With smiles for sunshine, tears for showers, I'll water, watch and guard the flower.

W.G. Rountree
Swainsboro, Georgia
April 1, 1882

Let brotherly love continue.

M.R. Rountree (Manning R. Rountree)
Swainsboro, Georgia
November 12, 1892

Keep peace with each and every friend.
Keep full in view the final end.
Keep pure they deeds to honor bright
Keep strong by faith in God and right.

I.W. Rountree,
Swainsboro, Georgia
December 16, 1883

I desire you to remember, I have good confidence in you as being kind and true to all your brothers and sisters. I hope you may so continue through life and when your work is done on earth, I hope you may be crowned with an angel in heaven,

Your Brother,
E. D. R. (Ebenezer Durden Rountree)
December 17, 1883

Submit yourself to God.
Resist the devil, and he will flee from you.

Your Brother,
A.J. Rountree
March 15, 1883

Dear Brother,

While traveling along the journey of life, may you meet with all the pleasures and success that is necessary for your welfare here on this earth, and finally, when the hand of death lays his cold, icy grip on you, may you then be transformed in that beautiful home above, where I hope we may meet –

J. B. Rountree
June 1, 1884

Dear Brother,

*Always bear in mind that a sweet and gentle spirit is the priceless
estimation in the sight of God.*

Your Devoted Sister,
Sarah
December 26, 1885

*I wish you much happiness and prosperity and a long life, and when
done with earth's trials, troubles and tribulations, may you be as an
angel crowned with heaven's brightest laurels. Sharing...but such
will make life a bliss complete.*

Your Sister,
Mary M. Rountree
March 8, 1885

Launched on Life's Tempestuous Sea.
May the Great Ruler of Heaven defend you from all evil.
May you never know the frowns of adversity.
And may your happiness never have an end.

Your Sister,
Jane Barwick (Jane Rountree Barwick)
August 19, 1882

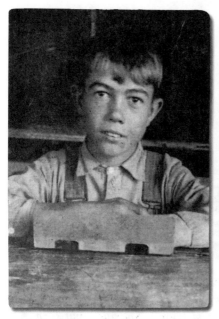

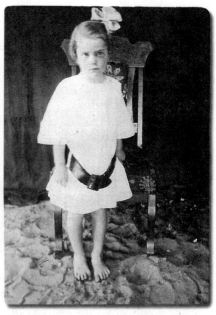

Josh Rountree, younger brother of Otis.

Emma Rountree, younger sister of Otis.

CHILDREN

The following entries in the autograph book are from Wash's children – Otis, Emma, and Josh. It should be noted that Otis was eight years old when he wrote this to his Daddy.

Dear Papa,

May you have a Happy, long life is the Desire of your son:

Otis
September 26, 1896
Swainsboro, Georgia

Dearest Papa,

I know that you never dreamed of me writing in your album, and I am only here wishing that I may fill my place in life as well as you have yours. May you have many happy birthdays.

Emma R.
May 10, 1922

As I read the writing in this book
I think of those who wrote them,
Some are alive, some will never look
But think where they were then
I hope that they have come true
But if they haven't
I will write them anew.

Your Youngest Son,
S. H. Rountree (Josh)

CLOSE RELATIVES

Here are a few of the notes written by close relatives.

Dear Uncle Wash,

When you and your sweetheart does agree,
I hope you will remember me.

Felix M. Rountree
December 18, 1883

Dear Uncle Wash,

I wish you much joy,
All the days of your life,
Make a good husband,
And get a good wife.

Your Loving Niece,
Mary Annie Rountree
October 26, 1882

Dear Uncle Wash,

May your life be a long sweet dream.

Your Loving Nephew,
Sammie

CLOSE FRIENDS

These are notes written by close friends.

I wish thee health.
I wish thee wealth.
I wish thee gold and store.
I wish thee heaven at the death –
What can I wish thee more?

Your Sister,
Edgealine Rountree
Swainsboro, Georgia
November 12, 1882

May you be successful in all your undertaking.
May the flowers bedeck your pathway
While on this earth, and after death, may you
Reach that celestial shore where parting
Is no more.

Is the sincere wish of your cousin,
Dora V. Rountree
Math, Georgia
September 4, 1883

Indulge the true ambition to excel.
In the best art – the art of living well.
Teach thee to shun the dangers of the main,
and how at length the Promised Land to gain.

Your Sister,
Sallie Rountree
December 17, 1883

Cousin Wash,

Tis sweet to love, but oh how bitter,
For you to love a girl and then can't get her.

A.D.
Bay Branch, Georgia
July 22, 1885

Cousin Wash,

I will a little pilgrim be
Resolved alone to follow thee
Thou Lamb of God thou now art gone
Up to the everlasting throne.

America Sutton
Bay Branch, Emanuel County, Georgia
July 23, 1885

Dear Old Uncle,

It is of no use to wish you continual happiness here below, for I
know it cannot be. But this much I do desire: That you may be
happy hereafter.

Your Loving Nephew,
Bob
Rogers, Georgia
February 21, 1887

Uncle Wash,

May the garden of your future destiny be strewn with roses of
friendship; and the auspicious star of Bethlehem, finally guide you
to the blissful shore of Paradise.

Is the sincere wish of your niece,
Mollie
Rogers, Georgia
February 21, 1887

When passions cross the wavering mind or adverse storms attend.
I will not fail through every scene to prove thy faithful friend.

Ridge (Flanders)
Flanders, Georgia
August 22, 1887

May there be just cloud enough in your life to make a beautiful
sunset.

Your Friend,
Mollie Flanders
Wrightsville, Georgia
August 22, 1887

DURDEN (DARDEN) DEKLE

(RELATED TO MARTHA WASHINGTON)

To use a cattleman's expression, I am double-bred Durden and my sister Lillian's children, Christy and George Darden, are triple-bred. Our line goes back twice to the Revolutionary War soldier, Captain John Darden, Sr.

L to R - Christy Darden, George Darden, Buddy and Lillian Darden, and Dorothy Budd, campaigning for Buddy. Buddy had a distinguished career in the U.S. Congress. A friend, Christopher Carpenter, said that it is a shame that the people of Georgia no longer benefit from Buddy Darden's representation, a statement to which I concur.

Until the family moved from Virginia to Georgia its surname was Darden. After the move, Jacob and John Darden changed their name to Durden. Some records show that the name had been changed back and forth previously. This could be due to poor record keeping or poor spelling.

The first Darden of our line to come to America was Stephen Darden. In 1640 he emigrated from Lancashire, England, to Nansemont County, Virginia, having received a land grant of one hundred fifty acres as recorded on November 11, 1640. A son, Jacob, accompanied the family to the New World.

It must have been quite a struggle to make a living in this new land. Why did they come to America? In 1640, the English Civil War was beginning. This would be a bloody affair. In reading the history of Lancashire it is patently evident that during this bloody fight this area was hotly contested. Stephen Darden could have been in disagreement with the rest of his community or he could have had his property destroyed and was trying to improve his lot.

Stephen's son Jacob had two sons, Jacob, Jr., and Richard Stephen. Grandfather Stephen Darden had purchased four hundred fifty acres in Isle of Wight County, Virginia, on which Jacob, Jr., settled after inheriting them. Jacob, Jr., was the father of Captain John Darden, Sr.

John, Sr., was born in 1710 on his father's property. He made his living farming and served as a citizen soldier. Commissioned a captain in the Virginia militia, he later served in the Continental Army and is listed in the *Historical Register of Virginians in the Revolution, 1775-1783*.

In a paper written for the Daughters of the American Revolution (DAR), Ada Jewel Rountree Kent states that Captain John Darden, Sr., "trained a young surveyor named George Washington." They both fought in the French and Indian War. Two generations of Darden families are intermingled with the George Washington family (Kent). John, Sr., became related to him through marriage to Elizabeth Dandridge. Her younger sister, Martha Dandridge, married Daniel Parke Custis and after his death she married the promising young surveyor and military leader.*

Elizabeth and Martha were daughters of John Dandridge (1701-1756), the son of an English merchant. As a teenager he emigrated from England to New Kent County, Virginia and in 1730 he was appointed county clerk. The same year he married Frances Jones (1710-1785), whose forebears had been early settlers of Williamsburg, Virginia. Her father was Orlando Jones and *his* father (Elizabeth's great-grandfather) was Roland Jones, who had emigrated from Oxfordshire, England. Reverend Jones served as the first rector of Bruton Parish Church from 1674 to 1688. In Volume II of his book *George Washington,* Douglas Southhall Freeman says that the Dandridge family was well liked but not wealthy (Freeman, p. 296).

Captain John Darden, Sr., had two sons, John, Jr., and Jacob. I am descended from both men. During the Revolution, John Darden, Jr., served as an ensign and, in 1781, was promoted to second lieutenant. He served under Nathanael Greene in the fierce fighting that took place in North and South Carolina.

John, Jr., and Jacob Darden had a close association with Stephen Heard, an early Georgia governor and the man for whom Heard County is named. The Scots-Irish Heard had been born in Ireland and immigrated to Virginia and then to Georgia, having been forced to leave Ireland when his father attacked an Anglican priest with a pitchfork. Stephen fought with George Washington in the French and Indian War, after which he moved to Wilkes County, Georgia, and established Heardmont, a large agricultural operation.

Stephen married a Miss Guerney and also sided with the Patriots in the American Revolution. When the British took Georgia and the Carolinas, Tories burned Heard's home and forced his wife and children to deal with the elements. Mrs. Heard died in a snowstorm from exposure.

While fighting in Georgia, Heard served under General Elijah Clarke at the Battle of Kettle Creek in Wilkes County, one of the key Revolutionary War battles in the state. He, along with twenty-three other Patriots, was captured, tried, and sentenced to hang forthwith. But Kate, a family slave, heard about her master's plight and took action. She was a large woman, standing over six feet tall, and Heard was a very small man. Kate appeared at the jailhouse door with a large box on her back. She told the jailor that she wanted to deliver some clean clothes to Mr. Heard. He countered that the prisoner would not need them as he was to be hung the next day. Kate persisted and the guard finally relented, allowing Kate into the cell where she had Heard change clothes and climb into the box. She covered him with the dirty clothes and carried him and the box out on her head. They then escaped on two Arabian horses, Star Heels and Lightfoot, which Heard had purchased earlier from General Washington (McCullar, p. 243).

"You saved my life, Kate. I free you," the governor said. "But I don't free you, Master Stephen," Kate replied. She remained with the family for the rest of her life and is buried at Heardmont on the same property as Heard's father-in-law, John Darden, Jr. (McCullar, p. 243).

John, Jr., and Jacob moved to Georgia after the Revolution and settled

Kate rescues Governor Heard by carrying him on
her head. Drawing by Kyle James.

first in Wilkes County and then in Emanuel County. After the war, John,
Jr.,'s daughter, Elizabeth, married Governor Heard. Jacob married Mary
Hilliard, the daughter of Colonel Elias Hilliard, a Patriot soldier who also
fought in North Carolina.

John, Jr.,'s son William married Mary Dekle, the daughter of John
Leonard Dekle, who emigrated in the late 1700's from Hanover, Germany,
through the port of Savannah. He was said to have been accompanied by
his brother. Dekle was an enterprising fellow. He acquired farmland on
the banks of Reedy Creek in what was then Montgomery County, later
became Emanuel County, and today is Candler County. More than two
hundred years later, that acreage is still in the possession of family heirs,
owned by Jim Thurmond, a direct descendant of John Dekle. William and

143

Mary Dekle Durden acquired more than one thousand acres of land near Norristown in Emanuel County. Their sixth child, Lucinda Durden, would later marry Manning Rountree.

The Durdens are perfect examples of Continental soldiers of English descent who moved to Georgia and adopted the Scots-Irish ways. Several times the Durdens married Scots-Irish and, in addition, the Durden family were leaders in Old Canoochee Primitive Baptist Church. They also embraced the Celtic practice of running herds of cattle, sheep, and hogs on their one thousand acres of wiregrass. This free running style of animal husbandry was quite characteristic among Scots-Irish southerners and was also commonly utilized by those of German and English descent.

*For a description of the events surrounding Martha Dandridge's first marriage to the wealthy Daniel Parke Custis, read Volume II, pages 290-299, of George Washington by Douglas Southhall Freeman. Some of it reads like a modern-day soap opera, especially the episode of Custis' father falling in love with a young slave boy and changing his will to leave his huge estate to the lad. After much wrangling, the family finally prevailed on Mr. Custis to limit his largess to granting the slave his freedom and a life estate in a rather opulent home.

Durden Reunion, about 1880. Notice the syrup pot that is used to cook Brunswick stew. Used with permission of the Georgia Archives.

SOPHIE WILSON HOLMES

When you get to be my age two things become quite apparent. The first is that one's existence on this earth goes by very quickly and the second is that there are certain people who impacted your life. Sophie Donna Wilson Holmes is, for me, one of those people. My great-grandmother was not only a very strong individual but also a person from another era – and as a child that really fascinated me.

I can see her now, sitting in her front porch swing on a hot Vidalia summer's night gently rocking one of my younger siblings while singing, "Go to Sleep." I would be sitting on the front steps and she would intersperse her lullaby with tales of what it was like during the very difficult Reconstruction period.

Sophie Holmes was born on Wednesday, January 23, 1868, just two years and two months after Appomattox. When Sophie was five, her mother, Kathryn Morrison Wilson, died after giving birth to her brother, D.Q. Wilson. Three months later, Sophie's grandmother, Mary Wilkes Morrison, died. This must have been a terrific shock for a five-year-old. Sophie's grandmother lived down the road, and I am sure she was a big part of the young girl's life. A year and seven months later, Sophie's father, Wallace R. Wilson, married Margaret F. McQueen. When Sophie was sixteen, Margaret McQueen died.

Sophie had an older sister, Mary Ella (Cummings), and a half sister, Kate (Vann). She also had two brothers, William Louis and D.Q. Wilson. Another brother, William Wallace Wilson, died while he was a baby.

Sophie was a very bright young lady. According to my mother, she was the top student at Walker Bridge School. When Sophie graduated from Walker Bridge, she was appointed teacher – April 15, 1886 (Davis, p. 361).

Kay Messink said that, after graduating from Walker Bridge, Sophie lived with the Peterson family. She was charged with walking the Peterson children to school. The story goes that this was necessary because of the Petersons' fear of snakes.

Sophie grew up in the Higgston community, near Vidalia. Her father was a prosperous dentist and farmer. Sophie and "sister Mary" played a big

Robert B. Holmes, husband of Sophie Wilson Holmes.

part in managing the Wilson household. On November 24, 1889, Sophie married Robert B. Holmes from Stellaville, Georgia. The wedding took place in Washington County, Georgia, most likely in Chalker, Georgia. Wallace R. Wilson was then living in Chalker. Stellaville was one of those places that if you blink, you'll miss it – I did. The small hamlet was just across the Jefferson/Washington County line from Chalker.

Dorothy Rountree Budd said that Sophie and Robert met while Sophie was in Washington County visiting her family. The story goes that the train was taking on passengers and Sophie was seen hanging out of a rail car window talking to some young friends. Robert was nearby and commented to an associate, "Who is that big-mouthed girl?" He was told that it was Sophie Wilson from Higgston. Robert promptly went over and introduced himself. The rest is history.

Robert B. Holmes was born October 16, 1860, to Robert W. and Lavinia Rainwater Holmes, who lived in Jefferson County, Georgia, west of Louisville. In that year's census, he was listed along with five siblings: Nancy J., David S., Lucinda, Alexander, and Caroline. Caroline later married Henry Parrish, the son of Jonathan Huff Parrish, a prominent Baptist minister.

During the War Between the States, Robert W. Holmes served in the Twelfth Georgia Regiment, Georgia Militia. In 1864, he took part in the defense of the Ogeechee River. After the war, he moved the family to Stellaville, most likely because the Ways Baptist Church there boasted an excellent private academy. Devout Christians all, Robert W., Lavinia, and their children were active members of Ways Baptist. A fascinating publication, *Ways Baptist Church Minutes 1817–1900, History 1817–1917*, tells an interesting story of the Holmes' family involvement.

During the nineteenth century, it was common for churches to discipline their members. This could be for various indiscretions including nonattendance, drinking, profanity, or dancing. On July 1, 1871, "Sister Aldrich, through her father, Brother R.W. Holmes, made acknowledgement to the church of having engaged in dancing since the granting of her letter of dismissal. She asked the church to forgive the offenses and requested the renewal of her letter. The church granted the application made in behalf of the Sister" (Smith, p. 66).

In the December 1881 minutes, Robert B. Holmes stated to the church that "he still wished to be excluded from the church on account of his unworthiness." It further stated that "the pastor requested to see the young brother and advised with him and 'C'" (Smith, p. 91). We do not know who "C" was. Apparently, Robert had had a disagreement with "C," and the pastor served as the mediator. It is interesting to note that some members seemed to come before the church quite often. Brother Oliphant was not only a leader but constantly appeared before the church body. When he asked for forgiveness, it was always given (Smith, p. 92).

On the other hand, the church made a great effort to take care of Saints in the community of faith. Before the War Between the States, blacks and whites worshipped together. Sister Hannah, "a free person of color, a member of this church, was in an afflicted and helpless condition and in need of some attention. A committee was appointed to give her relief. They voted to give her five dollars per month" (Smith, p. 97).

In the January 1879 minutes, it was reported that Sister Asenith Kendrich was without lodging. A committee was appointed, and sufficient housing was obtained. Another instance was that of Sister King, who was confined to her bed, and asked the membership to celebrate communion in her home. This was done (Smith, p. 97).

The fellowship was also very missional. This was quite remarkable when you consider how little they had. Ways Baptist Church was constantly sending funds to various mission projects, including the new Mercer University. I wonder if today's Mercer students realize the sacrifice that was made by countless Georgia Baptists.

The May 1884 minutes show that Robert B. Holmes was granted dismissal, apparently to join another church with his new wife Sophie. It was at that time that Robert became a Methodist. Robert and Sophie had six children – Jewel, Alex, Fred, Pierce, Clyde, and Kathryn.

Jewel left the family at a young age and struck out for California. About 1932, he drowned in a boating accident. Dorothy Budd still remembers Sophie's grief on hearing of her son's death. Jewel's son, Eldon, later worked for his uncle, Alex, a short time.

Alex attended Gordon Military College in Barnesville, Georgia, and

Alex Holmes (right), brother of Clyde.

148

graduated from the University of Georgia. After World War I, Alex was part of the U.S. and British Expeditionary Force that was sent to Russia in a feeble effort to quell the Bolshevik Revolution. It was at that time that Mr. Holmes developed an interest in furs and fur trading. Alex later married Leila Jardine from Douglas, Georgia. The couple traveled the Orient and Russia in search of furs. I have pictures that Alex took during the Bolshevik Revolution showing emaciated bodies piled as high as a ceiling, hundreds of them. Alex wrote on the back of one of the photographs that the people shown had died of starvation, disease, and gunshot wounds. Dorothy Budd said that Alex would send such interesting Christmas presents, including furs and Oriental rugs. Their business was first in San Francisco and later headquartered in Seattle. Alex and Leila had one child, Betty. Betty became an outstanding physician. She never married. Tragically, Betty was murdered in 1979 in a much publicized crime.

Fred became was a prominent Naval officer. Like his brother Alex, he attended Gordon Military College where he roomed with Richard B. Russell, later the prominent U.S. senator from Georgia. He graduated from the U.S. Naval Academy and served in World War I, earning the World War I ribbon with one star.

Fred was very generous in helping his sister, Clyde, and mother, Sophie. Dorothy Budd said that Fred owned the building occupied by the Vidalia Barbershop. The rent was fifty dollars per month. Clyde often had difficulty finding employment. During this time, the Vidalia public schools had a policy of not hiring locals. So Clyde would have to drive long distances to places like Center and Alston. Fred turned the barbershop rent over to his mother and sister, and Dorothy Budd says that many times, the rent money was the only thing that kept them going.

In a letter written for this book, Fred Holmes, Jr., - who also had a successful military career – indicates that although his father loved his family he had very little contact with them, a fact partly attributable to his active military service. Fred, Jr., notes that, "He [Fred, Sr.,] did not take me to his home in Vidalia to visit. My only visit to Vidalia was in November of 1956."

Between the world wars, Captain Fred Holmes, Sr., served on several battleships and also at the Pensacola Naval Air Station.

According to his son:

"During the early part of World War II, Dad served in the Fiji Islands running coast watchers in an effort consisting of covertly putting small

Fred S. Holmes

teams ashore on enemy islands to watch enemy shipping (and any other activity) and report by radio. For this service, Great Britain awarded him 'Night Commander Order of the British Empire.'"

Captain Holmes also served on Admiral Chester Nimitz's planning staff for the invasions of Iwo Jima and Okinawa. Later in the war he commanded the *USS Barrow,* a troop ship.

"Dad liked to tell the story that he got to pick the date for the invasion of Okinawa and picked it for my birthday, April 1."

Captain Holmes retired in 1949 and spent the rest of his life trading in real estate and antiques. He died September 21, 1970:

150

"He was in Providence, Rhode Island, with Mother at an auction. Mother said he all of a sudden made a funny noise and just keeled over. He never regained consciousness. I was at MIT just starting work on my Ph.D. and my family and I were living in Wheland, Massachusetts."

Pierce Holmes, a bachelor, became an attorney. He lived for a while in Savannah, Georgia, before moving to Houston, Texas. He experienced recurrent health problems, including bouts with alcoholism, and died on December 21, 1968. Like his brothers, Alex and Fred, Pierce made an effort to help Clyde and Sophie. One Christmas when the children were young, Pierce offered to bring the Santa Claus gifts. Clyde agreed, and Pierce promised to arrive at her home with the gifts on Christmas Eve. Clyde related how she waited all night for Pierce to show up. As the night passed, she became more and more concerned that Santa Claus was not coming. About seven a.m., the sun was rising and the children could be heard from their bedroom saying, "Can we get up now?" Clyde was getting desperate. Finally, she heard the sound of Pierce's car. The presents had arrived. Clyde said that after this harrowing experience, she would never again trust Santa Claus to anyone else.

Kathryn graduated from Wesleyan College in Macon, Georgia, and moved to Winston-Salem, North Carolina. There she met Kelsey Messink, a tobacco dealer with the R.J. Reynolds Tobacco Company. They married and moved about because the tobacco markets were held in different Southern towns. After World War II, they purchased a home in Vidalia on Jackson Street. Ann Messink Ross, their older daughter, graduated from Wesleyan College and married Dick Ross. They have three children and live in Memphis, Tennessee. Kay Messink, their younger daughter, graduated from the University of North Carolina at Chapel Hill and is a retired schoolteacher. She also lives in Memphis.

Dorothy Budd says that the home in which they lived on Church Street belonged to Grandmother Holmes. Mother says that not once during her childhood did Sophie ever mention that she owned the home and not Clyde. This was their home.

During the Depression, the Messinks also lived with Mrs. Holmes. This was not uncommon – families living together in order to save money. Thus, Ann and Kay Messink grew up well acquainted with their grandmother have vivid memories of her. Kay describes her as a "fantastic lady" and says that she "impacted so many of us."

Ann Ross said that Grandmother Holmes had a garden located by the ice plant. "I would accompany her to her garden, just a block from the house. She used an entire city block for the garden. She contracted to have it plowed, and then she would plant her seed. Sometimes she would let me plant some seeds under her watchful supervision. I can see her now in her big straw hat with her hoe, walking down the street to her garden." Kay wrote that Grandmother Holmes had a "large garden raising tomatoes, corn, potatoes, green beans, peas, and butter beans." (Ann also remembers her growing crowder peas, black-eyed peas, and onions.) She must have also grown cabbage, because she made kraut. Ann related that "as a child, I could go to the garden with her but couldn't do anything but pick bugs off the potatoes and tomatoes. During World War II, a canning plant was built, and Grandmother made good use of it. All of the 'girls' (Kay, Ann, Dorothy, Virginia, and Christine) would be shelling peas on the back porch, and she would say, 'Shell faster, girls, shell faster.' She had to get to the canning plant by one p.m. in order to finish by closing time.

She would stand on the front porch watering the yard while it was raining. When you asked her why, she would say it wasn't going to rain enough. She also raised chickens, and during World War II she canned chicken and sent packages to Virginia and James when they were overseas."

Frank Cummings, grandson of Q. Wilson, told me that the progress of their respective gardens was one of the favorite topics of conversation between Sophie and her brother Q. when he would visit her in Vidalia – which he did often because he loved his sister dearly. Once, Q. ventured the opinion that his garden was faring much better than hers and wondered out loud why this was the case. After some moments hesitation, Sophie replied that she bought all her seeds from Mr. Hastings in Atlanta. Then she added, "And you know he's a Republican."

At that time there was no government social safety net and the task of feeding the hungry fell to churches and individuals. Kay Messink remembers how people often knocked on Grandmother Holmes' back door seeking food. Kay said she never, ever recalled Sophie turning anyone down. If there were hungry people in Vidalia, I asked Kay, why didn't Grandmother Holmes have vegetables stolen from her garden. Almost indignantly, Kay answered, "Because people did not steal back then. It just wasn't done."

Among Kay's memories: "She loved babies, but especially baldheaded babies. Ann had a head of hair, and Grandmother would lay her across her lap, stroke her hair, and say, 'You'd be beautiful if you were bald.'" And: "She would not take a trip out of town. She would go visit Aunt Kate (Kate Vann) every Sunday, and she would walk down the street to visit Aunt

Sophie Holmes, early fifties. Notice Mr. Cullens' store in the background. As children, we loved to visit Mr. Cullens.

Alice, her sister-in-law. She would not go to visit her sister, Mary, or her brother, Q., both of whom lived in Washington County. She would say no before you got it out of your mouth."

Ann reminisces that "when I was ready for bed, I would crawl up in Grandmother's lap while she was sitting in her rocking chair in front of the fire. She would read me the funny papers. Her favorites were 'Rex Morgan, M.D.' and 'Brenda Starr.' Also, the last thing she would do was to sing me a lullaby, 'Go to Sleep, Little Baby.'" In the letter she sent, Ann included the words to this lullaby. It is amazing to me how all who knew Grandmother Holmes remember that song.

Ann tells how "sometimes she would make kettle tea for us for breakfast. It consisted of hot milk, vanilla flavoring, and sugar, with about a teaspoon of tea in it." I remember how Grandmother fixed breakfast toast. She would use real butter, no margarine. She would put one large glob of butter right in the middle of the bread, then put it in the oven. The buttered bread cooking made the kitchen smell wonderful. After putting jam or jelly on the toast, it was necessary to bite it in such a manner that

Grandmother Sophie Holmes.

you got just a little bit of the butter each time. You would end up eating the toast in a circular pattern. Ann says that "when Grandmama called us to eat, she would immediately tell us to 'go wash your hands.'"

Ann also relates how "when I had the croup, she would rub my chest with Vicks and put a square of flannel she had warmed by the fire on my chest, and I would go to bed. Good remedy." She also remembers "seeing

154

Sophie and her sister Kate, in Mrs. Holmes' bedroom, taking their hay-fever treatment together. It was a powder in a tin can. They would put some powder in the top of the can and set it on fire, then sat and breathed in the smoke. Did it stink!"

As was common during hard times, not only did Clyde and her four children live with Grandmother Holmes, but Kelsey's and Kathryn's families lived there also. There were two double beds and a single bed in Clyde's room. My mother recalls how Clyde and her three daughters slept in that room. Uncle James slept in a small room off of the back of the house. Later, as many as five females slept in Clyde's room. Kay told me that they all got along and that everyone did their part.

One of Christine "Chrissy" Anderson Williams' memories when visiting Vidalia was the big black skillet placed under the outdoor faucet to catch water for the animals. When she returned as an adult, she was surprised to see that it was such a small frying pan. Maybe the phrase, "You can't go home again," means that when you do, things will not be the same.

As Ann sums up: "Grandmother was a remarkable lady – smart and independent. Her husband died when my mother [their daughter] was only two years old. She had six children to look after and educate. Someone told me that every time one of her children went to prep school and college, she would sell off a piece of land to pay for it. She really believed in education. In an age when this was very rare, Sophie Wilson Holmes had five of her six children graduate from college."

Author's Note: Below is a letter written on Mother's Day 1955 by Alex Holmes to his mother Sophie Wilson Holmes.

Seattle, Washington
May 8, 1955

Dear Mother,

Something you should know and that I should tell you every day of your life. You are a very wonderful person. Now on Mother's Day I want you to know what a wonderful mother you have been to your own children, your grandchildren, and great grandchildren – you were the same to your father, your brothers and sisters. Your devotion and sacrifice to five generations where you have been a mother to all of them certainly must be rewarded in heaven. I want it to be a comfort to you at all times. You are grand.

Hope the day will be pleasant for you. I would love to be with you on Sunday. Will certainly be thinking of you. Am sure that you will have a good many of the family with you. Sorry that Leila and I can't be there (you are the only mother she has ever known) and loves you very much.

With every wish for your health and happiness in which Leila and Betty join me.

Your Son,
D.A. Holmes

"GO TO SLEEP"

Anyone who knew Sophie Holmes as a child remembers the lullaby, "Go To Sleep."

I always thought that this song was local to Vidalia and the family; however, I was recently in Camilla, Georgia, and heard my friend Jim Joiner

Go To Sleep

Go to sleep, Go to sleep. Go to sleep-y lit-tle ba - by.

Ma-ma went a-way and she told me to stay and take good care of the ba - by.

When she comes back she'll gimme piece of cake. An lem-me go to Meetin' with my dad - dy.

Baaah black sheep. Where is your lamb? Way down yon-der in the val - ley.

Buzzards and the butter-flies. Peckin' out his eyes. An the po' lil' thing cries "Mam - my!"

Horsey Hold Your Tail Up

Hor - sey hold your tail up. Hold your tail up. Hold your tail up.

Hor - sey hold your tail up. Keep the sun out-ta my eyes.

singing, "Go To Sleep." He told me that he had heard it as a child and had sung it to his daughter, Amy, who did not like the violent references. I would guess that the song's origin may be African or possibly Celtic, because it resembles an Appalachian lullaby discovered by my daughter, Becky.

"Horsey, Hold Your Tail Up" is a little ditty taught to my mother and her sister, Christine, by their uncle, Josh Rountree, who was about their age. Mother said that Clyde did not approve and thought the song naughty.

GLEANING

Gleaning is the gathering of leftover crops after harvest. Leviticus 23:22 commands a farmer to leave gleanings for the poor. In what is a beautiful love story, Ruth met Boaz while gleaning his fields.

It has not been long since our family engaged in the ancient practice of gleaning.

After the War Between the States, Georgians were economically devastated. Towns like Sandersville, the county seat of Washington County, were almost totally destroyed. In addition, farms, crops, and homes had been laid waste.

At this time, my great-great-grandfather, Wallace R. Wilson, married Kathryn Morrison and started his family and set up housekeeping near Higgston, Georgia. The land on which the community had been built had been donated by Wilson's father-in-law, D.Q. Morrison. Part of an original land grant given to the Morrison family by the State of Georgia (Davis, p. 270), the town was named after James Higgs. He, like many other early Montgomery County residents, was a descendant of a Revolutionary soldier who had migrated from North Carolina. Higgs lost his leg in the War Between the States. After the war, he married and fathered five children.

In 1881, the *Montgomery Monitor* stated that "wood and cotton are the principal articles of export...[Higgston] has a steam grist mill and gin and a Methodist church...James Higgs, P.M. Higgs Grist Mill, McIntyre, A.J. Constable, W.R. Wilson Dentist" (Davis, p. 270).

Because of the grinding poverty produced by the war and Federal impositions, there was a great need for social services. One-third of southern white males between the ages of seventeen and twenty-eight had been killed in the war. As a result, there were many orphaned children.

South Georgia Methodists responded by founding a children's home in Macon, primarily for the displaced children of Confederate veterans. Money was not available to fund the home so the idea was floated that each community give a day of work each year, gleaning cotton fields. The slogan was, "Pick a bale of cotton for the orphans' home." Later, a matron at the South Georgia Children's Home, Miss Annie McDonald, coined the phrase "work day." The term is still used today when Georgia Methodists collect money for the South and North Georgia Children's Homes (Keith-Lucas).

While looking through a recent issue of *The History of Montgomery County,* I discovered a picture of members of the Higgston Methodist Church picking cotton for the children's home. There, standing in the back row, sixth from the left, was my great-grandmother, Sophie Wilson Holmes.

I have studied this picture many times and find it to be intriguing. Who is the nice looking man to Sophie's left rear? Who is the other nice looking man, third from the right? He looks like he is kin to the man standing behind Sophie. You will notice that the men do not look downtrodden or beaten, but quite sure of themselves. Look at the young boy on the front row, far left. What is on his mind? Why is the woman in the middle sitting sideways? Check out the woman on the far left, wearing a bonnet, or the woman seated in front of the lady holding a baby. What kind of stories could they tell?

Leviticus 23:22, "When you reap the harvest of your land, do not reap to the very edges of your field, or gather the gleanings of your harvest. Leave them for the poor and the alien."

Cotton picking for the Methodist Home.

WHAT IT WAS LIKE

We need to remember was that the living conditions of late-nineteenth- and early-twentieth-century Georgians were unimaginable to the generations that followed, especially our own.

There was no Marshall Plan after the War Between the States as was implemented by the U.S. after World War II to help a devastated Europe recover. The Federal government had waged war on Southern civilians in a manner never seen before or since. During the 1864 Shenandoah Valley Campaign, General Phil Sheridan bragged that he had burned one thousand barns and homes. General William T. Sherman was no better. Georgia civilians had their livestock and crops destroyed, barns and homes burned, and the populace displaced. Great-Grandmother Sophie Holmes told me that after the Yankees came through Washington and Montgomery counties, there was nothing left to eat, not even salt enough to gather from the smokehouse floor.

Sherman's troops cut a sixty-mile-wide swath from Atlanta to Savannah. Swainsboro and Canoochee were in the middle of this path. One hundred twenty thousand Yankee troops lived off the civilian population. They ate what they wanted and destroyed the rest. This not only fostered bitterness that has lasted through the years; it also created unparalleled economic hardship.

Most people think of the Great Depression as lasting from 1929 to the onset of World War II. I contend that, because of the War Between the States, Georgia suffered an economic depression from 1865 until 1940.

It is remarkable how Georgians were able to survive after the war, particularly when you consider the policies instituted by the Federal government that added to the plight of all southerners. There was no availability of capital and, consequently, it was difficult to start new business ventures that could employ the young.

My great-uncles – Alex, Fred, Jewel, and Pierce Holmes – are examples of young southerners who left Georgia looking for better opportunities. In a letter to his sister Clyde dated October 1937, Alex Holmes shows the feeling the Holmes boys had toward conditions in the South. He writes from Seattle, Washington, about James Rountree, Clyde's son:

"James' health is better than when he came out here. Not knocking the South like Fred does, but must say that most people are malarial, and therefore, slow. It takes a year to get over this and develop the energy that is shown in the east or north. Your son will go places as well as the girls."

Part of Alex's complaint could be blamed on economic conditions and part could be laid to culture.

In his book *Cracker Culture*, Grady McWhiney points out that the War Between the States was not as much a fight of "brother against brother" as it was of culture against culture (McWhiney, p. xiii).

What Alex referred to as "malarial" was a difference in lifestyle between the more laid back southern culture and the Yankee, English, capitalistic way of doing things. The latter placed value on work and the accumulation of capital and as a virtue. Celtic southerners were more prone to value quality of life. This is one reason Celts were stockmen growing only enough food for family consumption. Raising stock on grass was a tradition brought from Northern Ireland and Scotland. It also allowed for a more relaxed lifestyle as the cattle only needed to be "gotten up" about twice a year.

In a 1928 letter to Clyde concerning James' applying to the U.S. Naval Academy in Annapolis, Fred writes:

"Vidalia High School is accredited, but I am told that the high schools there are worthless as prep schools...I know any smart boy who will get going, can pass a year of general high school in one month."

We must remember that Vidalia had no running water until 1920, although some citizens had electricity around 1905. Canoochee had neither until much later. There was no electricity in the countryside until the Rural Electrification Administration was formed in 1939.

While many of the Rountree-Holmes ancestors were teachers, the vast majority were yeoman farmers. Yeoman farmers were small, independent-minded people who worked and lived off their own land. What was their life like?

I had a fascinating interview with my dear friend and cousin, Sarah Underwood. She describes what it was like growing up on a yeoman farm in the very early twentieth century. Sarah, age ninety-three, was Otis Rountree's first cousin. Her father, Eugene Flanders, and Otis' mother, Zannie, were siblings. Sarah said that, when she was a young girl living near Canoochee, there was no telephone, electricity, or running water. She related how the family took a bath on Saturday night. The children bathed one after the other in the same water. The water was warmed either by the sun or near the log fire, depending on the season.

An example of how almost everything was handmade was the spoons and forks that Sarah still keeps. The forks are handmade and are worn on the left side. This is because everyone had their own fork and a metal plate. A right-handed person would wear the fork down on the left side.

Canoochee and Swainsboro were part of Georgia's wiregrass country. Wiregrass was used to graze cattle and sheep for nine months in the year. The other three months, the animals were turned out to glean the cotton and corn fields. In the early days, livestockmen drove their cattle to market, cracking their whips over the animals heads. Thus, the name "Crackers."

Because this land had abundant grass and a sandier soil, it did not have the large plantations of central Georgia. The yeoman farmers in the wiregrass country made their living off of a few cattle, hogs, sheep, and small crops of cotton. Corn was grown for the livestock and family consumption.

Each December when the temperature dropped the hogs were killed. Every part of the hog was used, from the bladder that was enjoyed by the children as a football, to the hams and shoulders that were salted and then placed on pine straw to dry. After drying, they were hung in a smokehouse. Even the intestines were either ground for sausage or washed for chitlins. The chitlins were served boiled or fried. If you have never tried chitlins you surely ought to experience them one time. My wife says don't bother. I prefer them boiled.

The corn was gathered dry. Corn cobs were used for fire starters and ground for feed. Before killing time, the corn was fed to the hogs. Chickens were housed in a coop and used for both eggs and meat. Surplus eggs were sold in town.

Sarah related how her father, Eugene Flanders, would get up early on Sunday morning, kill a chicken, and serve it fresh with biscuits for breakfast. I know she is correct in saying that no commercial chicken ever tasted so good. She also said, "My father was a mighty good man."

The family also kept turkeys and ate squirrel and rabbit. A small patch of sugar cane was also kept. In the fall, the farmers would bring their cane to one location and have a cane grinding. This was a grand social event and you will find this mentioned in several of Otis and Clyde's letters. The cane was used to make Georgia cane syrup which is still the best syrup

Cleaning chitlins - circa 1946 - E.I. Fordham Farm. Used with permission of the Georgia Archives.

there is. In addition, cane was also used to make sugar and cane juice. Cane juice is only good when fresh, and is quite delightful.

The job of a farm wife was particularly difficult. The wood stove had to be lit each time it was used, and that created summer time heat. Soot from the stove would permeate the kitchen, and since there was no refrigeration, meals had to be prepared daily.

Water had to be hauled from the well, and in the summer, canning was a very hot, difficult job. Boiling water, canning peaches, pears, apples, tomatoes, okra, peas, and beans, took constant attention to the stove in a sweltering house.

Washing was a weekly chore, usually done on Tuesday. Scrub boards, either metal or wood, were used. The clothes were washed outside in a big vat using homemade lye soap.

The predominant material used in farm clothes was chembrey, a rough type of cotton. Everything had to be ironed. The six pound iron was heated either on a stove or near the fireplace. The irons had to be constantly reheated. Ironing a typical man's shirt took two heated irons. Because of the rough material, even pillow cases needed to be ironed. No wonder southern women called irons "sad irons".

The result of all this backbreaking work was that women aged way before their time. The workload, coupled with medical problems associated with childbirth, meant that Southern rural women also had a shorter lifespan than their husbands. My great-great-grandfather, Wallace R. Wilson, lost two young wives. Both died from complications associated with childbirth.

This is the world into which young Dr. James Otis Rountree established his practice. Sarah said that Otis encouraged the people of Canoochee to dig deep wells so as to improve sanitation. He also promoted the first use of aspirin. This was in reaction to the flu epidemic, which swept through the South shortly after he began practicing.

You will see in the article on "Nineteenth Century Cures" that Dr. Otis Rountree had a lot of superstitions to overcome.

CANE SYRUP

Our grandson, Andrew Rich, enjoying sugar cane while sitting in the door of a restored 19th century house. Taken at the Jarrell Plantation at Travelers Rest Historic Site.

Most families who have lived in an area for any length of time possess certain fixtures and traits that run through the generations. What I would call a fixture is an item that is typical of the area, not just one family. In our case, it would be cane syrup, because from 1800 to 1940 cane syrup was a fixture in the lives of our forebears.

Cane syrup is a dark brown sweetener made from sugar cane. It has a very distinctive flavor – and I love it. If God made anything better than cane syrup, he would have kept it for himself. My wife Courtenay's biscuits, with real butter and cane syrup, are something to experience. Actually, you have to eat them in private or you will embarrass yourself.

This past week, we had four friends who are also New York Life

Insurance Company agents to dinner (the midday meal), to meet our new managing partner, Amy Scott. All of the guests were Southerners, with the exception of my good friend, Tim Chisholm, a Canadian, who works harder than anyone to be a Southerner. Courtenay put on the feed – country-fried steak, creamed corn, mashed potatoes, black-eyed peas, collard greens, fried okra, squash casserole, pecan pie (pronounced PEE-can pie), and sweet potato pie with real whipped cream. We have always had a bottle of cane syrup sitting on our table. Keith Mitchum, Tim Ellen, Chris Cuneo, and Burke Murph got into the cane syrup and biscuits. They, along with the others, consumed the entire bottle.

Courtenay and I have been diligent in seeing that our five children were raised with a proper appreciation of their South Georgia heritage. That is why I have always made sure that our family was amply supplied with cane syrup. Consequently, my children have taken up the tradition.

From the time that our family came to Georgia until World War II, our ancestors grew sugar cane and processed it into cane syrup at great social events called cane grindings. You will read in the letters how, in the fall of the year, people gathered and a farmer would make the syrup. Keep in mind that it takes about one hundred stalks of sugar cane to produce one gallon of cane syrup. It was a laborious process. The cane first has to be

Boiling cane syrup.

168

grown, no small task in itself. When it is mature, it is ground to squeeze out the juice, which is put in a large kettle and cooked down to about ten percent of its original volume. During this process, the workers "draw off the skimmings," which is any solid matter left after the grinding. The trick is to take up the syrup when it has *just* the proper consistency. It takes many hands, but it is always great fun and people enjoy getting together. Referring to cane syrup, South Georgian Janisse Ray, in her book *Wild Card Quilt*, wrote, "If our history had a taste this would be it!" (Ray, p. 68). I wholeheartedly concur.

LONGLEAF PINE

For seven generations my family has had an association with the longleaf pine and wiregrass. Around 1790, when Francis Richard and Nancy Jordan Flanders came to Georgia, south Georgia was a virtual sea of huge, old growth longleaf pine. The trees were not jammed together as is currently the practice, but were randomly spaced by nature. The forest floor was covered with wiregrass – a type of grass peculiar to the longleaf pine ecosystem.

During this period, numerous writers commented on the beauty of the primeval pine and wiregrass forest. In March 1828, Basil Hall, a British soldier, traveled inland from Savannah. He found roads to be almost nonexistent but he discovered this area to be quite beautiful:

> "I don't know exactly what was the cause, but it was a long time before I got quite tired of the scenery of these beautiful pine barrens. There was something, I thought, very graceful in the millions upon millions of tall and slender columns, growing up in solitude, not crowded upon one another, but gradually appearing to come closer and closer until they formed a compact mass, beyond which nothing was to be seen. Not even a ray of the sun could pierce this gloom; and the imagination was at liberty to follow its own devices into the wilderness, as far as it pleased" (Dorsey, p. 32).

After The War Between the States, the longleaf pine was almost completely removed and, over a period of about seventy years, the wiregrass surrendered to cropland and "improved grasses." Having raised cattle for twenty-five years, I can tell you that these so-called improved grasses demand water and fertilizer that was not necessary with wiregrass. With wiregrass, cattle could be run on a woods pasture almost year round without the extra demand of heavy fertilization.

The old growth longleaf was replaced with pine plantations that contained as many as nine hundred trees per acre. These are no more forests than are fields of cotton or soybeans. They are a crop. And because the sunlight cannot reach the ground and pine straw becomes quite thick, seed-producing plants do not grow and wildlife has nothing to eat. This is one of several reasons so many species have declined. In addition, the once beautiful wiregrass country with its stately five hundred-year-old pines does not have the serenity it once had. But of course, a pine plantation is certainly preferable to asphalt.

My mother, Dorothy Rountree Budd, tells a tale of Rocky Creek, a spot near Vidalia, Georgia, owned by a Mrs. Peterson. Mother says that it was as beautiful a place as you could imagine. She describes it as "gorgeous." She says that on her birthday and other special occasions, she and her friends would picnic there, and pick violets and make bouquets. She also says that if you lay in the wiregrass, you could hear the trees singing. Years later, when mother returned to Vidalia for one of her annual visits, she and her friends – Louise Jones, Jane Jackson McNatt, and Jean Jones Tolleson – visited Rocky Creek. It had been stripped of its timber, and track housing had taken its place. The violets were gone, and even the creek had dried up. Apparently, Mrs. Peterson had died, and Zenobia, her daughter, had sold the land. Its new owner had cut the timber, and you know the rest. Today, this part of Rocky Creek is a fishing pond.

Perhaps Zenobia needed the money. The primary reason for the demise of the longleaf in the first place was that, after the War Between the States, people were broke and they needed income in order to feed their families. As a result, northern capitalists descended on the South and took advantage of its cheap labor in wantonly developing this huge resource. They created a mini economic boom that collapsed as soon as the longleaf was gone.

One example of this is Chalker, Georgia, long ago situated in northeast Washington County near the Ogeechee River. My great-great-uncle, Q. Wilson, owned a store there. The town grew up around the timber industry and it was said that the sawdust piles were higher than two-story buildings. The Ogeechee River Swamp eventually was denuded of its old growth timber – hardwoods, cypress, and longleaf pine. Once the timber was gone, Chalker ceased to exist.

Much of the old growth longleaf pine was literally stolen from the people of Georgia. After the War Between the States, a northern businessman named William E. Dodge moved to what is now Dodge County, west of Emanuel and Montgomery counties. Since he did not drink, smoke, or work on Sunday, the community thought him to be a pious, decent man. Events were to prove otherwise. William E. Dodge, along with his sons, as well as a W.P. Eastman and a William Chauncey, established a vast timber operation. They used every method possible to lay their hands on trees to feed their mills, generally by obtaining improperly titled land and thereby robbing the rightful owners of their property. The landowners whose families had settled the Three Rivers region early in the nineteenth century resisted as best they could but the clout of the Dodge Company, combined with the Federal government, then in its "reconstruction" mode, was too powerful (Morrison, p. 112).

Lawmakers appointed by the Federal reconstruction government dominated the state legislature. As a result, the Georgia House and Senate were not freely elected, and Dodge and other unscrupulous carpetbaggers got their way. In addition, when Dodge encountered difficulty in getting the local courts to rule in his favor, he formed his own county – Dodge County – by using the corrupt legislature to carve it out of surrounding counties. Dodge is the only one of Georgia's one hundred fifty-nine counties that has the dubious distinction of being named after a carpetbagger.

The landowners did not knuckle under without a fight. Lucius Williams, a former sheriff and an ex-officer in the Confederate army, was one of those who resisted. But Dodge had deep pockets and he was not above using violence to obtain his end. He had Federal marshals kill Williams while he was asleep on his porch. His home, with his family huddled inside, was riddled with thirty-two bullet holes. This was one of many shameful instances in which violence was used to intimidate the local populace (Morrison, p. 132).

The result of these tragic events was that three hundred thousand acres of old growth longleaf timber were harvested. Many of the logs were floated down the Ocmulgee and Oconee rivers to the Altamaha River, and ultimately to Darien, Georgia, on the Atlantic coast. There, the timber was cut up and most of it sent to Europe. The environmental damage to Dodge, Telfair, Pulaski, Laurens, Wheeler, and part of Montgomery counties was incalculable.

Travelers reported that, in just twenty-five years, Georgia's pine belt was transformed from an exquisite forest to a land of cutover timber. The region was reported to look like a moonscape with stumps as far as the

Cousin Leonard Rountree's sawmill, located between Twin City and Canoochee.

eye could see. With no longleaf, the ecology of the whole region changed. The sand hill crane, the indigo snake, the red-cockaded woodpecker, the wood duck, and the gopher tortoise, to name only a few species, dropped precipitously in numbers. Erosion became a problem and the loss of topsoil produced a long-term negative economic impact. It is estimated that the Three Rivers section lost almost a foot of topsoil (Trimble, p. 142) while Little Saint Simons Island – off the Georgia coast – was reported to have grown almost a mile in length as a result of this erosion (Rogers). The three rivers remain filled with sediment today. Sediment still is "arriving" at the Georgia coast one hundred twenty-five years later (Rogers).

It is interesting to note that the site of Epworth By The Sea, the well-known Methodist campground on Saint Simons Island, was once owned by the Dodge Company. At its height, the company mill on the island sawed more than one hundred thousand feet of lumber daily (Martin, p. 39). Walking in the water at low tide, one can see the waste that was typical of that time, for even today there are hundreds of long slabs that were simply discarded. My cousin, William Dopson, a well-known forester, told me that only a small portion of each of these magnificent trees was actually used once it was felled. I guess it would be comparable to cutting the heart out of a watermelon and throwing the rest away.

When the Flanders and Rountrees settled in Georgia, the southern coastal plain contained ninety million acres of old growth longleaf pine. Now there are about three to four million acres. This important ecosystem contains wildlife that is highly dependent on the longleaf pine and wiregrass for survival. The wiregrass must be burned yearly in order to maintain the delicate balance between it and the trees. This process also enables the plants upon which wildlife depend to regenerate, and it assures that wiregrass predominates on the forest floor. Before the white man came, American Indians realized the importance of this cycle. If lightning did not do the job, then they burned the forests themselves.

The settlers of the Three Rivers area resisted Dodge because they had a lot more invested in their property than mere money. The Three Rivers area encompasses the land on the west bordered by the Ocmulgee, on the east by the Oconee, and on the south by the beginning of the Altamaha. This is the region that experienced Georgia's most severe battles between white settlers and Indians. Carlton Morrison, in his book *Running the River,* points out that settlers in this area were more interested in survival than "legal niceties" (Morrison, p.116) – the very thing that enabled Dodge to steal their property out from under them. After all, these people had given their blood and had settled an area that was, at best, harsh and unforgiving.

An incident involving my father's great-great-grandmother, Rebecca Pridgen Swain, exemplifies frontier rigors. Her father, Mark Pridgen, had been captured and killed by Indians in 1815. Rebecca was living in Jacksonville, Georgia, with her husband, Thomas S. Swain, a Telfair County office holder and prominent citizen. Their tract was at the big bend of the Ocmulgee River. At that time, whites occupied the eastern or "county" side of the Ocmulgee while the western side was considered Indian territory. Rebecca's sister had married Ludd Mobley, who owned a store on the western side of the river. He traded with the Indians and was considered an honest merchant. When the Indian trouble started, Rebecca crossed the river traveling in a one-horse cart to urge her sister to come to Jacksonville for safety. Several white families had been massacred, and Nancy had just had a baby. Nancy, however, would not leave her husband and was afraid that the journey would endanger her newborn.

Early the next morning, Indians in war paint appeared at the Mobley home. Ludd thought the best thing to do was to play along, so he warmly greeted them and invited them to sit down for breakfast. The Indians immediately accepted and went to Ludd's well and washed off the war paint. After eating, the Indians asked to see Ludd's new baby. They entered the room and confronted a terrified Nancy holding the child. The Indians said, "Me not hurt Mobley baby, me not hurt Mobley wife." They then repainted themselves, went about a mile down the road, and massacred an entire family (Morrison, p. 117).

Indian atrocities in the Three Rivers area began again in the spring of 1818. In March of that year, my father's great-great-grandfather, John Willcox II, heard a knock on his door. It was Littleton Burch. He and his father, Joseph, had crossed the Ocmulgee River and were no longer in Indian territory when they had been attacked while sleeping. Joseph Burch had been killed, and Littleton had been scalped while pretending to be dead. Littleton had placed moss on his head to relieve the pain. It had taken him two excruciating days, to make his way to the John Willcox house. After a long recuperation, Littleton finally returned to health and lived a long life.

This news spread among the settlers, who congregated at nearby Fort Adams for safety. They appointed Major Josiah Cawthon to head a militia force of thirty-four men to cross the Ocmulgee and attack the Indians. The militia surprised about sixty Indians eating breakfast at a creek now known as Breakfast Branch. A spirited engagement ensued. My ancestor,

Wiregrass. Courtesy of The Nature Conservancy.

175

John Willcox II – for whom Wilcox County is named – and his son, Mark, took part in this battle.* Mark had a long-time enemy, Nat Statham. In fact, it was reported that they were carrying weapons with the intention of using them on each other. When the whites attacked, Mark was shot in the head and it looked as if he would die on the battlefield. However, Nat picked Mark up, placed him on his shoulder with his rifle in tow, and in a hail of bullets carried his former enemy to a canoe. Nat, along with the other whites, was forced to cross the Ocmulgee. Five whites and four Indians died in the engagement. Among the whites to die was Michael Burch, brother of Littleton Burch, who was fighting to avenge his father and brother.

Mark Willcox would later become a member of the Georgia Legislature and a general in the Georgia Militia.

I am sure you can understand that, because of the sacrifices they had made, these settlers weren't real keen on Mr. Dodge's taking their property. This was particularly so because of the underhanded way in which he acquired their land and timber.

After Dodge swindled the people of the Three Rivers region, he moved his operation to Arizona. There he practiced the same tactics, taking land from settlers and Indians, this time for mining operations. Phelps Dodge Company, one of the largest copper extractors in the world, was formed out of this mining operation (Douglas).

To this day, there are land-title disputes in the Three Rivers area, due in part to the activities of the Dodges, and the environmental legacy left to us is more than burdensome (Rogers).

That's the bad news. The good news is that organizations such as the Nature Conservancy and the Woodruff Foundation, in tandem with the State of Georgia, are attempting to save the last remaining stands of longleaf pine. The State of Georgia, in cooperation with the Nature Conservancy, recently obtained large tracts of longleaf pine in Appling and Coffee counties. These forward-thinking groups realize that there is tremendous value in preserving the longleaf so that future generations may enjoy their majesty.

I recently visited the Joseph W. Jones Ecological Research Center at Ichauway Plantation. Ichauway, located near Newton, has one of Georgia's largest concentrations of longleaf pine. On each of the two mornings I was there, I arose before daylight, put on my exercise shoes, and walked on one of the four hundred miles of dirt roads that crisscross this twenty-nine thousand, four hundred fifty-one-acre plantation. The early December air was refreshing but it was the listening that was captivating. The sounds of the awakening day were akin to being in church. My friend, Noel Holcomb, had told me that to experience an early morning walk through the longleafs is to realize that, despite the issues facing us, the sun would come up, the birds would sing, and God would remain on His throne. Russ Harden, who works with the Woodruff Foundation, told me that a grand cathedral cannot offer a better place for worship. As the sun rose through the crowns of the longleafs, I felt God's presence in a very profound way.

* Another of John II's sons, Woodson, my great-great-grandfather, had seventy-eight sons, grandsons, and sons-in-law serve the Confederate cause. Of the seventy-eight, twelve died while fighting for the South (Evans, p. 2).

Otis Rountree and Clyde Holmes, surrounded by wiregrass

THE LETTERS OF CLYDE
HOLMES AND OTIS ROUNTREE

We are most fortunate that Clyde and Otis' daughters, Virginia, Dorothy, and Christine, saved their parent's letters. My cousin, Becky Waldron, called these correspondences family treasures – and they certainly are. Clyde and Otis wrote to each other between 1911 and 1920. Their epistles are funny, instructive, and prophetic. Reading them allows us to step back in time and get a glimpse of the life and trials of two young people falling in love.

In 1911, Otis was attending school at Atlanta College of Physicians and Surgeons (later Emory Medical School), and Clyde was beginning her studies at LaGrange College, a Methodist liberal arts college for women in LaGrange, Georgia. Otis was not only attending school, studying, and keeping the company of friends, but was also having to deal with his

James Otis Rountree   Clyde Holmes

recurrent stomach ailments. Clyde stayed busy teaching piano, going to church activities, and socializing, as well as keeping up with what was going on back in Vidalia.

As you read these letters, please remember that Clyde and Otis were very young. Secondly, I would urge you to interpret their words in the context of the times in which they were written. We should not judge persons living in the early twentieth century by the notions of the early twenty-first. After all, Otis, while in high school, was as close to the War of 1812 as we are to Otis.

It is obvious to me that Otis was his family's shining star. He was not only focused on his medical career but was a leader in his medical fraternity. He was loyal and smart, had a great sense of humor, and enjoyed a healthy social life. I never knew my grandfather, but having read through his letters and diaries several times, I feel a close kinship to this "forever young" man.

To describe Clyde, I will use Otis' own words. She was "a fine little girl, practical, smart, pretty. In fact she has all the attributes that go to make a good wife" (Diary, September 9, 1912). She later also proved to be very tough and resilient. Clyde was a testimony to the Proverbs' admonition that "her children rise up and call her blessed" (Proverbs 31:28).

As I read my grandparent's letters, I could not help but think of the ancestors long gone who helped shape the characters of Clyde and Otis, and who formed in them a strong sense of faith and family. I remember reading of the deep faith of John R. Flanders, Jr. as he gathered his family around their burning home. I thought of the perseverance of Sophie Holmes raising six children alone, and the determination of Williams Flanders and Nancy Chesnut as they walked home from war. I also recalled D.Q. Morrison's strong reserve after losing his wife, daughter, and grandchild within a year. May you enjoy reading of two families shaped by their past and *Rich Beyond Price* who come together and become one. Much joy and sorrow is captured in the pages written by Otis and Clyde and lovingly preserved for us by their children.

1911

The year 1911 found Otis Rountree attending the Atlanta College of Physicians and Surgeons, which was later named Emory Medical School. He lived at 35 Cone Street and was a member and later President of Phi Chi Medical Fraternity. He weighed one hundred fifty pounds and was five feet eleven inches tall. His expense and receipt book showed that, like his grandson, he enjoyed cigars. He also gave to the church and went to the "show" often. He kept diaries that are treasure troves of information.

On New Years' Day, 1911, Otis went hunting and killed two quail. He then left Cobbtown for Atlanta. His first day at school was occupied by trying to stay awake in class. His diary reports that he was "sleepy, sleepy." His diary also says that he was studying very hard and that he was drinking many "Dopes" (Coca Cola).

Otis Rountree and Vera Jenkins, about 1911.

On January 7, he attended a fraternity meeting. Sunday, January 22, he had "wine and cake" with his friend, Milner. He also attended the Park Avenue Methodist Church. January 19 is the first time of many he reports being sick with his recurrent stomach problem. Consequently, he cuts the next days' classes. The following day he visited Maude McLamore.

On March 9, Otis went to hear Teddy Roosevelt speak at the city auditorium. On March 10, he went to hear Woodrow Wilson. On April 10, he was sick the day before his embryology exam. He wrote that he "didn't sleep all night." He then reported that he was too sick to take his minor surgeries exam. He told his diary, "I think I'll go home. Went to see Dr. Pierson, also Dr. Derr, who took a radiogram of my stomach." Pierson said, "Do not go home," but he did go home to Cobbtown.

The diary for 1911 then stops.

Vidalia, GA
August 18, 1911
Friday P.M.

Dear Mr. Rountree,

Doubtless you have already put me down as a very poor correspondent but really my intentions are good. I wrote a letter to you last evening as it was raining so I could not go to prayer meeting. This morning I thought of several other things that I wanted to tell you so here I am writing again.

We certainly do miss you, Mr. Rountree. You were very nice to us all during your stay in Vidalia. Miss Lowe spent the day with me last Tuesday and spoke of how we would miss you, spoke very highly of you. Vidalia's society life is still somewhat gay, the picture show seems to be the main attraction. It is very entertaining this week and is being well attended. Probably you saw the advertisement of "Hazelle the Baby Wonder" who was to appear during this week.

She is only five years of age and seems to be a real wonder, especially at dancing and singing. I have only been one night. Alice and I went Tuesday night after the league.

Mr. Foy Powell came over last Friday night and carried me. He brought me the song "The Rosary" and I am just <u>crazy</u> about it. I believe you have read the book, have you not? I don't think one can appreciate the song unless they have read the book.

We enjoyed the party at Mrs. Lee's very much. Was awfully sorry you could not be there. Mr. Allcum is real nice I think. That is the only time I have been with him. I appreciate all the nice things he said about me, especially the one about having <u>some</u> sense. But you know I am afraid his mind has changed long ere this.

Mrs. George S. Rountree has been real sick all this week. She is at Mrs. French's and Mr. and Mrs. French are away so Mrs. Dickerson, the nurse at the Sanatorium here, is nursing her. I think that she better stay in Vidalia yet. I am sure I shall be delighted if our date can hold good, that is good if I can spare the time. Yet, you would enjoy going to . . . meeting that day and it comes only once each year. I would hate to deprive you of that pleasure where our date could be filled most any time. What do you think of it? Mr. McMillan left us last Monday afternoon. It seems real lonesome since <u>you and he</u> left.

I certainly appreciated all those nice things you said and spoke of hearing about me while here but feel very unworthy of them all. Only wish I could live up to them. Also I appreciate the many kindnesses you showed me. Don't think your conscience should hurt you for consuming any of my time for I assure you the pleasure was <u>at least</u> mutual. I am expecting to take supper at Mrs. Meadows with Miss Lowe tonight, as I want to get up town in time to get this in the 5:00 mail. Guess I had better close.

Sincerely,
Clyde

182

Otis (front right) with his high school graduating class.

Vidalia, GA
September 9, 1911

Dear Mr. Rountree,

It seems to be my failing to begin a letter several times before I am able to finish it. I began a letter to you last night and took such an awful headache I just could not write. So I am taking advantage of my first opportunity this afternoon.

Guess I had better tell you all the latest news of the day before I go any further. Mr. Adams and Kate Brown married this morning. The Vidalia crowd became so excited and enthusiastic over it that they had to go through the country to Higgston to take the 10 o'clock Seaboard. My brother has just come to dinner and says *that he heard they had "3 breakdowns" before they arrived.*

Well, I guess you already know about my Swainsboro call this afternoon. Mr. McMillan just told me that he would be over here tonight. You all had better be careful about that wonderful club you have organized around at your boarding place. I know you have a lively crowd around there.

The Williams girls did not come until Saturday night and stayed over until Monday afternoon. Letha, the older one, sang at the Methodist Church Sunday night. They are such sweet nice girls. I am sorry you did not get to see them.

Louis Thompson passed through here last Saturday on her way to Swainsboro. She is just up from a spell of fever and looks a little thin.

Mr. Rountree, it will suit me exactly for you to come Tuesday. I shall be glad if you can come over on the G&F Tuesday morning but if you cannot I shall expect you Tuesday night. Let me know exactly when you will come.

What day do you go back to Atlanta? You have decided to wait until about Saturday or Monday, have you not? I don't blame you at all for seeing what good shows you can during the year. I certainly wish it were possible for me to have that opportunity. You will have to tell me about them when you come to LaGrange. Wonder what Mr. Rufus W. Smith would say if I should ask him if you could come when I begin telling him about what a nice, good young man you are. He would say, "Yes, honey, that will be alright, he can come". He is a good old gentleman and just like a grandfather to all of us.

Alex left for Barnesville where he goes to attend Gordon Institute, yesterday I certainly hated to see him leave and yet was very glad for him to go.

I saw Mr. and Mrs. George S. Rountree in the post office last Sunday and they both said I must come around to see them before I leave. Mr. Rountree said he had a bug to put in my ear. I would like to know all about it so I think I shall go soon.

Am expected to take dinner with Alice tomorrow. She says she isn't going to give me much to eat though, that she is going to try to starve me...

There was a lecture over at the school auditorium last night, given in honor of the UDC, or rather to raise funds for the erection of their monument. I did not go but heard that the crowd was rather slim.

I guess I had better close this lengthy epistle, as I want to get it off on the five o'clock mail.

Sincerely,
Clyde

LaGrange College
LaGrange, GA
October 2, 1911

Dear Mr. Rountree,

We have just come upstairs from Mr. Smith's room where he had a whole bundle of letters which he had kept out of the mail. He read them out down at prayers and told the girls to come to his room and claim them. When all were in the room he gave a short talk on writing so many letters to young men, flirting, the reputation of the school, etc. Now what do you think of that?

But I think if they all wrote as <u>often</u> as you and I do, he would not be troubled a great deal keeping out letters, don't you think? Now really don't you think we are wonderful correspondents? I waited and waited for a letter from Mr. Rountree but no letter came until last Tuesday morning. So now I am writing you in a little less than a week's time since yours came. But you know I feel I will have to excuse you under the circumstances.

Was very sorry to hear of your accident with your unpacking. I certainly hope you and your friend in Tyler recovered and that your eyes are not troubling you now. It was too bad to celebrate your hearing good news from your exams by such an accident.

Am glad however, that you came out well in your exams. Feel sure it was out of (pity and tender consideration of your feelings of fright and anxiety) that they gave you a clean card. Well, alright, if you feel that way about it.

Guess I am doing very well in my work now. Am having to do some real hard studying as I am doubling in English as well as Music this year. The English course is so hard here and we are required to take German this year before graduating in Music. So you may imagine how busily engaged I am. Would you have thought of me doubling in my English course this fall? I have an oral debate tomorrow on the question of abolishing capital punishment. Now what do I know about capital punishment? Nothing whatever and more than that, I don't know how I'm going to manage, but I am just calmly sitting here writing and making mistakes as you have doubtless already observed.

Well Mr. Rountree, I am sitting right by the window where I get the full benefit of some good music right across the street, and now they are playing "Goodnight" (no, I am not going to tell you good night right now), but it reminds me of being at home in the parlor playing, etc.

But I don't know what to tell you about coming down here. You know I would be awfully glad to see you in that new brown suit but I am afraid Mr. Smith would object. I don't want to do anything that would be against his wishes and, honest Injun, some of the girls have already tried and I'm afraid. One young man came to see one of the girls yesterday – was in town all day yesterday and today and Mr. Smith would not let her see him at all. "Ain't it awful" though? So I guess we had better wait until about Christmas, don't you think so…

Well, I must close and study for a while. Send my mail to LaGrange College instead of Southern College.

Sincerely,
Clyde

P.S. Please pardon the mistakes and I will try to do better next time.

LaGrange College
LaGrange, GA
October 11, 1911
Dear Mr. Rountree,

Have you again decided that I am sick and had your decision confirmed when you saw the handwriting? I was surprised when you wrote me about what you had decided because I never once dreamed of anything of the kind. I will tell you the reason the handwriting looked so "foreign" to you. Vera addressed the envelope and insists on doing so each time and changing her handwriting – now, what do you know about that?

Last week when your letter came I resolved to answer it immediately but had a hard examination to prepare for and stand together with my other work. I studied yesterday afternoon and heard from it this morning. So tonight I feel free and lighthearted over having passed. Isn't it a relief to hear something like that when so much depends on it.

I guess you enjoyed going to the shows you spoke of. I certainly wish I had the opportunity of seeing some of those musical comedies. But anyway, I am glad to hear about them even if I can't see them. Everything here is just the same old story over and over each day. It gets a little monotonous sometimes, especially to "Vieve". We have not even been up town since we hit this place. Have only been to church every Sunday and once in the week to a wedding and to walk every afternoon.

Then the weather has been awfully warm for October, don't you think so? So very dry and dusty we could hardly live. But it rained last night, has been cloudy all day, and is raining now. So after it fairs off probably we will have some cold weather.

I guess you have heard of the strike on the G&F Railroad, have you not? Isn't it awful – oh, the trouble <u>we</u> do have with those G&F Trains [from Swainsboro to Vidalia].

How do you like your new abode? I think from what you have told me that it must be a much more desirable place than the other up in the city. Probably you will <u>miss</u> hearing the little lady play "Ocean Roll" and "Alexander's Rag Time Band" though, are you grieving about that part of it? It has not been convenient for me to go up town yet, but I shall be glad to exchange pennants with you

Vera Jenkins and Mattie Kate Brown, friends of Clyde.

as soon as I can go and get one. I have not had the photos made yet but you know I think your room will really look more "artistic" without that likeness of myself. The pennants look so nice without pictures. By the way, Setha Williams came up to see us last Friday. Her brother Bob married one of the LaGrange girls and Setha and one of her married sisters came up to the wedding. After the bride and groom left they came up here to see us. Said they saw just lot of Vidalia folk when they passed through there. I felt very much like going back with them Saturday morning.

Mr. Rountree, have you fully decided on the route to go home

Christmas? Vieve and Vera want to go by Macon so they can do some shopping. Of course, it is immaterial with me except on account of the trains being late. However, we have plenty of time yet to discuss the different routes. Don't you think so? I am very sorry you can't come down to see the club now but think it will be lovely to have you come by LaGrange Christmas. Shall be glad to see you during the holidays. The very idea of my having dates ahead already – absurd.

Vieve is telling me to quit writing and help her with her English lesson. So "good night".

Sincerely,
Clyde

LaGrange College
LaGrange, GA
October 29, 1911
Sunday Evening

Dear Mr. Rountree,

Wonder what is the trouble with you Atlanta people or did you expect to hear from me again before you wrote? I received your pennant last Monday morning and am crazy about it. I certainly do appreciate it and think it will add a great deal to our line of pennants. Doubtless you are beginning to think that I am not going to send you one, but just let me explain. I went uptown to get one and they had sold out, but said they had some nice ones ordered and would let me know when they came, so I am expecting to hear from them at any time. Just as soon as I do, I shall send you one.

Uncle Rufus is on another one of his "letter-writing spells" this week and has been for nearly two weeks. He kept out some letters last week and I'm afraid one of mine was in the bunch, so I want you to let me know if you received my letter and if so, about what time during the week. I am beginning to decide you did not get it as

I have not heard from you...

I don't know of any unusual happenings in these parts except I have senior privileges at present and chaperoned a crowd of girls out in the woods on a little picnic. We had a lovely time and made some real cute little pictures of the crowd. Now just imagine me being a dignified senior – can go uptown with another senior and am fairing very well now. Several of the girls with a teacher went out to Dixie Cotton Mills last night and had a little concert in the church. We had several readings, vocal solos, and a talk by one of the pastors in town. I had to play accompaniments for the girls. It is about two miles out there and we had more fun walking out there and back...

I want to thank you again for your pennant.

The light bell has rung so guess I'd better tell you good night.

Sincerely,
Clyde

LaGrange College
LaGrange, GA
November 13, 1911

Dear Mr. Rountree,

Wonder how you Atlanta people are feeling on this cold Monday morning. Is everything up there frozen like it is here? It rained all last night and yesterday until about dinner time, then the wind began to blow and this morning my, my, my, we can hardly put our heads out the door, it is so cold...well, back to the point. I was awfully sorry you didn't get my other letter, but if anyone read it, I hope they are satisfied. Of course, there was nothing in it that I would mind anyone seeing except that I don't care for any and everybody to know my affairs, do you? But poor old Mr. Smith is getting so childish and has broken so much in the last year. I feel like he can't last much longer. Mr. Rountree, let me tell you something aw-ful. I am in just lots of trouble. Guess you are wondering what next, are you not. Well it is merely this, and nothing more. I am on the Public Debate Team from the Irenian Literary Society and the more I study about it, the more I feel my inability to debate. The subject is "Resolved: That Senators should be elected by popular vote" and I am on the "affirmative" side of the question. You know I never was a "politician or a _suffragette_". So how can I discuss such political questions, please tell me?

But why should I be telling you about my troubles. I just wanted to know if you knew any lawyers in Atlanta, or anyone else who might give me a few points. I hate awfully bad to ask of you, but certainly would appreciate it if you can and will. Well my colleague and I, are up against two of the smartest girls in the school and we just must win.

Well, Vera, Guenevieve, and some of the other girls are waiting on me to go to walk, so had better close up. Please excuse the quality as well as the quantity of this letter but we don't have any news up here. Don't see any nice shows like you do.

Sincerely,
Clyde

Otis and friends. On the back of the picture is written, "Swainsboro, Ga., May 1907, Sadie Smith, Clair Kicklighter, Winey Coleman, Otis Rountree, Essie Ford, Levy Thompson".

LaGrange, GA
December 19, 1911

Dear Mr. Rountree,

Hope you will excuse my long delay in writing you about our plans but we were late deciding what date to go. I think though that we finally have decided definitely on going Thursday morning. We leave here at 6:30 and arrive at Macon at about 11:50, I think. We have about four hours and a half, I think, as the M.D.& S. leaves about 3:30 that afternoon.

We are expecting a great time while there. Mrs. Jenkins is going to meet Vera and we are going to do some Christmas present shopping. We are expecting to see some of Vieve's friends from Shorter, and the Bessie Tift girls, Anna and Vivian, are going to join us there. So, with all this crowd we are expecting to have a dandy time, don't you think we will enjoy it?

Hope everything will be conveniently arranged for you so that you will not be put out any. When do you get out of school?

The Riverside boys are already out but the Gordon boys do not go home until the twenty-third, so Alex wrote me. I don't know when any of the others are out. The school at home closes Friday and I hear they are going to give a recital on Friday night. I certainly hope they will have something nice.

And O., I hope the picture shows will be good while we are at home. Am just hungry to see another good show.

Well, yes, it was a big joke on me about sending your letter to Marietta but really it was only a mistake in addressing some envelopes. I'll tell you all about it later. Vieve is calling me to come on and go down stairs with her so will close

Sincerely,
Clyde

1912

Nineteen-twelve saw Woodrow Wilson, a man with Georgia connections, elected President. Tom Watson, a redheaded, firebrand populist would lead Georgia to vote for Oscar Underwood of Alabama.

Juliet Gordon Lowe of Savannah, Georgia, founded the Girl Scouts, March 12, 1912.

The "unsinkable" Titanic sank on April 14, 1912.

Joseph Meriweather Terrell of Greenville, Georgia, who had been appointed U.S. Senator by Governor Joseph Brown, died in 1912, and

Otis Rountree with Hattie Mae Mulling, Summer 1912.

was replaced by Hoke Smith. Nineteen-twelve also saw the re-election of Governor Joe Brown.

This period of Georgia history was marked by very sharp political rivalries between the factions of Hoke Smith and Joe Brown. You will notice Clyde and Otis commenting on these events.

Otis lived at the Chi Phi House, 152 Forrest Avenue (now Ralph McGill). His telephone number was 6658.

OTIS' 1912 DIARY

During this period, Otis' time was spent studying, going to class, playing cards, writing and visiting the young ladies.

On Monday, February 26, Otis wrote in his diary: "At all classes, to seventh anniversary of Phi Chi banquet at Piedmont Hotel. Several faculty members present and some of the boys got drunk. We went afterwards to take on the town. To bed at 2:30."

The next day he told the diary that he attended all classes. On March 3-6, Otis was sick with his usual stomach trouble. He reported on March 8 that he was still sick. Said he took a walk, came home and was "sick all night."

Vera Jenkins visited Otis and his roommate, Dr. Sauls. They took walks together and he reported, "Sick all night" on March 20.

March 21, he took his last exam, and the diary skipped to April 16.

He arrives in Cobbtown on April 19 and reports that his mother has a new baby [George].

On May 4, he reports that he went down to Lyons in the p.m., called up Letha Williams and went to see her in the evening. "Fairly good time. She seems to be a good, sensible girl, but so nervous, she gets me the same way."

On May 18, he reports, "Birthday, Clyde. I found out later, too late to send her anything. Will make up for it next year. Wonder if I really will – if it will be of any interest to me then?"

May 23 – "Received grade card from Atlanta College of Physicians and Surgeons. Passed all – clear card to senior class – JOY!!!"

June 16 – "To Vidalia with Clyde in p.m. To walk and to ride." During this time, Otis was working at the Bank of Emmanuel in Swainsboro and

Vera Jenkins and Otis Rountree - Grant Park, Atlanta, March 1912.

living with his grandfather, John R. Flanders, Jr.

June 26, a very revealing comment – "Went driving with Clyde in p.m. Nice time. I'm going to stop going over so much before I get too far gone to stop. Went to moving picture show with C.H. this evening."

August 6 – "Ridge and I went to Canooche River fishing, spent the day at and near Gator Lake. Caught 30 fish."

195

August 8 – "Ridge and I went fishing again and it rained on us nearly all day. Caught 22 fish, some good ones."

August 12 – "L. from Clyde – very short. Not at all satisfactory. Spent night with grandpa."

About the August 15 letter, his diary said, "Got letter from Clyde – a very nice letter. Hattie Mulling on train from Stillmore [see picture]."

August 31 – "Fishing with Joe to Canooche. Was good luck, but it was Joe's unlucky day. Hogs got the fish. He shot to scare them, killed one and disabled another. We caught some fine Jack, Pike and Perch. Home at 5:00 o'clock p.m. Mama gone to Swainsboro."

September 4 – "Papa, Sam, Joe and I went to Canooche – Gator Lake to camp out. Got in about 4:30 p.m. Papa and I caught some nice Pike in nets. Joe was cook and we had a fine supper. Put out 30 cat hooks and caught 26 cats and two eels first round. Good night for camping."

September 5 – "Fished all morning and between us, caught good mess to carry home. Went to gator caves and swamps, known only to Joe, but too much weather to catch many there. Rain came up and we had to leave without dinner."

September 8 – "Went to Vidalia at 10:46. Dined at Colonial Hotel. To Sunday school and to walk with Clyde. Dr. May lent us his car to go to ride – kind of him. I ate supper with Clyde and they had a good meal, too. Believe me. To preaching at Methodist Church. Left at 10:45."

September 9 – "Left at noon accidentally. Met Clyde in p.m. S.A.R. train and saw her home in buggy. To see Clyde eve. Almost lost my head and told her something, but I'll wait awhile. She is a fine little girl, practical, smart, pretty. In fact, she has all the attributes that go to make a good wife. If I thought I could carry out my part of the contract, had any means of support and could win her, we'd be wed at once. Everything is dark ahead though and I'll have to wait awhile – two or three years looks like."

September 10 – "Called Clyde and told her I might be back before school starts."

September 12 – "Ridge left the night before for Athens to enter sophomore year at [the University of] Georgia."

Friday, September 27 – "Package from Clyde express. Sofa pillows as donation to Chapter house."

Saturday, October 19 – "Ridge came over from Athens. I cut classes and went to Georgia-Vanderbilt football game. Game 46 to 0, favor Vandy. Smoker in chapter house tonight, but I had to entertain Ridge so he and I went to Grand Theatre getting in for tail-end of smoker. Retired at 1:30."

Tuesday, November 5 – "Crowd was celebrating Wilson victory in presidential race."

Saturday, November 16 – "Went to Georgia vs. Tech football game in p.m. Georgia beat Tech 20-0. A good game."

Thursday, November 20 – "Thanksgiving. Holiday. Slept late. Got little enjoyment out of day [he was apparently very homesick]. Ate dinner at Folsoms' about 4:30 – the worst Thanksgiving dinner I ever ate. Back home and to study."

Sunday, December 8 – "My birthday. 24 years old...."

Tuesday, December 10 – "Rather sick. Bought calabash pipe in p.m."

Wednesday, December 11 – "Sick and out in a.m. Barnette gave a class

Joe and Vera (Jenkins) Jackson before they married. Vera and Clyde were close friends. Joe and Vera's daughter, Jane, was Dorothy Rountree Budd's best friend. Jane married Billy McNatt of Lyons. Billy and Jane's son, William, was an outstanding wrestler at Briarcliff High School. Joe and Vera lived most of their married lives in the home of Mrs. Jenkins, Vera's mother. After Mrs. Jenkins died, her home, one of the most beautiful in town, was sold and a grocery store erected in its place.

Clyde (Left) with her first cousin Lucille Parrish.

exam to school in p.m. Westmoreland amputated leg -- sarcoma just below knee. Studied obstetrics. To bed at 11:30."

Saturday, December 14 – "My last meeting as presiding senior, Jim Pitman elected in my place."

Friday, December 12 – "Had all classes. Fowler gave exam, which I barely passed. To clinic in p.m. Left at 9:45. One-and-half hours for Macon. We played get back all the way. Stayed at Brownhouse, to bed at 2:30. Slept till 9 a.m."

Saturday, December 21 – "Walked around Macon till 11:30 when I left for Vienna, reaching there at 2 o'clock. Dined at Virginia Hotel. To see Dr. Williams in p.m. Supper at Mrs. Roberts. Back to hotel and called up [Dr.] Sims at Cordele."

Monday, December 23 – "Over to Southern Cotton Oil Company

place and worked with Sims a little. Dined with him. Left at 2 o'clock s.a.l. Reached Vidalia at 7 o'clock. Telegraphed Clyde and went over to see her after just seeing George's baby. Had a right nice time. Left at 10:45. Spent night at Colonial Hotel."

Tuesday, December 24 – "Home in a.m. Little Jordan girl on train. Walked around Collins with her. Spent day at house with the folks."

Wednesday, December 25 – "To Vidalia to see George and Mae Dee, then ate dinner with Clyde. Vieve French and Anna Currie there for dinner also. Excellent dinner. Very nice to us. Took Kodak pictures in p.m. Clyde went to church. Christmas tree. Met Vera with crowd and she went with us. I stayed at Clyde's till 11:45. Had a good time. She gave me photo."

Thursday, December 26 – "To Collins. Ate breakfast. Met Papa and he would have me go to Reidsville with him. He is drinking and wants me to stay around all the time. Dined at Roger's house wrote to Clyde. Papa decided he could not stand it down there, so we drove 15 miles back to Cobbtown. Dark drive and almost gone by the time there."

Friday, December 27 – "Around home all day. In p.m. had telegram from Jake Sauls stating he would come Saturday a.m."

Saturday, December 28 – "Up at 5:30. Drove to Collins and met Jake. Fine drive back home, though cold. We met Papa at Collins coming in from Savannah en route to Reidsville. Around the house all day. Went hunting with Jake. He got one bird. I got two. Papa came in on the train. Mary Lou played for us."

Sunday, December 29 – "Jake and I studied it a little. Had excellent turkey dinner. In the p.m. to walk with 'B'. I called up Clyde and we tried to get Vera but failed. We met Sam coming in from Ailey on train. Went to house and studied some more then to bed."

Monday, December 30 – "Up early. Cold and very windy but Jake, Joe, Sam and I went hunting. Found plenty of birds but too windy to shoot good. Jake, Joe one each only. Called up Grandpa [John R. Flanders, Jr.] after administering to Papa. Jake and I went to Swainsboro. Spent night with Grandpa."

Tuesday, December 31 – "Around town with Leon Bell. ... left for Vidalia. Reached there at 12 o'clock. Dined at Colonial. Raining and raining. Jake to see Vera and I to see Clyde. Nice time. After Jake and I went to see Clyde till 8:30 he left for Vera's. I stayed with the dearest lady till the old year went out. Proposed to her, got no answer. Guess I should have waited, but don't regret it a bit. This is a day that means something to me. Leave p.m. for Atlanta. To bed at 2 a.m."

Author's Note: Apparently this is the first time that Clyde called Otis by his first name.

LaGrange, GA
January 8, 1912

Dear Otis,

What do you think about that? May I have the privilege, although you are so many years my senior? It may sound a little rude but I can always talk more freely to anyone when I call them by their names, can't you? No, I much prefer my name without the title…

We had a very nice time at Marie's party on Friday night. Am awfully sorry you could not go. No, I did not see you at the picture show, although I don't know why because I saw Colonel Patillo and Mr. George Rountree. You must have just made your retreat when I looked back.

I received the music alright and certainly appreciate it. I am so very fond of music anyway and think all these are so pretty. Will take your advice and try to be prepared to play them for you next June.

Sincerely,
Clyde

LaGrange, GA
February 11, 1912

Dear Otis,

I had fully intended waiting two weeks longer to write you, as you treated me so nicely, but after taking a second thought I decided you might forget my address and also that I might lose yours, so I say here goes. Now really, I think you are the limit, only two letters since Christmas and this is February. But, still, if you prefer to do that way it will be perfectly alright with me.

It has been raining and snowing just a little for the last few days so we could not go to Church today. But this afternoon a Mr. Hawkins, a man traveling for the Orphans' Home, was kind enough to come up and give us a talk, pass around cards for subscription, etc. Of course, we were required to go and listen. It was very good, but I had a splitting headache and...did not enjoy it much.

Two of the girls and I all read a book this morning "When Woman Proposes" – and I have been mad ever since. Don't you hate to be disappointed in a book? When I first started reading it, I thought I would like it, but it ended positively silly...

The Georgia Glee Club came last Tuesday night but I was not among the lucky few who had the opportunity of going. You can't imagine why, can you? No, I did not make A or distinction in deportment, because I did not come back on time after Christmas. I could not have gone anyway because I had to study. But last Thursday afternoon, "Vanity Fair" was shown at one moving picture show and "The Last Of The Mohicans" at the other. We went and saw "Vanity Fair" which was real good but did not have time to go to the other one.

No, I am hardly a lawyer in any degree – the sad news of our

Otis (Left) - someone wrote on the back of this photo, "Feb 22nd, Hauling wood for Board money". It doesn't say when or where.

defeat in the debate will prove that to you – but think I will be able to give my piano recital some time real soon. Otis, think of the consolation (not much), but although it did most kill me to lose I am trying to stand it. The other society had their public debate last night and it was real good. The subject was "Resolve That The Classical Course in College is Best Adapted to the Average Girl" – one that appeals to, and interests us all.

A long letter from Alice revealed to me her new occupation. Do you know she is traveling for the Practical Reference Library? She wrote me from Baxley and is going to Willacoochee tomorrow. I think it is awful, but just anything to get away from Vidalia suits her. She told me about what a nice time she had in Atlanta. She said you came around and carried her to the moving pictures, I believe it was.

Guess you enjoyed "The Pink Lady". You are certainly lucky to be convenient to so many good shows.

There are several girls in here talking and laughing. They all say to tell you hello.......

The supper bell has rung so, goodbye.

Sincerely,
Clyde

Author's Note: Apparently, even in the distant past, depression affected college students.

LaGrange, GA
February 27, 1912

Dear Otis,

Despite the fact that I am a little bit tired from taking gymnastics, I am attempting to write you this afternoon. I was sick Sunday and was busy all day Monday, or Monday morning and went to the picture show in the afternoon... There are about a dozen girls in the room talking and laughing, excuse all the mistakes will you?

We had a grand time at the moving pictures yesterday. Mrs. Parsons, one of the voice teachers, carried her pupils and although I am not one of her pupils now, I was last year so she sent me a special invitation to go. We saw East Lynn and it was real good. I have seen it played a long time ago but sat up there and cried during it all, what do you think about that? Did you see the piece in the paper about Miss Randall from Greensboro killing herself? She was up here last fall and we knew her very well, she was an orphan girl and was subject to depression spells. They said the cause of her trouble was that she wanted to marry and her people objected on account of her age. I think it is one of the saddest cases I ever heard of. She was a beautiful girl.

Well, Otis, I certainly enjoyed your visit last Thursday, really wouldn't it have been fine? No we did not have holiday or even half holiday for Mr. George Washington's Birthday. Anyway, you wrote me so late that I wouldn't have had time to let you know. You must have thought of that and done it on purpose, now honest, did you?

But really, I would have been mighty glad for you to come but could not very well arrange affairs then even if Uncle Rufus had consented.

Otis, I want to ask a favor of you. Please send me the little note that was sent in my last letter I want to read it, they will not tell me what was in it and I am awfully worried about it.

I think it will be fine for your roommate to come down to Vidalia to see us next summer, hope we can make him enjoy himself. Tell him I think his heart is in the right place exactly.

I have given up the idea of being a lawyer, am afraid I would make a failure. However, I hope the other girls will succeed.

But I must close now and study for a while.

Sincerely,
Clyde

LaGrange College
LaGrange, GA
April 3, 1912

Dear Otis,

...Yes, you are very nice to tell me to go to Atlanta to see you. Really, wouldn't it be grand? However, I think I know something still nicer. But remember, it is a great big secret. I think probably Mr. Smith will let you come down here on the 21st if that time still suits you. I will ask him, and let you know definitely next time.

We went over to the Baptist College Monday night and saw the play given by the expression pupils. It was a real good play, but the acting was not so good. However, we enjoyed it very much. Just anything for a change.

Yes, I received a letter from you while Vera was in Atlanta, and was very glad for that was the only way I heard how she was getting on...

Did you see my big brother's [Jewel] announcements in last Sunday's Journal? And my sister-in-law had her picture there to adorn a part of one page. Now, won't that seem strange for a member of our family to marry and leave home?

...I am sending you a program of my recital, thinking that probably you will be interested enough to read it over. I came out very well with all my pieces. Although I did take a big dose of ammonia to steady my nerves before I played.

I must stop now and study awhile. Again, let me thank you for the candy, and tell you we certainly did enjoy it.

Sincerely,
Clyde

LaGrange College
LaGrange, GA
May 5, 1912

Dear Otis,

I am expecting to be away tomorrow, so that is why I'm writing you this afternoon. I'm going to the great city of -- did you say Atlanta? -- Why, no. Standing Rock, of course. You are familiar

Jake Sauls and Vera Jenkins, taken at Grant Park in Atlanta, March 1912. Both were close to Clyde and Otis. Vera, from Vidalia, attended LaGrange College with Clyde, and Jake was Otis' fraternity brother in medical school.

with the name and the place. One of the girls has relatives there, and she invited me to go down and spend the day with her. They are to have a big church day and dinner on the ground. Isn't that interesting? Suppose you come up and join us. Now what do you think about that?

Otis, I am very, very sorry that your home affairs were such that you had to hurry home, and could not come by here. Not only because I was disappointed but because I hate for your people to be sick. Certainly hope your mother, father, and little brother are much improved long ere this. Probably everyone will be well and I shall see you often during the summer months, hope so anyway.

Where do you think you shall be, Swainsboro, Cobbtown, North Carolina, Vidalia, or New York City (please take notice of the contrast will you)? Guess you have fully decided have you not?

One of my uncles who lived in Augusta died last Tuesday with paralysis. He has been in poor health for a good while, but the end came unexpectedly. He was the last one of papa's brothers. One blessing, however, is that his children are all grown, educated and doing well...

The house in Vidalia. It is now a Re/Max Real Estate office.

Well, be good, continue your reform, and don't wait to get home to write me.

Sincerely,
Clyde

May 1912
Sunday P.M.

Dear Otis,

This is commencement Sunday at the Southern College so we were not required to go to church this morning – any who wanted to could, but that was only four, I think. So we have had the entire day to use as we chose. I will agree what a delightful time we have had cooking candy, etc. We have not had time to get lonesome at all.

Wonder what one young man, Mr. James Otis Rountree is doing this afternoon just at this time – 3:00 never mind, do you realize we only have two more Sundays here? Then we can go home and have some Sunday afternoon to use at our own disposal – want that be a dandy though?

I don't know anything unusual that has happened up here recently except that we went to a party last night. Yes, a real party and that is not at the college – what do you know about that? One of the town girls, who comes to school up here, and I have the same birthday – May 18th, so she took me by surprise and entertained in <u>my honor</u> last night. The lady principal let us all go. Wasn't that nice? Of course, there were no town people there, nothing but college girls but we certainly enjoyed it. We got some real sweet little presents, nothing expensive, however. I certainly enjoyed it and appreciated it.

The Ladies Missionary Society of the North Georgia (Methodist) Conference held a convention here last week and we certainly had a siege of company – some delegates and some just visitors of the

207

Genevieve French, Otis, and Clyde. This picture was taken before Otis and Clyde were married. Have you noticed how young people back then had style? See how Otis is decked out in his hat, three-piece suit, and cigar. The ladies donned hats and elegant dresses. Even the plant to Otis' left had style!

girls – and missionary services. The services are very interesting but more interesting was the reception out on the campus on Monday afternoon. The seniors and junior . . . were invited to serve and to help entertain very much to my joy. I only had to serve at the punch bowl, which suited me exactly. Of course I became quite thirsty occasionally. I beg your pardon, I did not mean to say so much about the convention, etc. etc., I know all that is of no interest whatsoever to you...

It is real sad when you think of it to leave these girls, many of whom we will never see again. Guess Genevieve and I will stay through commencement and may go home by Atlanta – don't know yet however. Edna is going next week, she wants to get home for the U.C.L. commencement. I wish I could get home in time for some of those Sunday school .....they are having. I am sure they enjoy them very much...

I think I am using the only pen on the hall and as Vera is waiting for it I had better give it to her. So good-bye.

Clyde

Vidalia, GA
June 4, 1912

Dear Otis,

. . .I shall be very glad to have you come over next Sunday, and, if I live and nothing prevents, I shall be right there at Sunday School when you come. I will have to play Sunday as Alice is not to be here, but will see you after the services anyway.

Hastily,
Clyde

Vidalia, GA
July 2, 1912

Dear Otis,

Yes, I know it is my time to do the apology after waiting so long to answer your letter. I don't know how to apologize – anyway, I hate apologies, don't you? But I just want to say it wasn't my fault. You will have to blame the District Conference [Methodist], all those delegates, and the presiding Elder for having so many meetings.

We are not through with preaching services yet, by any means. Dr. Carey, an elderly gentleman from Atlanta, began yesterday a series of doctrined sermons which he says are not intended to offend anyone but are to turn up Methodists and show them just what beliefs are. They are very good indeed, especially interesting to Methodists. His sermons last an hour or more making the services at least an hour and a half. Don't you want to go tonight?

Clyde

Vidalia, GA
August 10, 1912

Dear Otis,

I received the piece of music you sent and like it fine. Think the chorus is very pretty. Hope I shall be able to play it for you when you come again. I certainly do like it and appreciate it much more than I can express.

I gave up my trip to Covington, although I saw in the Constitution where Vera and I both would attend. I was real anxious to go but could not. Hope you enjoyed your fishing while at home.

Sincerely,
Clyde

Vidalia, GA
August 15, 1912

Dear Otis,

...*I am feeling a little bit tired and bad tonight. Alice and I went out to Mrs. Darby's burial this afternoon, and it was such a long, hot, dusty tiresome ride that I feel tired and my eyes burn awfully. Suppose you come over and doctor me for a while. Really, if you had been here yesterday I might have given you some professional work. My head just ached perfectly awful all day and nothing would relieve it until I went to sleep last night. Do you think you could have helped the cause?*

By the way, Herbert Bailey asked me to tell you that he had found your pipe. Says you can get it by coming immediately.

There is to be a picnic out at Tiger Springs tomorrow afternoon – come over and go, won't you? Or do you prefer only meeting the train tomorrow night? I don't think I shall go as tomorrow is my day at Higgston, you know. They were to have it last week but postponed it on account of the funeral of Mrs. Darby.

I had begun reading "The White Mice" and like it fine as far as I have read, but have not read very far. Haven't had very much time recently, have been serving some, and have been sitting up with the corpse some...

I have an invitation to go over to Wadley Friday afternoon to see a cousin of mine, Dr. Holmes. There he is to take us over to Mount Moriah Campground near Louisville, in the car Saturday. Stay over there Sunday and come back Monday, what do you think of it? It would be a nice trip for me and I would get to see just lots of Papa's relatives but don't see how I can go. Mama wants me to go but I don't think I can.

Hope you are enjoying yourself and your work. Write me real soon.

Sincerely,
Clyde

Author's Note: This letter was written to Otis in Cobbtown. Apparently, he was just preparing to go back to school.

Vidalia, GA
September 2, 1912

Dear Otis,

I was very much disappointed this morning when I received your note stating that you could not come tomorrow. However, I guess it is best, because I am almost sick tonight and have been feeling badly all day. So feel sure that I, at last, would enjoy your visit more when I am feeling better – looking at it from a selfish standpoint. However, I am glad you have decided to make two more visits instead of one before you go back to school. Keep that idea in your mind...

What would you say if I were to tell you that I would leave in a few days for Sparks to accept a position as teacher in Sparks Collegiate Institute, to be a literary teacher of the Fourth and Fifth grades getting a salary of $50 per month. I had an offer of the place. Had a letter from the President of school yesterday. He was our pastor for four years – was pastor when I joined the church. It certainly is a good offer, but I wrote him today that I could not accept it.

I have finished reading the "White Mice" and like it just fine. Have read about half of "Freckles" and like it very much so far. Think it is much like those others, "The Harvester" and "A Girl of the Lumber Lost." I shall expect you real soon. Must close now as I am feeling so tired.

Sincerely,
Clyde

Vidalia, GA
September 12, 1912

Dear Otis,

    I certainly am due you a letter and a real nice long one, too, so here goes a feeble effort. I'm staying home from prayer meeting tonight to write you because I just must tell you some things without waiting any longer.
    First, you are entirely too good to me. If you were not the best boy anywhere, you would not have gone to so much trouble to get here Monday. You don't know how I did hate your not getting my message – then your getting left in Stillmore. You certainly were good to come on in spite of it all, and I appreciate it more than I can express.

Clyde, probably taken in Canoochee.

Speaking of dreams – but a good part of Monday night seems very much of a dream to me. I remember very distinctly what you said to me, but you took me very much by surprise and I hardly remember one word that I said. However, I'm glad you opened up your heart and told me how you felt. And remember although you made no promises you are going to have a good year, and a successful one if my hopes and good wishes avail anything.

Mama was awake when I came in Monday night and didn't say a word about your staying late when I told her all your "adventures" of the day. Said you got here too late to be <u>run off</u>. I think she thinks you are a pretty nice fellow anyway. I was glad to wait with you as long as I could but people are so prone to make remarks, etc., etc.

You know people around here know more about your affairs than you do. They are continually asking me about not going back to school and telling me what my plans are, et cetera, et cetera. I just let them talk and say things to keep them guessing – isn't that alright?

Am glad you had a good trip to Atlanta. You must have had a sleepy time of it unless you had several dopes in the meantime ["dopes" are Coca-Colas].

Am sure you all have a nice, convenient place out there at your Chapter House. I certainly hope it will be a complete success. Yes sir, you may enroll me as one of your Phi Chi members now and count on me as being a loyal, true one with your interests at heart.

It was very kind of you to say that your only objection to Atlanta was [illegible] and a very great objection, I'm sure. I wish we were situated so I could see you occasionally at least. For I didn't realize how much I enjoyed your company and how much I would miss you until you left to be gone until Christmas.

Write me real soon for I'm always glad to hear from you.

As Ever,
Clyde

Vidalia, GA
October 16, 1912

Dear Otis,

It seems that no matter how sick your patient gets, you just will not suggest a remedy for her illness. I have had La grippe for nearly two weeks but have been feeling so very badly today that I could hardly stay up. This afternoon I decided to take my temperature. My face seemed so hot and flushed. It was only 100, so I have been taking Quinine ever since. So you may imagine how I feel tonight and in hopes that I shall be all right tomorrow.

I am still going to Higgston, but the weather is getting so bad and the train is so late coming at night, that I have been considering giving it up. I mentioned it to some of my pupils last Monday, and they were almost ready to mob me, so I should probably continue until Christmas anyway.

I was to lead the League tonight, but I couldn't face the small ratchet after I found out I had some fever. The weather is so disagreeable that I don't expect anyone hardly will be there. I saw Vera and talked with her for quite a while Sunday morning. She asked me Dr. Sauls' address about a half dozen times and then wrote it down for fear she would forget. So I guess another heavy missive will be coming forth real soon. Vera says she is going back to school after Christmas and I hope she will – so many people seem to doubt it after she has stayed out all the fall. She said she is not going to Atlanta this fall, is only staying home wearing glasses.

Tell Mr. Sauls I certainly appreciate his kind offer of his services up there this year, but be sure that you don't ask him what he offered to do for me.

Guess you boys are living high out there, but you had better be careful about other people's property. The first thing you know some of you will be in police court for malicious mischief. Aren't you afraid? Did you make the three boys recently initiated do the milking of the cow?

Are you coming down to Macon to the fair? I don't suppose that is very interesting to you though. Alice has been insisting on my going up with her the latter part of the week and staying for about two days. I don't care especially about going though, there is so much sameness about a fair that where you go once, you see about all there ever is to be seen. Don't you think so?

Then, you remember I am to stay at home all the fall, so I can go up to Atlanta to the opera next spring. I heard there were some doubts about their having it next year that they did not come out on it last spring. Is that true or have you heard anything of it?

Guess I had better tell you good night as I seem to be so dull I can't write without making mistakes.

As Ever,
Clyde

Vidalia, GA
Fall 1912

Dear Otis,

Doubtless you will be a little surprised at my staying at home instead of going to Church this evening, but the weather is most too inclement. However, your patient is recuperating rapidly from her La Grippe. My case was not very serious after all, only had to be very careful from the very first. After this I think I shall try to act with more prudence so I will have no more luck like that.

Fred Darby came down to Macon yesterday, saw the Mercer-Georgia Tech football game, then came down on the seaboard to Vidalia this morning. He carried us to ride in Frank's car this afternoon, came on over here and stayed until about 7 o'clock, then went home expecting to take the 9 o'clock train and return to Atlanta. Says he will reach there at 7:30 a.m. just a half hour before his class. Don't you imagine he will feel like work after two sleepless nights.

Well, how did you enjoy the fair? Am sure you and I were both greatly benefited by going, aren't you? But really I wanted to go after I've received your letter. Did you expect a telegram from me anytime

Friday or Saturday? Wish so much that I could have seen you but I could not go to Macon. Anyway, it will be only about two months longer before you will be home for a while and then what?

Received your souvenir of Atlanta this morning and appreciate it very much. Have enjoyed looking at the scenes especially those with familiar names. Am sorry one picture is lacking and shall expect the Kodak view.

How are you enjoying your work, I feel sure that I can testify to your good attention during lectures.

Hope you all had a dandy time out there Saturday night, am sure you did though. Sure I shall be delighted to be your guest at your Fraternity Dance. I don't know anything about dancing – but that will be perfectly alright, it's very nice to be a "wallflower". Where is it to be, I must learn to dance gracefully before then...

Hope your Goryga [what is a Goryga?] is much better ere this and you are enjoying life to the fullest. Hope you have not had any more fever.

As Ever,
Clyde

Vidalia, GA
November 4, 1912

Dear Otis,

Here I am attempting to write to you tonight with people talking on all sides of me. So you need not be surprised at mistakes in spelling, rhetoric and punctuation.

Have been up town for quite a while this afternoon, chasing around with Vera and Eleen [word unintelligible] so I am rather tired. By the way, Vera told me to ask you if you still have the negatives of those pictures of you all while she was in Atlanta. If you have, I think she wants them.

Otis, it seems that I have gone back to my same old occupation – you wonder what that is? Well, when certain young couples in Vidalia have misunderstandings, and the young man wants to go with some other girl for spite – I'm the girl to come in. Guess I had better be "once in a while" than not at all where it seems to have no steady at all. I feel sorry for TH though, he was so crazy about Vera and still is, and she treats him like a little dog. He can't even go to see her now.

Vera entertained at a Halloween party Thursday night, and we had a delightful time. Not such a large crowd there, just enough to have a good time. We were well entertained in very much the usual manner of such parties...

It is about time for me to leave so will ring off.

With Best Wishes,
Clyde

Vidalia, GA
November 22, 1912

Dear Otis,

Your long expected letter came last night but I did not get it until Tuesday at noon. If you will stop and think for one moment, probably you can imagine at what rate of speed my mind has already begun to travel, can you not?

I certainly am sorry you were sick and hope you are entirely well and back at work long ere this. I sympathize with you most heartedly for I know what a lonesome job it is. You can just sit down and think, and think and think, but my, don't you feel lonesome with it all?

Speaking of spending the holidays up there, you make me feel real blue and lonesome. I know of just lots of things to tell you but had everything planned for your visit Christmas. I expect though that when all the other boys start home, you will be among the first to the train.

No really, I was only joking. I don't blame you at all for taking advantage of every opportunity to improve yourself and your abilities, although we would be disappointed at not seeing you, you would have a very short while to stay after all.

Have you entirely given up the idea of taking the hospital course next summer? As to your locating in Mexico, I shall be delighted to give you my view on that subject right now. I shouldn't think it would be best to go south at all. Why not consider Greenland or Iceland?

Guess you have heard all about Mr. Rountree's brother being killed in a wreck. I have not seen the paper to get a full account of the accident, but have heard that about eight people were killed.

Vidalia is right in the midst of a siege of revival meetings. The Primitives (Primitive Baptists) have been having services all this week beside protracted services at the Presbyterian church. A two weeks meeting just closed at the Methodist church Sunday night. We had good services, good preaching and good attendance, but only three accessions to the church. One that you will probably be interested in was T.H. Johnson.

Fred left about two weeks ago for Gordon Institute, rather a jumped up affair, but he was so anxious to go. Our family seems rather diminished with Fred and Alex both gone. My, doesn't it seem strange when you are accustomed to such a crowd.

What have you planned for next Thursday? There seems to be nothing doing here but cane grindings. I think that is the program for Thanksgiving as well as every other day...

Let me hear from you as soon as you feel like writing. Hope you have entirely recovered from your illness.

Sincerely,
Clyde

Vidalia, GA
December 3, 1912
Dear Otis,

...*What kind of time did you have Thanksgiving? Was sorry you could not be with us but guess you had a more enjoyable day than we did. It was very cold early that morning until the sun melted the snow off the ground. In the afternoon Mr. Powell, Mrs. Smith, Mr. Yomans and I walked out to Mr. George Matthews's farm. We went down the railroad, took pictures, shot targets and finally drank cane juice. We had a delightful time but I almost froze stiff especially coming back home.*

I'm so glad you decided to come home for the holiday. Think it will be good for you to have a change and a rest for a few days don't you? Especially if you will come to Vidalia and take Christmas dinner with me (conceit where art thou). What do you say about coming sure enough?

Alex has been at home for the last few days but is at Ailey now. Don't suppose he will buy anymore cotton this year. He did very well at Broxton but Mr. Jones told him he could barely make expenses from now on, on account of the crop being so short so he is working with Mr. Peterson in a dry goods store. Says he is to room with one of your brothers, the youngest I suppose.

Fred was a little homesick when he first went to Barnesville, but seems to have the Gordon spirit as he expressed it, at present. His last letter was football, football and then some more football...

Let me hear from you real soon. Guess you will be home in about three weeks, then I can whisper all my secrets, can't I?

As Ever,
Clyde

Author's Note: Sarah Underwood told me that the word "chance", used by Wash Rountree, means a crop abundant enough to last a year.

Cobbtown, GA
December 11, 1912
Dear Otis,

> *Your ma and the two babies are at Lucian Durden's today. Mary Lou and myself keeping house. I would have gone with them, but wanted to do some writing. All are well here, except your ma has a cold and almost cough. Ridge writes me he is much improved. We are through grinding cane, and we made a nice chance of fine syrup. They have about two bales of cotton to gather yet, and this is the last of the gathering this season – only hog killing and maybe you will all be here to help with that insofar as the eating goes. It will be but a few days now before you are out for Christmas.*
>
> *Mary Lou arrived from Swainsboro last night and says your grandpa [John R. Flanders, Jr.] is in his usual health. He was real sick. Nothing preventing, I intend going up there tomorrow night. Bob Sutton got dangerously shot Thursday night in a row with some other boys in a cane grinding near Stillmore. He was cut about the face and shot just above and below the heart. Condition is said to be critical. David Kerow, who shot him. Glad some of Ebb's boys were not in it. Guess you are familiar with the fact of Jack's death. His remains were brought here, but I did not find out until after they left, not expecting it and not being at the depot. Everything is moving along about as usual here. Hope you are better off.*
>
> *May add a little more before sealing if I hear anything from Bob's condition.*

With Best Wishes,
Your Pa

Vidalia, GA
December 17, 1912

Dear Otis,

Wonder what you are doing and how you are feeling on this Monday morning of your last week before the holidays. Do you feel like entering very heartily into several days work or have you very much of the Christmas spirit? It is certainly hard to realize that the time is so near.

I suppose a great many people feel just like I do about it. I have intended all the year to do so many things and accomplish so much before Christmas, but the time is nearly here and I'm not nearly ready for it.

How long do you intend staying in Vienna, or rather what time will you reach Vidalia? Hope you and Mr. Sauls, if he comes, will spend quite a good part of your time in our little city, although I must say it has been very dull here all the fall. Am glad you accepted my invitation to dine with us, although you accepted on condition.

You should have been here yesterday, our pastor, Mr. Williams, preached his first sermon and Mr. Dumas actually gave way and brought his flock up to hear him. Everybody seemed very much surprised at him for he never was known to do anything of that kind before.

Guess I shall be quite busy this week as I am on the Committee to collect funds for a Christmas tree. Mr. Rountree and Mr. J.C. Adams were appointed and those two were to select two ladies to assist them. So Mr. Rountree told me last night he thought I would have to help. So there it is, I don't like to do that, but will do what I can.

I don't know any news to tell you, so will wait until you come. Let me hear from you real soon, I want to know your plans.

Sincerely,
Clyde

222

1913

We wonder where Otis got the money to attend medical school. We surmise that Wash, who was a farmer, footed some of the bill. We also know that when Otis graduated, he owed some money.

May 12, 1913 – Otis Graduated from the Atlanta College of Physicians and Surgeons.

Wednesday, January 1 – "Beginning at Vidalia, Jake and T. We missed 9:35 train. Called up girls, Clyde and Vera fooled around town all morning. In P.M. to walk. Took Kodak pictures. Vieve lent me horse and buggy and I took Clyde home. Came back to Mrs. French's. After supper to see Clyde. Was about left. Jake and I, with Dr. Selman, to Helena at 9:20. Played cards till 1:00 a.m. Took Southern to Atlanta. Arrived at 6:00 a.m."

Sunday, January 5 – "Up at 9:00 a.m. To town for breakfast at 11. Came back, studied Elkin. About three o'clock, Wright took Bill Roberts, Lake, McClure, and me up to Georgian Apartments to see Misses Brooks, Eula Harvey and Spradley. E. Harvey looks very much like Clyde – like her only in looks though."

Monday, January 6 – "Stood Elkin's exam. Made at least a 90. Out to Mrs. Watkins, studied Pat's notes with Pat. At 2 o'clock, took Pullian's exam. Made a B. Back home and studied till supper. Wrote V. French. Sent her Kodak pictures. Studied till 1:30. Lost fountain pen today."

Thursday, January 16 – "Feeling very depressed for some reason."

Friday, January 17 – "Sick with stomach trouble, but all classes in A.M. No breakfast or dinner. At Robert's clinic. Cut Barnett's and went home. Up to Scherer's for a little supper. Got a haircut and rode home. Feeling a little better tonight..."

Saturday, January 19 – "To all classes, to McRae's in P.M. but sick and went home before through..."

Sunday, January 20 – "Report sick...wrote Clyde returning enclosures – a hard letter to write" [what happened there?].

Friday, January 24 – "Letter from Clyde which helped me muchly.... in P.M. to see patient with Jake and Pat – bled her."

Thursday, January 30 – "Letter from Papa. Sent him a book. Wrote him and also a note to Clyde; cut Burnett at Grady. Supper at Scherer's. Home and studied."

Thursday, January 31 – "...to all classes...studied till 12 o'clock. Smoked my last cigar till 22 or 23 of February. Then no more till March 1. That cigar smoked mighty good. Went to Atlanta 'Honey Boy George' Minstrel Fair."

Friday, February 14 – "Sent Clyde box Liggett's [chocolate candy] today. Letter from Vieve French this morning."

Thursday, February 13 – "To Leland for B. To all classes. Burnett did Caesarian section at Grady Hospital on Hunchback and KK Pelvis. Time 1 hour, 5 minutes. Operation highly successful. Dr. Goldsmith saved child..."

Monday, February 17 – "To Leland for B. To all classes. To Scherer's for dinner. In P.M., gave Negro woman anesthetic for 2 hours. Operation by Barnett – Osphorectomy. My first anesthetic. House and studied some. Wrote to C.H. and to town for S. Back and to bed. Jake slept most of the night w.o. undressing."

Tuesday, February 25 – "To all classes. Another done for my tuition which was due January 1."

Sunday, March 1 – "Paid tuition."

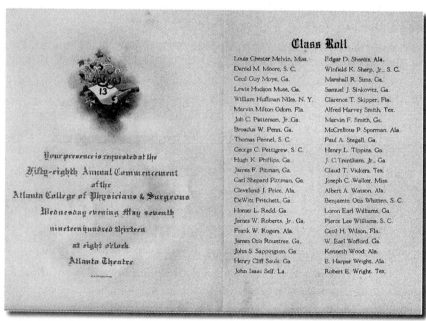

Class Roll

Louis Chester Melvin, Miss.	Edgar D. Shanks, Ala.
Daniel M. Moore, S. C.	Winfield K. Sharp, Jr., S. C.
Cecil Guy Moye, Ga.	Marshall R. Sims, Ga.
Lewie Hudson Muse, Ga.	Samuel J. Sinkovitz, Ga.
William Huffman Niles, N. Y.	Clarence T. Skipper, Fla.
Marvin Milton Odom, Fla.	Alfred Harvey Smith, Tex.
Job C. Patterson, Jr.,Ga.	Marvin F. Smith, Ga.
Broadus W. Penn, Ga.	McCrellous P. Sporman, Ala.
Thomas Pennel, S. C.	Paul A. Stegall, Ga.
George C. Pettigrew, S. C.	Henry L. Tippins, Ga.
Hugh K. Phillips, Ga.	J. C.Trentham, Jr., Ga.
James F. Pitman, Ga.	Claud T. Vickers, Tex.
Carl Shepard Pittman, Ga.	Joseph C. Walker, Miss.
Cleveland J. Price, Ala.	Albert A. Watson, Ala.
DeWitt Pritchett, Ga.	Benjamin Otis Whitten, S. C.
Homer L. Redd, Ga.	Loron Earl Williams, Ga.
James W. Roberts, Jr., Ga.	Pierce Lee Williams, S. C.
Frank W. Rogers, Ala.	Cecil H. Wilson, Fla.
James Otis Rountree, Ga.	W. Earl Wofford, Ga.
John S. Sappington, Ga.	Kenneth Wood, Ala.
Henry Cliff Sauls, Ga.	E. Harper Wright, Ala.
John Isaac Self, La.	Robert E. Wright, Tex.

Your presence is requested at the

Fifty-eighth Annual Commencement

of the

Atlanta College of Physicians & Surgeons

Wednesday evening May seventh

nineteen hundred thirteen

at eight o'clock

Atlanta Theatre

Otis Rountree's graduation invitation from the Atlanta College of Physicians and Surgeons, 1913.

Saturday, March 8 – "…back home and to Phi Chi banquet at Kimbell House 4:00 p.m. Good time and stayed painfully sober. Helped Willis Westmoreland home in cab. Rest of crowd hilarious – to bed at 2 o'clock."

Sunday, March 9 – "Up at 9:30 to First Baptist Church…Bill and I stayed home with Chitwood. Stopped at Durand's for supper and ate $3.50 worth of food – damn fool. Back home at 9 o'clock. To bed at 1:30 – NEVER AGAIN."

Wednesday, March 12 – "Letter from Clyde and answered it, I wish I had it back."

Sunday, March 23 – "To Sacred Heart Catholic Church with Way – pretty Easter service."

Wednesday, April 2 – "In P.M. to Georgian Hospital with Shanks. Dr. Barfield gave me a place as intern there…April 8, moved out to Georgian Hospital today to serve a year as House Physician beginning May 15…"

Sunday, April 20 – "…in P.M. had a patient baby, 1 1/3 years old intestinal indigestion and collected my first fee – 50¢. Studied till 11:30 – to bed at 2:30 – Shanks and I called to see a case of arebro-spinal meningitis. Back to bed at 4:30, to see patient again at 8:00 a.m. Monday."

The diary ends here for 1913.

Author's Note: This is the only letter we have written by John R. Flanders, Jr., and was written to his grandson, Otis. The words in parenthesis we assume to be correct.

Swainsboro, GA
1913

Dear Otis,

I received your letter several days ago. And was glad to hear from and hear that you was making such progress in your studies. The resen I have written you no sooner is I have been so unwell till I have not been able to write and still unwell yet. I thought I was going to die about two weeks ago but I am gaining some strength. It is my hart and I believe it is caused by (stomach ache). I (can't) eat nothing only soups and the like. I am so week till I (ache) I have been to the office only a few times now it is cold till I am shut in we are frozen over (here) I guess you are.

Otis don't expect a long letter from me this time I have not heard from Cobbtown since you wrote me. Be a good boy and come and see me when you get out. Write soon. Nannie says howdy Otis.

Your Grand Pa,
John R. Flanders

Author's Note: Like her daughter Dorothy and her granddaughter Lillian, Clyde loved chocolate.

Vidalia, GA
January 4, 1913

Dear Otis,

I can't say how you will enjoy this letter but you need not be surprised if it just a little "sweetie-sweet". You wonder why? Because I have a great big box of Nunnally's right by my side – you understand? Come over and help me enjoy it, it is really and truly Mr. Youmans' candy this time.

Your letter came last night and I was not at all surprised that you and Mr. Sauls were sleepy and tired when you reached Atlanta. Hope you came out all okay in your exams Friday.

You can't imagine how glad I am that you were well as much as you were during the holidays and how much I enjoyed being with you. I have certainly missed you since you left, didn't know I could miss anyone and be so lonesome until last Thursday. I slept very little Wednesday night and felt miserable all day Thursday.

Forgive me for saying all this but it comes directly from my heart. You say there are thousands of points against my marrying you. I know our time was limited when you were here, but won't you please tell me what you have reference to. It is very likely to be quite a while before we see each other again, so we can discuss it freely. You certainly are fair and just in your proposal, which makes me think more of you, but I am not ready to say positively, I think I need more time to consider.

I am looking over an old Designer. I found this little poem which I enjoyed and will possibly appeal to you. In closing I want to say one thing you must remember. Among the different young men that I have been with, you always seemed to be different from others and they tell me that it is love. So, if I know my heart tonight, I do love you and will do all in my power to be true to you in every way.

Let me hear from you when you have time to write. I am real anxious to see our pictures. Wishing you and Mr. Sauls much success in all your work this spring.

Sincerely,
Clyde

Author's Note: Remember that during the silent movie days, pianos were used to accompany the movie to denote action or romance, etc.

Vidalia, GA
January 7, 1913
Tuesday P.M.

Otis Dear,

I would give most any old thing I know if I could have a good long talk with my sweetheart this afternoon. Why can't you come over and spend the afternoon with me, am sure you could cheer me up. I'm desperately ill so you see I need the doctor. I have the worst case of blues I've had for quite a while. Let me tell you what I have gone and done. Don't let it shock you though, you had better sit down so you won't fall. I've made arrangements with Roy Page to play down at the picture show all this week. I managed to get

*through with last night but have the rest of the week before me. If I
ever do get out of this, it's "never again" for me...*

*I like my pin better every day, the more I look at it the prettier
it gets. It certainly is pretty at night and shows off beautifully...will
write you more next time, must go and give a music lesson now.*

Love and Best Wishes,
Clyde

Author's Note: Clyde agrees to marry Otis.

Vidalia, GA
January 25, 1913
Wednesday Evening

Dear Otis,

*...I wish so much that I could see you and talk with you tonight
– I often think of your short vacation Christmas and wish we
could go over it again. I think of so many things we should have
discussed. You certainly have been candid and honest with me, and
I believe you are sincere in all that you say. I don't intend to leave
the impression that I doubt your sincerity at all.*

*It must be, as you say, that sometimes I doubt my own heart.
But if I know my heart tonight, I love you better than anyone in the
world – there, I think that you and I ought to feel that we belong to
each other. So I'm going to promise you tonight what is so sacred
to us, to share your lot in life. Your offer is all that anyone could
ask, for worldly goods are not happiness in this life by any means,
do you think so? I like to think that we have something to look
forward to and ever build air castles probably, for all we get a great
deal of pleasure out of anticipation. So be a good boy and remember
someone is counting on you and is interested in all your work.*

I am quite tired and sleepy so will tell you "good night". Hope your headache has decided to leave you and you are feeling much better ere this.

With Love,
Clyde

Vidalia, GA
January 27, 1913

Dear Otis,

Hello you. Wonder how you are feeling and what you are doing this gloomy, cloudy Sunday afternoon. Wish you were right here in the little town of Vidalia, Georgia, and well, I won't say what part. I have just come in from Sunday school, came directly on home to write you my sweetheart – now what do you think of me? Do you believe in fortune telling? I have about decided there is something in it, although I have never had any experience except once in my life. Several years ago I had my palm read and the lady described my disposition to a tee, then she proceeded to tell me of my love affairs. She said I had never loved anyone up to that time, that I would not love anyone for some time but when I did fall in love, I would love very <u>hard</u>. She said I would finally marry a man whose name should begin with "<u>R</u>" and that I would be very happy. That I would not be wealthy but would have plenty to live on, etc. etc. – now what do you think about that? I have thought of it several times, especially in the last few weeks.

Anyway, I'm glad you woke and found that the letter you mentioned was only a dream letter. And I'm happy in your love and over our engagement. As to our keeping it a secret, I certainly wish it to be so, as you say, for the present and I shall consider my promise to you more sacred than anything else to me.

I am glad you look at it in such a practical light and don't expect me to quit going with other boys, yet I know from the very first that you would. And of course I shall not expect you to quit going to see other girls – I don't think that is the right way to look at

229

it at all. Mama has often told me that there is many a slip between the cup and the lip and we never know what may happen. However, let us hope and trust that our lives will be spared and that nothing will ever come between us. Oh, how I do wish I could see you and have a long talk with you tonight! I feel so much more like talking freely with you now...

I must go now and eat supper, it will soon be time for preaching. I have written this very hurriedly and with children talking all around, so pardon my mistakes. Write me real soon.

Love and Best Wishes,
Clyde

Author's Note: Did you know that Clyde enjoyed Ragtime? Otis had been offered a position at the Georgian Hospital.

Vidalia, GA
February 10, 1913
Monday A.M.

Dear Otis,

...We had a big minstrel show at the Opera House last Tuesday night, which was very good. It was a company of 25 men, some of whom had very good voices and the orchestra was real good. I certainly do enjoy good music, ragtime as well as classic, don't you?

They sang several songs that you sent and they sounded very good indeed, "That's How I Need You", "Till The Sands of The Desert Grow Cold", and "When Uncle Joe Plays A Rag On His Old Banjo", I believe were all. One that I liked very much was "Waiting For The Robert E. Lee", sounds very much like "Mammy's Shufflin' Dance".

I have not thought much more about teaching yet, have hardly had time to think recently, but I really think that plan will be best for both of us, don't you? Dr. Thompson asked me about you yesterday and, when I spoke of the hospital proposition, he said be sure and

On the back of the picture is written, "Otis and ?, Prince (the horse)".

take it. Said you would be so much better prepared when you began practicing regularly.

I know it will be hard for both of us to have to wait another year, but probably we will be nearer and can see each other more often than this year. Anyway, we have a duty to perform, we owe ourselves and our parents so much, and that must come before pleasure. I know that you are anxious to begin paying up those debts, and I think you are right, but I think you ought to get the best preparation while you are at it. Still you know best, you know more about how to get the best results than I do, for I don't know much.

Have you seen anything more of my double? I think I have seen your double now, only at a distance, however. Do you suppose any of your brothers were over here a week ago yesterday? I did not see his face very well for I couldn't afford to stare, but I saw his back and never did want to ask a fellow his name as much. He was just about your size and walked just like you...

I was just about to forget something, can you guess what, it's very important? I'm glad you have stopped smoking and hope you will keep it up. Quite a number of the boys here have quit entirely. Spurgeon Meadows quit on January 1, Will Thomas, Herbert, Mr.

Yeomans, Alex Holmes, and others have quit. I don't know how long the reform movement will last, though.

Be good, and don't kill any of those sick Negroes that you have to walk so far to see.

With Love,
Clyde

LaGrange, GA
February 28, 1913

Dear Otis,

...I was not in the best of spirits, I read both letters over and over again, and then just sat down and built a few "castles in Spain" – I thought of the past, of the many happy hours which seemed like seconds that we have spent together, and then I thought and planned for the future.

Otis, I am looking forward to the time when as you said "we shall begin a new life". I feel then that all the shadows will be changed to sunshine. It will be great to have someone whom you love better than anything else on earth with you for all time, through joy and sorrow and to know that this one loves you better than anything or anybody on earth. I tell you love is a great thing and though we grow awfully inpatient sometimes we can live on hope until we realize our dreams...

Your brother [Ridge] certainly has a terrible time. I was so much in hopes he would do better after his operations. I surely would go to him if I were you, especially if he does not intend to let your father know about it.

It is nearly 10:00 so I must tell you good night. Be good and remember your little girl loves you with all her heart.

Sincerely,
Clyde

March 1913

Dear Otis,

...You ought to be here now to drink milk and eat butter and clabber. We get about four gallons of milk a day, and I fed lots of it to my pigs. You ought to see them! Five gilts and six males. Will ship two gilts to Vidalia in a few days, one to Ike and one to Geo Raiford, but both in one box. All five are taken up, or have been spoken for, at $8.00 per, and they are now nearly big enough to shift for themselves, being one month old and a few days over.
...Well, we are soon to have a full-fledged M.D. in our family! Success to you, Doc. Wish we could have the benefits of your services when we need a Dr. Guess you will be home to visit Gator [we do not know who Gator was] before entering into active service? Hope you are doing well, and will come out with banners flying and horns tooting.

Your Pa

Vidalia, GA
April 16, 1913

Dear Otis,

You realize that the time is drawing near when your guests are to arrive in Atlanta? Yes, we are going to see you, so the public say, therefore are we not your guests? Anyway, according to our present plans, Will Thomas better known in these parts as "Little Willie", and I are to leave here on the noon train Thursday week arriving in Atlanta about 7:00 I believe...
Will Thomas has something planned for every hour of our time. I can't begin to name the things he has promised to take us to, but I will tell you a few that I remember. Friday evening we are to go to the theater, Saturday afternoon to the matinee, Saturday evening to

the opera, Sunday morning to the First Methodist Church, Sunday afternoon to the free concert, Sunday evening to the First Baptist Church, and Monday back home. Besides all this we have several other things to take in, so I think if our plans work we will have all our time very well occupied...

We certainly don't expect you to take up too much of your time with us, when your time is so valuable during the entire week. While I shall enjoy every moment you can possibly spend with us or with me I don't want you to feel under any obligations to see that we are entertained, etc...

Otis, I have often thought how happy I should be and am to be loved by so grand and noble a man as you are. That you love this simple little country girl when you might win beautiful wealthy girls there. Yet I do not doubt your sincerity, you are so honest, frank, and so true. I hope and trust I may never give you cause to regret your choice and that I may always be as true and faithful to you as I can be.

I am getting so dull and sleepy I guess I had better mark this "continued" in the next issue. Be good and write when you can.

Love,
Clyde

Vidalia, GA
April 22, 1913
Monday Evening

Dear Otis,

If I should telephone for my physician tonight a very urgent call, I wonder if he would be at my service. I must say that your patient feels quite indisposed on account of a severe cold, and also the thought of all those nice little doses Mrs. Holmes is patiently waiting to prepare her with before she retires. Mrs. Holmes says that if there is not a change for the better of course – there is no

Atlanta for Clyde, so you don't blame me for being willing to take most anything, do you?

But our plans now are to leave here on the Seaboard train Thursday morning, reaching Atlanta about 5 o'clock that afternoon. Vieve leaves LaGrange on Thursday afternoon at 4:20, and I think reaches Atlanta about 7 that evening. So we will get there before she does and Will Thomas will meet us here. So you will be relieved of that responsibility. The address of the family we are to stop with is 33 Poplar Circle, Inman Park. How does that suit your convenience?

I don't know how I would manage if Tommy were not going. He has looked up the schedule and planned everything for us. He had just gotten a diagram of the Opera House and my – I think we will have to sit in the gallery. I am certainly glad we decided to go to only two operas anyway.

I am so glad the time is so near where I shall see you and be with you again and I hope you can be with me most of the time at least and that you will not have to be busy much of the time.

I don't know much to write tonight except that I'm just waiting anxiously to see you. I want to prepare you for one thing though, so you will survive. I have fallen off and look so thin and bad you will hardly know me – so you may expect the worst. Be good until I see you. Good night.

Clyde

Author's Note: Clyde is visiting her friends at LaGrange College.

LaGrange, GA
May 1, 1913
Wednesday Evening

Dear Otis,

I have just been uptown with Vieve and one of the other girls – I being a teacher of course could chaperone them – and tell you

I certainly am tired. This place is just filled with high rocky hills and I always did tire quickly from walking on rocks than anything I know of. ....I think some of them (the pictures) are very good, don't you? Several of the girls up here have asked me if the young man with me is not my brother – of course I say yes.

Well, I certainly hope you have finished up those pesky old exams, and you can begin to have some rest now for you certainly do need it. You have been writing all along that you thought I was working too hard, have you not? Well, I have lost only about five pounds and I believe you said you were off about twenty, what does it mean? I certainly will be glad when all of those examinations are over and you can begin to feel free again, but most of all, I hope you made good marks on these and will come out all right on the others.

Otis, we certainly had a delightful time up there and appreciate every effort you and your friends put forth to make us enjoy ourselves. You certainly were a nice little boy and to show us around and keep us from getting lost. I can speak for one and say that I enjoyed every moment spent with you for as Vieve says, "Otis and Bubba know how to be so nice to you and make you have such a good time".

I enjoy being with you for other reasons as well though, sweetheart, because I love you. As I told you, I don't feel like I have hardly seen you at all, but we were in such a rush all the time. I do hope that you can get off for a short while, at least, during the summer where you will feel better and not be busy at all...

I think I shall go home Friday, so let me hear from you right away. The light bell has rung so all school girls must say goodnight.

Clyde

THE LETTERS OF OTIS AND CLYDE ROUNTREE

Author's Note: Apparently May 7, 1913, was the day Otis graduated from the Atlanta College of Physicians and Surgeons. You will also note that these letters continually mention his health problem.

Vidalia, GA
May 8, 1913
Wednesday Eve

My Dear Otis,

Your letter came yesterday and while I knew you were quite busy I could not help feeling a little bit anxious and impatient. I was about to fear that you had gone to California for your health, if you decide to go let me go too, will you?

No, really I felt perfectly easy about your examinations, although I was getting anxious to hear from you. How about that State Board business, has it come off yet? You can just bet your life you have my good wishes if that means anything. I guess you have had a very eventful day of it today, this 7th day of May 1913. How about the sounds of glory and honor -- guess it will always be a memorable day with all of you. I wish so much that I could have stayed over. I was certainly tempted to go back when I received that invitation last Saturday. I certainly did want to be there, though I expect it is best that I could not.

People here have been very much interested in my trip up there -- not especially about how I enjoyed the opera, but they want to know if I saw you. One lady was asking me yesterday if I saw you and I very calmly told her "No, maame." She says, "You needn't tell me that for I know better, you have had too broad a smile on your face since you came back." Must I wear a long face all the time on account of curiosity and gossip?

Vidalia is very much interested in the two weddings that are soon to come off. They are to be on the same day, June the 4th ... Ola is planning a very swell thing. She asked me to preside at the punchbowl, which means that I must have a nice green dress, and you may imagine how much like a pumpkin I will look in green. It certainly seems strange that so many of my schoolmates and close friends are married or soon will be -- makes you stop and wonder how old you really are anyway, doesn't it?

...I hope you are all doing nicely with your work and will soon feel care free and easy once more. Let me hear from you as soon as possible.

With Love,
Clyde

Author's Note: Kind of interesting, the social stigma that was in existence at the time between townies and country folk.

Vidalia, GA
June 9, 1913
Monday P.M.

Dear Otis,

...Well, the long expected weddings are now over and the two couples are yet on their tour, Ola's wedding was a very pretty one, yet a very serious and solemn occasion. I never have attended anything that seemed so much like a funeral ceremony, the wedding march sounded like a funeral dirge to me – nice way to talk about the ceremony of the happy young couple, isn't it? They sent out 150 invitations and I think their presents amounted to at least $400 or more. I guess I have quite long enough ahead of me to plan my wedding but unless I change my mind considerably, I want a big affair with all my friends and acquaintances present, don't you?

Last Saturday a week, the Chamber of Commerce gave a big barbecue for the farmers of the county, and you know everybody and all their family were here. They had several great speakers for the occasion, beside a brass band from <u>Cobbtown</u>, a nice little town over in Tattnall County, between Swainsboro and Collins. I did not go because there was such a crowd of country people here, I did not care to be there, but Mr. Rountree says one of your brothers was here, was a leader of the band, and kept trying to find me in that crowd all day. I'm so glad I didn't go...

When do you think you can get off to come home? I hope you can arrange to get off for two or three weeks this summer and that you will spend most of your time in Vidalia. Let me hear from you as often as you can.

Sincerely,
Clyde

Vidalia, GA
June 25, 1913

My Dear,

I don't think I shall ever make any more rash promises or statements about writing letters, would you? The meeting is still in progress, and besides, I have had company all this week, so I have had very little time at my own disposal. But I have thought of you every moment of the time, and have at last the pleasant task of writing to you.

Bless your heart, I wish I could see you right now and hear you say again and again, "Clyde, I do love you." I realize more fully every day that you are my ideal, the more I am thrown with other young men, the more experience I have with this world, the more I do realize that the hand of fate is surely kind.

Alice was here yesterday, and she told me that she and John Eli were discussing me and my prospects, and John E wondered when you and I would marry. She asked him if he knew that we were, and how he knew it. He said yes, he knew it, "Why Alice, they just looked like it. They looked like they were meant for each other." What do you know about that? I have been having a time this week trying to go to church, hearing music lessons and entertaining company. Next week I'll make up for lost time. I must go to church now.

Clyde

Author's Note: Sounds like there is trouble in paradise. This letter was written by Clyde to Otis while he was visiting Cobbtown.

Vidalia, GA
June 27, 1913
Thursday P.M.

Dear Otis,

I expected to get a letter from you this morning but, guess you are out on that fishing trip. How are you enjoying your vacation? I feel sure you enjoy being at home and hope you will go back to your work feeling much better and much more like work...

But now to the point, I had a special reason for writing you this afternoon. At the party last night, I talked to George Matthews for quite a while. As soon as he heard that you were to be here Sunday, he told me to write you that he wanted you to take dinner with him. I objected to that at once because we are expecting you to dine with us Sunday. Then he insisted that I write you today and ask you to take supper with him Sunday night, so you understand the program now, don't you? George said he would take you over to the New Vidalia, introduce you to that pretty widow, Mrs. Hayes, and then you would quit me. But if that is to be the result of my labors, you need not come down with me Sunday at all, just go out to the hotel and you will get to meet her a little sooner.

Otis, if you happen to have a knife, or a razor or anything of that kind near you, take it and cut a notch in something right quick, for I am not going uptown at all this afternoon, am going to stay right here at home. Am going to Prayer Meeting tonight, though I hardly think I can stand it if I were not.

Well, I started out intending to write you only a short note and here I have written a long letter. Remember your engagement for Sunday and write me your plans.

Sincerely,
Clyde

Vidalia, GA
July 29, 1913
Monday Evening

Dear Otis,

...But the meeting closed last night and I would be in such a rush all this week. We had a real good meeting, five services and good attendance. Had 16 accessions to the church, but that singer was the most disgusting piece of humanity I ever saw, I think. He wanted everyone to know that he was Mr. Mylam from Atlanta, that he had studied music in Chicago, and had composed several songs. He stayed here only one week and wanted $50 to stay the next – so he left. I'm glad the meeting has closed, because it was not raining and it was so very warm we could hardly live...

By the way, Otis, I had a long talk with your cousin, George S. [Rountree], last Sunday night. A terrible thunder shower came up while we were at church, the lights went out and Mr. Williams dismissed us. But it was raining so we could not think of leaving the church, so he talked with me for about a half hour trying to pick me, of course. He says, "You know, that looks mighty funny to me, him spending so much of his time over here – I tell you, Clyde, you all had better not keep me in the dark." It certainly is amusing to hear him talk when his curiosity is slightly aroused, isn't it?

I guess it is about time for me to bring this to a close so goodnight. Remember your little girl loves you and trusts you above anybody in this world.

As Ever,
Clyde

Vidalia, GA
September 1, 1913

Dear Otis,

Your letter came Wednesday morning and I think I have read it over at least a dozen times since that time. You wonder why I feel sure, but I can't tell you. I have also done some tall thinking and wondering, have even spent some sleepless nights since that time.

Why do I continue to place and "build air castles", why should anyone do that where it all seems to be in vain? It is just like blowing soap bubbles that burst as soon as the wind strikes them, yet when I was a little girl how I did enjoy it, and, how many scoldings I have gotten for that very thing. We all get a certain amount of real pleasure out of looking into the future and planning for the future, yet that is so much better than brooding over the past, isn't it?

Otis, I love you and it just seems to come natural for me to think of you and plan for our future happiness all the time from morning until night. I have never really cared for anyone but you, although at one time I thought I did, and it seems to me that I love you more and with a purer, stronger, truer love everyday of my life.

I was somewhat surprised to hear of your brother [Arlis] marrying, for I did not expect it this early. We heard that Clark Rountree and Mrs. Coleman were married at the same time, but the news came from a very uncertain source, so we don't know whether that is true or not.

How is your brother getting on now? Certainly hope he is still improving rapidly.

Our school opens Monday morning and they expect a large opening I think. All of the faculty are new teachers except Professor Ainsworth and Professor Guffey. Have not seen any of them yet but hope we will have a better looking crew than last year's, don't you wish that much for the benefit of those before whom they have to appear, in other words the pupils.

My music class continues to increase, I now have nine that have been taking nearly all the summer and will have at least six more next week. I feel real proud of that record, don't you? I don't mean to be boastful at all, but I do think it is real good.

It is getting late so I must go now. Be good and don't wait so long to write me, hear?

Sincerely,
Clyde

Author's Note: Apparently our couple had a little tift. Was Clyde out with someone else when Otis came to town?

October 1913
Thursday Eve

My Dear Otis,

I got your letter this morning as I started out to Mrs. Crawford's and read it on the way out there. I'm afraid my music lesson, as well as my other work, had very little spirit in it this time anyway, for I could hardly withhold the tears until I got back home. I wanted to see you standing there at the gate and hear you say again "Clyde, don't forget me, hear? And remember I love you."

Nobody in this world knows what I have gone through today, guess I have read your letter at least a dozen times, have thought, prayed, shed tears, and finally turned it over to Mama to read. She would not say much but now I feel better that she knows all.

Otis, I love you as only woman can love man just because you are so noble, so good and so strong and -- well, just because you are you and I love you, that is the only explanation. I have promised to share your lot in life because I love you, I'm sorry you are beginning to feel doubtful and wonder if my affection is not centered on someone else. Yet, I can only see how that might be, if you have paid the slightest bit of attention to ... gossip.

I have known this other gentleman for only about nine months, during which time he has been very nice indeed. When he first began showing me attention, I enjoyed being with him because he was very jolly and nice and was very good company. Then you were not here, of course I enjoyed going out to different things and could not well refuse to go. I never dreamed at that time that he would ever think anything of me except as a friend, but now I believe he is in earnest, though it is very hard for a girl to tell. You know yourself that you have been very careless about writing -- I do not think that I am unreasonable or expect too much -- but you have been more negligent about that than anyone I have ever known I think. What could I do, when I wrote you how people question me about you, my own family teased me about not hearing from you and that stung to the core, I don't suppose you thought of it, but you just did not seem to pay any attention to what I said.

It seemed that I had stood about as much as I could, you wrote me you could not come down here, then I jumped at the chance to go to Macon if you could be there -- I felt like I had to see you. Now that I have seen you I feel better over it if you don't.

Otis, dear, I'm sorry you think I am dissatisfied, don't you believe I would have told you Sunday night if I had felt that way about it? I intended to stop this other party, but cannot do it right at once -- can't you trust me to do that? I do not expect to tell him or anyone else of the engagement, although this bunch of loafers and gossipers seem to know more about my plans now than I do. Otis, sweetheart, you don't think I acted the least bit unconcerned or distant towards you, do you? Then take back what you said and tell me I'm the same nice sweet little girl like you used to every time you came to see me. I'm very sorry indeed that there was a misunderstanding, and I was not here when you came Sunday afternoon, yet I don't think you could censor me for that. I think you must have imagined all the chilly atmosphere after that, now really did not that have a great deal to do with it?

Yet Otis, you have taken such a broad view of this affair, you are always so reasonable and practical about anything. I only hope you will heed Dr. Sauls' lecture in the future -- he's all right for he's my friend.

I must go now, my eyes are burning red awfully. Hope you are feeling much better than you were Tuesday night, I am sorry for any trouble or worry I have caused you. Remember your little sweetheart loves you still.

C -

Fall 1913
Tuesday A.M.

My Dear,

You can't imagine the anxiety I felt until I received your letter yesterday at noon, unless you experience it while waiting for my reply last week, and I guess you did then -- what do you say about it? It certainly made me feel happy to know that you had not lost confidence in me, that you still believe me to be true as I have honestly striven to be.

Yet, I still don't understand why you doubted me unless, as I said before, you did heed the gossip of this place. Because I don't see how you could have expected me to stay down there and talk to you at the hotel any later than I did, no matter how much I wanted to, nor how lonesome you were. I could not afford it, now really do <u>you</u> think so? I want to know if you heard anything more about the other party than you told me Sunday night. You remember you said you were only judging from different little things these "prying" people had said to you. I guess though, that I have experienced about as much trouble from stinging questions and remarks as you did while here.

But you say you are going to do better about writing and I believe you are. You have made a very good beginning but tried not to verify the old adage about the good beginning and the bad ending, hear? That witch at the party knew what she was talking about all right, didn't she -- no matter where the information came from...

Tell Dr. Sauls I say for him to keep you straight and see that you heed his advice. Remember I love you and your letters mean so much to me.

Sincerely,
Clyde

Author's Note: Clyde's Prophetic Dream. Was God preparing her for the events of seven years, hence? This must have been before he had his first operation.

Vidalia, GA
November 1913
Dear Otis,

Your letter came last Wednesday and as you said, I was beginning to wonder if all those promises and resolutions were a thing of the past, again. I am sorry you are kept so very busy up there, Otis, while I am sure the experience is fine for you, yet I certainly wish you had more time to devote to one or two other things.

Before your letter came last week, I had an awful dream – do you believe there is anything in dreams? I think it was on Monday night, I dreamed that you were very sick and had one of the nurses to write me. Then, the next thing I knew I was there trying in my feeble way to do something for you, that you were seriously ill and all your people were there with you. Of course, my dream ended there and left me wide awake, thinking and wondering, Otis, I really wondered if you were to get desperately ill, would you write me or wire me, and would you want me to go to you? Heaven knows I don't know of anything that would keep me away if such a thing should happen.

But, let's change the subject and "never trouble trouble till trouble troubles you", isn't that a good plan?

...Otis, I think you are awful what you did with my last letter? Surely you are not quite so careless with all of them, are you? However, one question that I ask you has been settled, I think, I am more than willing to let our little misunderstanding drop and forget it entirely...

It is supper time now, and I must go. Be good and remember I still love you. Hurry and cure up your thumb so you can write me.

As Ever,
Clyde

Vidalia, GA
November 1913
Tuesday A.M.

Well Dear,

I can't begin to tell you how glad I was to get your letter without having to wait so long this time. I have often heard that if you have to wait for anything, a long time you will appreciate it more when you finally do get it. But I don't think it is true in every instance, do you? I certainly enjoyed your letter and appreciate your efforts to be more prompt with them.

How are you this time? Hope your neuralgia is not troubling you anymore. Wish I could have seen you when your face looked so much like a full moon or did it look like that?

Hope your patient is doing nicely now and that your work will not be all for "gratitude". How are you and your nurse friend progressing these days? Have you had anymore trouble or disagreements with her?

Otis, you did not know Dr. Huie's wife did you? She died last Thursday night with tuberculosis. It was certainly pitiful. She was nothing more than a girl when she married and was still young. She was a real pretty girl, but when she died was the poorest person I have ever seen. It was one of the saddest deaths I have ever known of. Everybody here thought so much of her and Dr. Huie too. Mr. Youmans has gone back to Cuba, can't you sympathize with me in my loneliness? He came to see me the night before he left but I didn't go to the train to see him off. I promised him that I would go all the way to Cuba to play the wedding march for him if he would send me an invitation...

Well, I had another dream last night, but I shall not relate it, it is too ridiculous. No, they are not caused from eating meat for supper, but from association of ideas. Write your little sweetheart real soon, hear?

With Love,
Clyde

Author's Note: This postcard was written to Otis by his good friend, Dr. Shanks.

Savannah, GA
December 15, 1913

Dear Buck,

I have just learned of your illness and I hasten to offer my sympathy and good wishes.
I am very sorry to know it was necessary for you to undergo an operation, but I trust you were benefited by same.
Hurry up and get well, and by all means, come to see me when you come to South Georgia.

Shanks

Author's Note: When Otis was in the hospital in Atlanta in 1913 for his first surgery, his "Pa" Wash wrote to him and told him of the hard times at home. Though the Wash Rountree family had little money, very few material possessions, and failing crops, they gained strength through their faith and love for one another.

December 1913

Dear Otis,

...We ought to be more thankful for we have good health, peace, and plenty to eat, no doubt would enjoy more in life with your present state of feeling, but I am committed hopelessly to the pessimistic side of things and am not fit to paint rosy pictures of the future under any conditions. Life and how to live it are serious problems. Years ago I thought I would one day reach the stature of a man, but I will never be anything more than a simple child. Knowing so well of the benefits I was deprived of in my young days, so far

as our means permitted, we have tried to place you all above them and your success in life will show to what use you have put them. We rise and fall with our children. To know you are all succeeding, industrious, honest, sober, and respected in your communities, will be enough to make up feel fully repaid for all cares and anxieties. Knowing the responsibilities of married life, I can only hope and pray that as you all see proper to mate you may be guided by the ONE who makes no mistakes; then it will prove a success. With the right companion I don't doubt but what it will be a help to you in many ways.

Well, my business is so tangled I can't find a way out just at this time. Have reached the point where I can't well help myself, much more others. May the good Lord guide me through safely and all the rest…

Your Pa

Vidalia, GA
Late December 1913

Otis Dear,

What in the world is the matter up there? It has been a week today since I heard from you, and I feel sure I would hear real often when you got able to write again. Are you not doing so well, or are you not ready to come home? I am anxious to hear how you are and if you received the package I sent you Christmas. I had it registered, however, so I guess it is alright.

If you will answer all the above questions for me, probably my nerves will be a little more quiet. Probably I can tell you sometime why I feel so very anxious about you at this time. Everything has been very quiet in Vidalia all during the holidays – nothing exciting that I have heard of. All the boys [Fred and Alex] have been here and my, what a difference it makes, they give me enough to do to keep me busy alright…

Of course, I still love you better than anybody, you know that, don't you? I do and want to see you more than I ever thought I could. I certainly hope you are still improving and that I can see you real soon. If you can't write me, get some of the others to do so right away, hear?

As Ever,
Clyde

1914

January 1914 saw Otis and Clyde secretly engaged but not having set the date. Otis was recuperating in Atlanta from an operation. This was the first attempt to repair his stomach ulcer. It was unsuccessful. Clyde was quite worried about Otis. He had undergone surgery December 1913.

Clyde was still having her dreams and teaching music.

Otis was working at the Georgian Hospital. During the winter of 1914 he set up his practice in Canoochee. Canoochee was a small community located in Emanuel County.

War clouds were becoming more ominous. It looked as if the U.S. would be drawn into World War I. This would also drastically affect cotton prices.

CURES

A country doctor in rural Georgia had to deal with numerous superstitions and novel cures. Elizabeth Rodgers compiled this list. It was obtained from the Georgia archives.

Cure to move the bowels: Take hogs' hooves, parch them, beat fine, mix syrup with them, mix flour, take three times a day. It will move the bowels when nothing else will.

Cure for mad dog bite: Take poke root and boil it in sweet milk. You must drink it for three weeks. You must not eat anything salty or greasy, drink coffee or tea.

Cure for the shingles: Take gunpowder and mix it in cream and rub it on and bathe it in by the fire twice a day.

Cure for the piles: Take a handful of persimmon root bark; stew it in fresh butter or mutton suet. Grease the parts with it. Take one teaspoonful of sulfur every day inward.

Cure for the fever: Take cow manure, take the manure that comes in May and dry it and keep it and make a tea of it and give it to the patient several times a day. It will break the fever. You may fool the patient with it by putting sage in with the tea or some other herb.

Cure for a sore: Bind warm cow manure to the sore. When you take off the poultice, wash the sore in red oak tea. When the tea is cold, make a salve, take wild arsenic and stew it in lard and grease it twice a day.

When a woman miscarries and the afterbirth don't come: Give a dose of castor oil and that generally brings it. And if that don't do, it won't hurt. If she ain't cleared in four or five days, if she was not gone more than five months and if she wastes too much, give her a little alum.

When a woman is pestered with humor in her privates: Take one handful of white planting, one teaspoon full of black pepper, quarter of a pound of mutton tala; stew it together and grease with it.

Cure for spitting blood: Ezekiel 16:6. Repeat it three times secretly. If you can't memorize it, get the Bible and read it secretly to yourself (Cashin, p. 170).

Taken from Otis' graduation invitation.

Author's Note: Clyde's brother Fred is admitted to the U.S. Naval Academy.

Vidalia, GA
Winter 1914

Dear Otis,

...Otis, do tell me this -- what railroad is Canoochee on? Vera and Dr. Thompson tried to rag me, in the drugstore a few days ago, by asking me how far it was from a railroad. They said it was five miles. Of course I did the best I could, but I knew very little about it so they had the advantage of me. So, do tell me more about it, hear?

...Otis, do you read the papers these days? Did you see where Fred passed his examination for Annapolis? It seems real hard when we think of his being away from home eight years and yet it certainly will make a man of him.

And those people out there think you are to be married right away, do they? Well, I guess they can just live and learn, probably you can surprise them in one way if not another.

Every time I see Mr. Rountree he asks me about you, says you won't write to him at all. He says you will be telling some of those people they had better get a doctor before long. He had better be careful how he talks to them like that though.

Now, don't wait a long time to write me sweetheart for I am anxious to hear from you.

Lovingly,
Clyde

Sunday P.M.
Winter 1914

Dear Otis,

Wonder how you are feeling this cold windy afternoon, also what are you doing with yourself sitting by a good warm fire smoking a nice cigar or cigarette from your collection. I have just come in from Sunday school, did not tarry on the way at all, decided the most comfortable place to be found was at home by the fire.

Otis, you did not think it strange of me writing you such an <u>unusual</u> *letter last week, did you? I seemed real anxious about you, so it seemed about twice as long to me as it really had been since I had heard from you. Then, too, my same old* <u>hobby</u>, *I had a dream which disturbed me quite a good deal. I will tell you about it when you come to see me.*

By the way, when is that to be? When you get strong enough to take the trip home, and another thing to be considered is the walk over here when you get to Vidalia. Otis, I am certainly anxious to see you, and hope you will soon be able to take the trip.

Mr. Rountree told me about his trip to Vienna and that those people seem to think that you had better get busy. Said two or three others were considering the place and that you had better leave the hospital as soon as you could. What other places did you have in mind, you have not been considering another Panama, Canada or Cuban proposition have you? I don't suppose you could begin to make any definite plans, though, until you are a little stronger, can you? ...

Hurry and write to me again Otis, for I am anxious to hear from you, want to know when you are coming.

Love Forever,
Clyde

Vidalia, GA
February 2, 1914

My Dear,

Guess you have at least reached the city of Canoochee and are "sitting out in front of the grocery stores whittling white pine" are you or are you not? Just the same, allow me to say that you are certainly being missed by at least one person back here in Vidalia. My, just the thought of how long it will be before you can come back to see me makes me feel real lonesome and blue.

It seems almost an age since last Monday night and to think that I couldn't be with you that afternoon and had such a short while that night. It was a shame to be treated that way the last few hours you were here wasn't it? But never mind, you be sure to bring a book of some kind, such as Ben Hur or an annual or two, one that you will have to come by for as you want to carry it home, every time you come. Those few moments are short but pleasant indeed.

Otis, we have had a terrible accident here since you left. I don't suppose you have heard of it. Do you know Mr. Will Shivers that married Will McMillan's sister? He and Mr. Cook were out hunting last Tuesday and Mr. Shivers accidentally shot himself through the bowels. He went to take his gun out of the buggy or rather to put it in the back of the buggy, which of course made him right at the gun.

They brought him here to the sanitorium and operated on him, though they had no hopes of his getting well. He died Wednesday night about 11 o'clock I think. I certainly sympathize with his family. His wife is certainly a sweet nice little woman, is left with four children and not a dollar to live on. He worked for the Dixie Cotton Company but always lived right up to his salary.

I saw Mr. McMillan and talked with him for a good long time out at Mrs. Crawford's yesterday. He told me all the news from Swainsboro even to the history of "Black Bess" where the name originated how she was lady-broke but brought hard luck to so many couples in the past etc.

Said he saw Nell Smith's announcement in last Sunday's paper, she is to marry a doctor over at her house. He is from Hartwell. I believe I am about to be the only one of my schoolmates left -- I will have a long, stringy neck and all kinds of crow's feet around my *mouth and eyes the first thing I know.*

Otis, when is your brother coming over here? I haven't seen anything of a tall handsome, redheaded man around here. Write me real soon sweetheart, for I love you and am anxious to hear from you.

As Ever,
Clyde

Vidalia, GA
February 1914

Dear Otis,

I have just had a long telephone conversation with Mrs. French, you know how interesting she is, so I stayed there so long I almost froze. We discussed not only our trip to Atlanta but plans for spending several days down at Tybee this summer. Says Will Thomas wants to take Genevieve and her if I will go and if we can prevail on you to take a few days off and go with us. Mrs. French says that W.G. said he could think of no one else he would like to go -- now don't we feel highly complimented? Guess we will have to plan all that later on in the year, though...

Don't you ever say again that I don't care whether or not you quit smoking -- for although I don't suppose it matters how I feel about it if you have made up your mind to begin again, I certainly do think it is a bad habit. So many boys say they get so much pleasure out of it, yet anyone can see the results and see that it is not only injurious, but a needless expense. But never mind, you know all these things and I didn't intend reading you a regular moral lecture.

Yes, it did look rather strange for me to go to the train with him (Mr. Youmans), didn't it? But you know he was going all the way to Cuba. I want to see you awful bad but I don't want you to go to Cuba at all, so I don't know so much about going to the train -- I can't go to the train with anyone except those who are bound for Cuba.

He is no longer a real estate man, he has gone back to the sugar mills but will no doubt be equally as prosperous if not more so. The night before he left he brought me some specimens of his sugar making. Four little bottles full, showing it in four different stages. Everyone here has been teasing me ever since, mama declares she is going to keep them and show them to you, but I'm going to destroy them before long...

I certainly appreciated the clipping from the Constitution regarding the opera season. You had better send me any information you can get for I need it all.

I have nearly frozen trying to write this letter. It's a wonder it is not covered with icicles, so I'm going to tell you goodbye. Please forgive this poor excuse for a letter and I'll try to do better next time. Be good and write your sweetheart real soon.

With Love,
Clyde

Author's Note: Clyde sees this new game – basketball. Black Bess was Otis' horse.

Vidalia, GA
February 26, 1914

Dear Otis,

Wonder if you people over there are having as nice cool weather as we are, it feels like we might be living right near the North Pole. Wish you were here so I could snowball you, and that we could take some pictures in the snow.

Your letter came yesterday and I am certainly glad to know that you are not disappointed in Clyde and your work there. Am glad, too, that you have been kept busy, hope you will still get plenty to do. People here are continually asking me about you and when I, too, am going to Canoochee. Doubtless you know something of the

257

disposition of one Mr. John S. Snead, do you not? He never sees me unless he has to say something about my affairs. As soon as he sees me coming, he gets that broad smile from ear-to-ear, and I feel prepared for most anything that may come. He told me a few days ago that he was very much surprised to see that advertisement in the paper. Of course, I asked him what, and he said Mr. McGhee was advertising for an organist. I told him he should not worry for I would be here for quite a while yet.

Otis, I saw part of the basketball game between the Brewton Parker Institute and Lanier High School in Macon, last Friday afternoon. Mr. Jenkins had to go to Mount Vernon on some business and Vera, Alice and I went in the car with him. We did not know about the game until we got there and did not have time to stay very long, but certainly enjoyed the little while we were there. Stayed just long enough to get very much interested in the game, I felt like a schoolgirl again…

I know you are glad to see your brother and his wife but am sure you did not appreciate any display of curiosity, did you? Well, it is perfectly natural for people to guess and wonder and want to know definitely. I would like to know definitely myself, wouldn't you? But, probably we can tell after a little while, and it will happen just as soon as possible so why should we worry.

Really, dear, I miss you so much and want to be with you all the time, I can't help feeling a little bit impatient sometimes. You may rest assured your little girl will remain true and wait for you. I'm sorry you felt the least bit doubtful of me the day before you left here, am sorry I gave you cause to feel that way which, I know I did. But you finally understood and saw that I was not to blame, didn't you? Be good to Black Bess, hear? Maybe my time will come later on. Wish I could take those long drives with you now, but – never mind.

Be careful and don't fall in love with any of those good-looking country lasses up there…

With Love,
Clyde

Author's Note: This letter was written by Clyde to Otis in Cobbtown. Apparently he had made one of his many trips back to look after his younger brother.

Vidalia, GA
1914

Dear Otis,

Your letter came this morning and indeed I have no scolding for you, for I must say you did well this time – wrote promptly in a perfectly nice letter. Am glad you found the little boy better, was afraid he was seriously ill, when they phoned for you to come home.

I am glad, too, that you were so fortunate in a professional as well as a financial way – guess it's a good thing you went home when you did anyway. No, I don't think you are conceited in the least, and I am very proud of you. We have to learn to "paddle our own canoe" in this world, and in my opinion you did exactly the right thing.

Otis, I don't know when I have ever felt as I did Sunday afternoon – guess I was just not feeling very well and oh, that dreary road we traveled – it was enough to make anyone feel downcast and forlorn. But the real thing that made me feel blue was that you had to leave that afternoon, I certainly hated to see you leave and was so lonesome for you that night…

I was uptown yesterday afternoon and everybody I saw nearly had something to say about you. Of course, it was "when are you all going to --?" "Where is he going to locate?", etc., etc.

Speaking of going to Canoochee, Otis, you know as I told you I don't know enough about it to say. But for some reason or other, I like Savannah, a place like Dr. Shanks is so nice, a good salary to begin with, too, don't you think? …Write me again soon.

With Love,
Clyde

Foreground - Otis and Clyde.

Author's Note: Apparently Otis was in Atlanta with Ridge who was being treated for his headaches.

Vidalia, GA
1914

Dear Otis,

I received your letter yesterday and again this morning – certainly am sorry to hear of Ridge's condition. Looks like he has a hard time, one spell right after another, I certainly do sympathize with him. Hope something can be done for him that will do him permanent good.

Otis, I am certainly glad you came over here and that you enjoyed your trip, would like to have it repeated often but I don't want to be frightened any more, like I was Thursday morning in the

260

parlor. It is funny when you think about it now, but I was so weak I couldn't stand up, and when I sat down so suddenly the chair rolled back and hit the wall – and my, what a noise it made. I thought you took it very calmly, but I don't think I ever have been quite as weak for just a minute or so.

Momma scolded me good because I did not ask you to stay to dinner, but really I did not think of it and then I knew you would not have time. I might have had a little manners though, and asked you anyway . . .

As Ever,
Clyde

Author's Note: Was this the first time Clyde told Otis she would go to Canoochee?

Vidalia, GA
1914

Dearest,

. . .Otis, I realize that it is perfectly natural for you to feel a bit despondent over losing a patient, but I don't think that ought to make you feel so badly after all. People get beyond medical aid and die sometime and doctors are not to blame at all. So in spite of the dark side of the case don't let that discourage you, hear?

Alice and I have been out walking all afternoon and had a very pleasant little chat and walked so much with new shoes on, that I was most passed going when I got home.

I went to Mt. Vernon Thursday morning and spent the day. Had a real pleasant time, it was like going to the country for a rest. The glee club did as well as could be expected, considering where it came from. I enjoyed it very much however, for it was something different from what I had seen lately (you know I have been to so many entertainments in the last few weeks).

There was a big singing convention at Lyons today, a crowd of countrymen with voices that almost split your ears. Quite a crowd from here went down to hear them I think, I did not choose the big business. I have heard them before.

Otis, I am so glad your work is progressing so nicely, but the loss of a patient must not make you feel badly. Your practice is bound to increase, for in the first place you know your business and then you are sticking to it.

I must go to church now, so goodbye. Be good and remember I still love you and would even go to Canoochee with you if you said so.

As Ever,
Clyde

Vidalia, GA
April 8, 1914

Dear Otis,

...Otis, let me tell you what I did this morning, probably you will be surprised, but I hope you will recover. For the last two months I have been aggravated nearly beyond endurance with, first, one music agent and then another. So this morning a man came with "exactly the thing I needed for my pupils, it would not cost me anything, I was to be their advertising agent", I did everything and said everything imaginable to convince him that I did not want the stuff but he still persisted, so I finally told him that I did not intend teaching but a very short while longer, that I was going into another line of work altogether. He said, "Well when you do that, you will not just sit down and hold your hands, you will want to do something to help your husband along, won't you". I managed to "shake him" but it was a hard task.

But did you think that I would tell him <u>our</u> secret, and especially to a perfect stranger. Well, I did not tell him directly but I led him to believe it anyway.

Otis, I'm so glad you are coming again, I won't say soon for the first of May is not very soon, do you think? Be sure to come by Swainsboro and bring that brother and sister of yours, will you, or rather let them bring you. You know I am anxious to meet them and know them…

It is getting late so I must say good night. Be good and remember I love you and want you more every day.

As Ever,
Clyde

Vidalia, GA
April 10, 1914

My Own Dear,

Wonder how you are feeling and what you are doing with yourself this terrible warm evening. Hope you have not been sick anymore or had anymore runaway accidents or anything of that kind.

I was certainly sorry as well as surprised to hear of Black Bess doing anymore such stunts as that, but I have always heard that it is a bad plan to always take the horse's bridle off so he can drink so there may be something in it, don't you think? You were certainly very fortunate not to have been hurt yourself and to have the buggy torn to pieces and the horse ruined weren't you?

…You are certainly mistaken about one thing though, I certainly do like to play tennis, always have enjoyed the game. I played a good deal the last year I was in school but have not played any since then, but you go ahead and get the court ready and I'll sure play with you when I move out there.

However, I don't know much about the horseback riding proposition for Black Bess is likely to become frightened again. You had better be careful with her and watch her, hear?

Anyway, speaking of tennis, horseback riding etc. I'm going to find a plenty to occupy my time when I go to Canoochee, keeping house, trying to make you happy and comfortable, and then I'll have that music class I'm going to get, don't you remember?

...You and your brother be sure and arrange that trip over here as soon as you can for I am anxious to see you dear. It is awfully hard for us to be separated so much but we will just have to live and hope for the time when we shall be together through the rest of our lives. I feel like we will all be very happy for love shall be supreme in our home.

You must write me as often as you can, everyday at least.

Clyde

Vidalia, GA
April 17, 1914

My Dear,

...Otis, I can hardly realize that you were here Sunday, it was for such a short time and I want to see you worse than ever if that is possible. Why is it that during the time that we have known each other best and enjoyed being together most, we have never been conveniently situated or so we could see each other often? But, I am looking forward to the time when all of this will be changed and we can be together for life for we shall belong to each other.

John Eli Matthews is here again, was here last week on account of the contest at Dublin, is here now to make a speech for Clements tomorrow. Think he expects to come again next week as he is to introduce the speaker, Colonel Safford, for Memorial Day [Confederate Memorial Day held each April]. Don't suppose he and Alice have any objection to his numerous calls home.

Went out to Mrs. Crawford's this morning and found them in much better spirits, Jack is feeling much better, was sitting out on the piazza when I got there. I got back from out there about one o'clock, ate my dinner, cleaned up the parlor, and had just lain down to rest a few minutes when the schoolchildren came. I got up gave four lessons and then went to choir practice tonight -- do you suppose I am tired now or not?

...As Ever,
Clyde

Author's Note: You see in this letter what a difference improvements in medical science have made in people's lives. The death of young children was not uncommon.

Vidalia, GA
April 26, 1914

Dear Otis,

...My, how I wish you were to be here tomorrow afternoon and night, but another such happy one as last Sunday night might ruin me. I did not realize that I loved you so much until you got out there where you are so near and yet so far. It really is not so far away, yet you can't come to Vidalia just any old time, and that is what hurts...

Otis, everything here has been gloomy and sad for the last few days, there have been several real sick babies, two of them have died and another is not expected to live. Mr. J.S. Jenkins lost his little two-year-old boy, Mr. E.S. Meadows lost one about the same age, and Mr. George Cannady's is not expected to live. There is a very sick one over on Oconee Heights, too. I don't know the name. Everybody seems to sympathize, especially with Mr. and Mrs. Jenkins, for theirs was all they had, they were perfectly foolish about him. They had lost one child before, about ten years ago, I think, it is certainly sad for them.

So you are really considering seriously going to war? I don't know whether I like that or not, it depends on what you get out of it, yet it would be awful for you to be so far away from home. How is it managed, do you have to stand an examination, or can just any

licensed physician enlist?
...It is getting late, and I am tired and sleepy, so will continue
this tomorrow. Pleasant dreams.

Your S.H.,
Clyde

Author's Note: Tybee Island is a beach community near Savannah.

Vidalia, GA
May 4, 1914

Dearest –

> *...Went to church this morning, to Sunday School this afternoon,*
> *and expect to go again tonight, have you done that well? I wish you*
> *had been with me this afternoon and have seen what a beautiful*
> *bunch of sweet peas I got. Kathryn Godbee brought me a bunch,*
> *almost large enough to cover over a good sized wash bowl. I put*
> *them in a vase at the church until tonight, am going to bring them*
> *home after church.*
> *We decided on a place and time for our picnic this afternoon.*
> *Decided to go to Tybee on the fifteenth of this month, the round trip*
> *fare to be $1.25 – I believe that is all we have decided so far. Do you*
> *think you could arrange to go there, it is just three days before my*
> *birthday, let's go up and celebrate, hear?*
> *I shall certainly be glad for you all to come next Sunday, but*
> *if that would interfere with your getting off on the picnic, don't do*
> *it until later, hear? For I certainly do want you to go to Savannah*
> *with me. Well, sir, who would have thought of me? Almost asking a*
> *man for a date, but you told me to let you know, didn't you?*
> *...Otis, I certainly did enjoy your letter this morning, it made*
> *me feel so glad and happy. I read it over and over again and wished*
> *for you, I believe if you had been here and said, "Clyde, come on and*
> *go back with me now", I would have done so without hesitating a*

266

bit. Don't you worry about my not liking Canoochee, for anywhere with you will suit me. And besides, all those other things we are to do, I'm going with you on some of those long drives. Probably I can learn to help you administer to some of your patients at least.

I must go now, just let me whisper this – "I love you with all my heart" and a goodbye.

Sincerely Yours,
Clyde

Vidalia, GA
May 1914

My Dear,

I have just been out riding with Dr. and Mrs. Thompson, had a very nice time, but those questions he asks are something fierce. He says, however, that he thinks you are such a fine fellow, that you are bound to make a success. He says, though, that he thinks you made a mistake by going to such a small place, and another thing, he can't see why we don't go on and get married. Says if he were in your place, and I would not live with you out there, he would not want me later - what do you say about that?

The people here are still interested and curious about our affairs. They still enjoy giving advice, but I guess they see that it isn't heeded…

…I went to the music club Monday afternoon, had a very pleasant time, the program was fine and the refreshments - well, we had ice cream with the purest strawberries in it. That speaks for itself, doesn't it? The Salamagundi club meets at Mrs. Schumperts tomorrow afternoon, but I don't know that I shall go.

Alice and I are planning to go to Mt. Vernon Thursday morning and spend the day at Uncle Willy's [Willy Wilson, Sophie's brother] and of course taking in the glee club that evening. I am not sure about it yet though.

My paper has given out, so there - what did we say about writing every day - shall I write you tomorrow or not?

As Ever,
Clyde

Vidalia, GA
May 12, 1914

Dear Otis,

...I received an invitation yesterday to a moonlight picnic out at Tiger Springs Thursday evening – what do you think of going out there on Thursday evening and then getting off on that early train Friday morning? That will be most too much of the big business, don't you think?

The schedule on the early Seaboard train has been changed as I told you yesterday so that it comes at 4:55 so we will certainly have to rise early that morning, won't we? I think quite a large crowd is expecting to go. Certainly hope everything will run smoothly and well and we will enjoy it immensely. We'll write Dr. Shanks and get it off this afternoon.

I'm sure you and I will enjoy the picnic just the fact that we are together will make us enjoy it. I am so anxious to see you and talk to you for a long time. I have something very important to tell you when I see you Otis, something which concerns you and me.

Remember dear, that I love you more and more if it is possible everyday and am looking forward to the time when we can be together for always can share each other's sorrows and joys -- then we will be supremely happy.

I shall expect you Thursday evening, and am expecting a great time Friday.

With Love,
Clyde

Vidalia GA
May 21, 1914

Dear Otis,

Well, how is my sweetheart this afternoon? I do wish I were out there driving Black Bess with you, it is so pretty and pleasant outside-just a little dusty, but the wind is not blowing so hard today. I have been here all day, right by my lonesome part of the time-if you were in Vidalia, you would not allow that would you?

But it seems that all of our entertainments are coming off at one time. Our commencement last through tomorrow night, making four nights in succession. Tonight after the recital at the schoolhouse, Mrs. Jackson is to have a theater party-now doesn't that sound big, "theater party". I have taken it all in so far, for we have so few things to go to. As soon as this is all over we'll have a complete rest for about six months...

Have you heard any more from Ridge? Certainly hope he is improving ere this time. I appreciate all those things he said about me but I'm sure he will change his mind about my being so quiet when he knows me better, aren't you? That was not a fair test when he and Fred got strung out that night...

Alice and Miss Campbell have told me about everything that happened at the picnic, although they did not get to talk to Dr. Shanks, they seem greatly impressed with his good looks. I hope he will go out to see you and the meantime, come to Vidalia...

It is getting late and I must go dress for tonight, so goodbye.

Sincerely Yours,
Clyde

Vidalia, GA
May 1914

Dear Otis,

...*Otis, Mrs. Jack Crawford died Saturday night – isn't that too bad, think of that little 16-month-old baby without a mother and almost without a father. They carried her to Wrightsville Sunday morning to bury her there.*

It seems that all over trouble is coming at once. This morning, Roy Darby was coming from Lyons on his motorcycle and ran into an automobile and was knocked senseless, the worst lick being on his head. They're not expecting him to live. Isn't it awful, I do hope he will get alright.

Tuesday A.M.

I did not get to finish this last night, was too sleepy. We have just heard that they operated on Roy last night and that his skull was fractured and the blood clotted around the brain, that he had revived from the operation and seemed some better.

It looks rain this morning and my, how glad I am. It is so dry and dusty and everybody feels so drowsy. I must cut this short as Kathryn is in a hurry to go to mail it. But let me just say this, "I'm still loving you as much as possible and want to see you so I can hardly wait".

As Ever,
Clyde

Vidalia, GA
May 1914
Monday Evening

My Dear,

Mamma had just come from up town and brought me the nicest kind of a letter from you. I have read it over and over again and enjoyed it more each time. You are exactly the right kind of sweetheart to have anyway. I had been here all by myself all the afternoon and your letter just made me feel good all over.

I'm so glad your patient is doing so nicely – hope he will continue so and that you will have no bad luck with him. Am afraid he was not very favorably impressed with Vidalia, however.

I don't know of anything new happening around here lately. There is to be a big double wedding at Mt. Vernon Wednesday – Miss Mamie Conner and Mr. Earnest Dixon and Miss Naomi Brewton and Mr. Tom Conner, you may know some of the parties concerned. It is to be a church affair and Miss Mamie invited Alice and me to go up and see them get "scared to death." I certainly hope I shall get to go. Think we need to take lessons.

Otis, you just ought to be here to listen to the music across the way with me. They are still very kind and accommodating about playing for me and this time they are using a harp with it which makes it very fine – just think of it, here?

The Baptist Sunday School picnic was postponed from last Wednesday on account of Roy being so badly hurt, and now they have set June 10th for the time – do you think you would like to go? I understand that the Presbyterian schools from Aimwell and several others are to unite with the Vidalia schools and go to Tybee on the 15th. Suppose we undertake another such trip.

No, dear, I agree with you fully. I believe you and I have gotten more out of things that happened unexpectedly, that we had not planned so far ahead. Yet we get a great deal of pleasure and joy out of anticipation – just so we are not disappointed in the realization.

I am not worried about how we shall arrange about my being left alone when I go to Canoochee, for I think we have plently of time for that yet. There is one good thing about it though Otis and that is I am not foolishly afraid when alone, like some people are, but I don't know so much about being left alone at night. I believe, though, that you have more calls at night than during the day.

With Love,
Clyde

May 27, 1914

My Dear,

    I have just been out to see Mrs. Crawford [Jack Crawford's mother] and the baby and my – what a pitiful sight that is. The baby looks so pale and weak and old Mrs. C – is hardly able to lift her at all. I sat there for nearly an hour hardly able to speak I was so choked up and once and a while the tears came in spite of me.

    Have not heard from Roy since about 3:00 this afternoon. They said then that he had two or three sinking spells and that he couldn't last long at that. They don't seem to have any hope for him at all...

    Pierce is in a hurry to mail this so I must ring off. He is getting so impatient.

With Love,
Clyde

Author's Note: Fred is leaving for the Naval Academy.

Vidalia, GA
June 1914

Dear Otis,

    I was not at home last evening so I could not write you, but you will get this tomorrow anyway, so here goes. Wish I could peep in this morning and see you cooking your perfectly nice breakfast, how about it? Why not let me come and eat with you?

    ...How is Black Bess now, have you had any more trouble with her, opening gates, untying ropes, etc., etc. I think she has been learning bad tricks.

    We are expecting a great time here on the Fourth of July, the men are planning the greatest celebration Vidalia has ever had. A big dinner speaking, automobile race, and well, I don't know what else. There is a big write-up in the last Vidalia Advance about it, but I haven't had a chance to read it yet. Yes, Otis, Fred has gone, if he passes the physical examination, for 15 months. It is right hard to think of his being away so long but it is the best thing ever could happen for him. He told me about telling you goodbye when you were here and telling you that he hoped to see you again when he came home, do you suppose he will?

A music pupil has come, so I must cut this short. Be good and let me hear from you as often as you can.

With Love,
Clyde

Author's Note: The quote attributed to Sophie Holmes is quite instructive. What a shame our society does not place the same emphasis on the word duty.

1914

Dear Otis,

Well, good morning sweetheart, how are you with this awfully warm weather? Hope you are not feeling as downcast and blue as this little friend of yours is. Wish so much that I could see you for just a short while – if I had the opportunity to open my heart and tell you all my troubles I think I should feel much better. But it isn't fair to burden someone else with my troubles is it?

But here's the cause of the whole trouble – I can't go to Covington – isn't that awful though? But you see it interferes with the meeting and "when pleasure interferes with duty, you <u>must</u> cut out the pleasure" – Mrs. Sophie Holmes. Vera intends going though, will leave here in the morning and go by Macon... I have been attending the meetings regularly all the past week, which of course has made *me feel very tired a good part of the time. We have certainly had some fine sermons, am sorry you could not stay over all the week.*

I hardly realize that it has been only a week since you left here for it seems like almost a month. Guess you are hard at work now though, so much so that you don't feel very much like you have been here. Do your very best up there Otis, but do not injure your health by hard work. For you know what that would mean.

I must go now and get ready for Sunday school, so we'll have to make this rather short. I'm going to write again though the first of next week or rather of this week. Write me real soon.

With Love,
Clyde

Vidalia, GA
June 9, 1914

Dear Otis,

...In the first place, Fred left this morning at 10 o'clock, I went down to see him off and had a <u>terrible</u> time. When I got back home, we had company so I helped prepare dinner and then took the responsibility of entertaining for a while. After that, I went to sleep and slept too late to go to the club. I was on the program so they say I will have to pay a fine of fifty cents, now what do you think of that? I just think that they can't get blood out of a turnip – do you believe it?

I went to ride with Vera and Mr. Jackson about six o'clock and have just gotten back. They tried to get me to go to the picnic Wednesday – but nay, nay for me...

Will try to write a long letter tomorrow but will have to stop this now. I am still loving you with all my heart.

As Ever,
Clyde

Author's Note: I see now where I inherited my love of buttermilk. Fred has arrived at the Naval Academy.

Vidalia, GA
June 16, 1914

Dear Otis,

...How do you like cooking in this warm weather? I think I had rather do most anything I know except split rails or play at the picture show, for it is certainly something awful. I haven't energy enough for anything, all I care about doing is sleeping and drinking ice tea or buttermilk.

Otis, we have some of the finest plums you ever saw, the large apricot kind. They are good when we let them ripen, but just get one a little bit green, and they are certainly sour. I will try to save you some until you come and have them good and ripe, as you don't like <u>anything</u> *sour, do you?*

Fred was admitted to the Naval Academy all right, but he said he was beginning to get rather discouraged, so many of the boys failed and he came very near it because he did not know the different colors, so many different shades got him all mixed up – then he got excited and the man got mad. Of course, he thought sure he was a goner then...

I shall expect you Wednesday, hear?

As Ever,
Clyde

Author's Note: Clyde mentions how hot it was in the house on Church Street and how the mosquitoes bothered her. I remember as a child going to sleep in that same room and she would bring in a large spray can of DDT and fill the room with DDT mist.

She also told me to sleep at the foot of the bed and I would be much cooler. She was definitely a believer in mind over matter.

Ridge is sick again. He must have really suffered.

Summer 1914

Dear Otis,

    I am feeling rather tied and sleepy tonight but am going to write you anyway – think I shall feel better after a little chat with you. I have not been working so hard to cause me to feel so tired, but did not sleep much last night or Saturday night on account of the mosquitoes and the heat. It is much cooler now though and I bought me some "Skee-Ter-Go" this afternoon, so I feel like I shall make up for lost time in a little while.

    Otis, how are you feeling now since your return to Canoochee, and how did you enjoy your trip home? Wish I could have gone with you – yes, I really do, but it seems to be our fate to keep waiting and building "castles in Spain" for a while longer. Never mind you have heard that "all things come to those who wait", haven't you? Of course, I don't believe absolutely in that expression but there is surely something to it.

    Pierce has just come in from up town and brought me your letter. You make me feel glad and happy because I am living when you write and such letters, Otis, of course, I believe you love me, haven't any doubt about that, but the happiest moments of my life are when I am with you and you are telling me that old story again and again. Then the next thing to that is having you write me about it. I am glad I told you how I felt about our arrangements for this fall, but why didn't you tell me how you felt when we were discussing the school problem? I didn't think you disapproved of it so much, I really thought the plan suits you pretty well. But anyway, I don't suppose we need to worry about that, do you? I am sorry you had to leave your work and go to Atlanta, but certainly am glad you stopped by to see me for I thoroughly enjoyed your visit. Wish you could come most every night.

    I am glad Ridge is doing so nicely, hope he will improve rapidly now, and have no more trouble. Guess he will be going back to Camilla just as soon as he is strong enough . . .

With Love,
Clyde

Ridge Rountree, brother of Otis. Ridge suffered from recurrent medical problems. He married shortly after Otis and Clyde. We see in the letters how he was constantly plagued by frequent debilitating headaches. He typically treated his headaches by lacing a towel with chloroform (available over the counter at the time) and placing it over his face for a few seconds then removing it, thereby relieving his excruciating pain. One Sunday afternoon Ridge was suffering from another sick headache, so he used the described treatment. Tragically, however, he left the towel on for too long (whether by accident or on purpose is unknown) and died.

Author's Note: The second sentence in the second paragraph is quite prophetic.

Vidalia, GA
June 30, 1914

My Own Dear,

> *Your letter has just come and sweetheart, I want you more than ever this afternoon. I believe if you were here now saying Clyde come on and go back with me today, I would not hesitate one second. Of course I hope I still have my practical sense or better judgment with me, but I believe that you could really be more successful in your profession if you were married. Then while I have always had enough to be comfortable, I know how to economize, I could and would be a help in some ways, don't you think?*
> *I don't mean to be throwing bouquets at myself at all, but I have enough confidence in myself and in you to believe that after all we could do better together. And I'm sure we will both be happier together, our life is before us but we don't have long in this world so why not be as happy as possible while here? So, I think that the only and the best thing for me to do is to just wait until you get in a little better shape and then go. I don't like the idea of your being out there by yourself and I don't think that there is much real true love in a case like this unless the girl were willing to sacrifice something, or to help bear the hardships as well as enjoy the pleasures of this life, so dear, when you get ready for me, just let me know, hear?*
> *...Otis, Mrs. Mosley and Mrs. Schumpert said all kinds of nice things about you yesterday, even told me how good you looked Tuesday night (like I didn't know it). They asked me how old you were, said you didn't look over 22 years old, what do you know about that? I told them not to tell any of your patients that you looked so young...*
> *Alex is going up to town now so I want to get this off.*

As Ever,
Clyde

Vidalia, GA
July 1914

Dear Otis,

...How are you feeling now, Otis? Hope you are staying busy and feeling fine as ever. Mr. Rountree came and asked me about you yesterday – he didn't like it because you didn't call him up last Tuesday night, said he would get you back yet. I told him that you found everybody sick out there when you got back. And he wanted to know if I thought that was good or bad. Said he was surprised at me when I told him I thought it was pretty good. Have you heard from Ridge since you left up there? Is your sister still with you? Ask her what she thinks of Canoochee as a place to live, if she thinks it is a very dead, lonesome place, hear?

Julia wrote me that her house party would not be until August, about the first, I think, so I shall be here all of July, I guess. Then I hope to be away all of August and take a complete rest. I believe I shall feel better afterward if I should do that. Not that I work so hard but the change would be good for me, don't you think so, <u>doctor</u>?

...Will write you again tomorrow if there is any possible chance.

Sincerely,
Clyde

Author's Note: Ridge had just had an operation. Clyde has applied for a teaching job at Graymont-Summitt, now Twin City. That's about fifteen miles from Canoochee.

Vidalia, GA
July 1914

Dear Otis,

...We certainly had a big day for Vidalia yesterday. Everything was good and well carried out and <u>everybody</u> in the whole country

was here. It is certainly a miracle that someone was not hurt for the people were just packed and jammed and the automobiles coming from everywhere. All the business firms were well advertised and the stores decorated with stars and stripes – wish you could have been here and seen it.

Don't know anything definite from Graymont yet, but keep in hopes, suppose you go over and put in a good word for me, hear? Think it would be great, don't you?

I must go dress for Sunday School, so be good and write me right away. Let me know how Ridge is getting on – also how lively your sister thinks Canoochee is, hear.

With Love,
Clyde

Vidalia, GA
July 1914

Dear Otis,

Please pardon me this time for waiting so long to write you, and I won't do it again, honest I won't. Will you risk it? It is just that same old reason, I won't say excuse for I don't like that word, do you? I am still awfully busy, I don't know when I am to go to Covington, except that it would be sometime the first week of August. I want you to come to see me before I go if you can possibly get off. I expect you had better come next week sometime, don't you?

I am hoping to spend some time in Augusta before I come home, and if I do, I can't say when I'll be back here. But if I can arrange that, I will come back on the GNF and you can meet me at Swainsboro, what do you think of that? And take me right out to Canoochee to your house - what do you say to that? "Let's change the subject right here," that's what you say I expect, isn't it?

...Mr. Rountree told me sometime ago that he wrote you to go to Statesboro and every time he sees me now he asks me if you have

said anything about it, so do tell me something to tell him. Says you will work yourself to death out there, and your wife, too, if you ever get one to go out there.

I must go now dear, will write more next time.

Clyde

Vidalia, GA
August 3, 1914

My Dear,

Have just gotten home from Sunday School, naturally feeling a great lonesome sensation for you, so the only thing I see to do is sit down and tell you about it. I feel that way most all of the time though, I do very well as long as I stay real busy and keep my mind well occupied, but on occasions like this especially, I think I would really like to live in Canooche. If you were to have any calls this afternoon, I could not go with you though, for it is thundering, lightning and raining. It has been awfully warm all day and rather stormy this afternoon. Looks now like it might rain all night.

I received your letter this morning and liked the new stationery just fine. Think it looks very business-like. Also enjoyed the letter as usual. You make me want to go out there right away. I am a good housekeeper and cook, too. I do have to say it myself.

Otis, I want you to come to see me real soon, I am expecting to go to Covington next Saturday if I can get off by then. If I can't, I'll go Monday – Julia wrote me to come on after the 8th, but I don't like the idea of traveling on Saturday, so I may wait until Monday. You let me know when it will suit you to come, just as soon as you can. I surely am anxious to see you, and hope you will have longer to stay this time than before.

How is Ridge getting on now, Otis? Hope he is improving rapidly – has he come out to see you yet? A trip out there might make him improve, think it would help me.

Well, dear, since we have made different arrangements for this *fall, I'm rather glad I did not get the place at Greymont. I never would have applied if it had not been for Miss Cowart and the idea of being near you, so you could come to see me often. It is not a case of sour grapes either, I just did not want to stay here all this year again and teach.*

Well, sweetheart, I have been interrupted several times, so it is real late now. It has stopped raining now, so I can go to church – wish you could come over and take me and make this evening one of perfect happiness. Remember, you mean more to me than anybody in the world, I love you and want you all the time.

Sincerely,
Clyde

Author's Note: Clyde took a trip to Covington to attend a house party given by her friend.

August 7, 1914

Dear Otis,

Well at last I am in Covington and really, it is a great place. The people are just grand and the town is so pretty. We went out for a ride this morning and certainly explored some nice country, I don't know where we went but we came back to Oxford and saw everything to be seen there. Mrs. Aiken gave us a reception this afternoon and I stood in the "firing line" until I felt like I would drop. There must have been 75 ladies and I remember about three of their names. Anyway, I am awfully tired and sleepy tonight, have had a very strenuous day of it...

Well, I can't write any more. People are talking at such a rate in my room. They all send you their love. Write me real soon in care of Mrs. Julia Aiken.

With Love,
Clyde

Author's Note: This is the first letter we have from Otis. Wonder what happened to all the other ones?

Canoochee, GA
August 11, 1914

Dear Clyde,

...Ridge is still up here with me and is doing well. He says that if he could stay up here, two weeks longer he'd be strong as a mule. I'm going to miss him when he leaves. I had not realized how much it meant to have some congenial party with you all the time.

Don't let any of those boys at Covington fall too deeply in love with you, but they can't help that though. Let me hear from you.

Train time, so goodbye.

Lovingly,
Otis

Canoochee, GA
August 1914

Dear Clyde,

Wonder what you are doing today? If you have already left for Covington and, if so, how you are enjoying your trip, also if there are many thoughts of your sweetheart inside that pretty head of yours? Don't you wish, Clyde, it were <u>our</u> trip and that we were going – well, no matter much where just so we had each other but on a trip for which we had plenty of time and with nothing to do but enjoy life? I want you to have a mighty good time while you are away, I hope you'll enjoy every minute of it, but to think that those people are going to have you with them for nearly a month and that I shall not be able to see you in all that time makes me right blue and envious of them. But you are going to write me every day, aren't you? That will help lots, but it's hard to realize that I must be away *from you a whole month. If I get too lonely you needn't be surprised to get a telegram that I am coming after you or coming to see you, anyway.*

Did you get my note of yesterday? Ridge and I rode down to Garfield to mail it. The note itself was not worth that, for there were only a few hurried lines, but I wanted you to know that I was thinking of you and wanting to hear from you.

Tuesday A.M. -

Well, Clyde, if I don't hurry I'm afraid you will not get the long letter I promised this week. I was interrupted yesterday morning by a fellow who had cut his hand badly across the back of it and it took me two hours to get through with him. It was cut into the bone and the tendon to his forefinger was severed, but I fixed it up all o.k. and believe that I'll get good results from it. I had a good day's work yesterday, including last night, for I was out from 10:30 to 1:00. If every day were as good as yesterday we'd soon be able to go to Frisco or most any other place in the U.S.

Ridge is up now and in good shape. I enjoy having him with me very much and wish he could stay here all the time till December. Yesterday he amused himself by catching bullfrogs, which we ate for supper last night. He came in just now, looked at your picture and said, "I don't see how you stay here by yourself with the picture of as pretty a girl as this always before you." He is going back to his work August 15th.

Clyde, did I write you of John Eli Mathews calling on me last week? He was going to Garfield to speak and stopped in at my residence for a few minutes. If he told you of it I don't suppose he could say much of the good appearance of things. Ridge had been very ill for two days and things were in a muddle all around. Think I'll have things arranged pretty nicely by the time you come; that is, nicely for Canoochee.

Has it been raining any for you lately? Judging from the first fourteen days of "dog days," the proverbial forty days of rain is with us. I'm without a buggy top just now, so I get into it often.

By the way, what is the matter with my letters from you? I thought I was playing the limit with my one little letter and one piece of one, but I have not had a scratch from you. Guess, though, you are pretty busy right now, aren't you? Hope I'll hear from you often while you are away.

With Love,
Otis

Author's Note: McKinney's Mill, mentioned in this letter, is still operating today as a restaurant. It is located between Swainsboro and Midville near the Ogeechee River. It has great food. The best fried bream I ever had.

Canoochee, GA
August 15, 1914

Dear Clyde,

The receipt of a letter from the dearest little lady in all this world made me feel mighty good today. I wanted to hear from you very much and, while I know you are busy as could be with getting away and then with getting "broke in" at the house party, I was somewhat worried about your not writing. But, "All things come to him who waits", if he do the right thing while he is waiting. I wrote you two letters from Vidalia which were forwarded to you, I suppose. Thought I'd wait till I had an answer before I tried again.

I'm glad you are having such a good time in Covington, and hope you will enjoy every minute of your stay to the utmost. But, don't tire yourself down, little girl, with all those joy rides, receptions, and the late hours that necessarily go with such things. Don't I wish I could be on a two-week house party with you, though! But to spend two weeks where I could see you several times a day, tell you and prove to you how much I love you, no matter whether it was at a gay house party or twenty miles out in the woods, would be the thing I had rather do of all others.

It's awful lonesome up here, knowing that my little sweetheart is way off up in North Georgia, for it already seems an age since I saw her. Clyde, dear, I love you all that is possible for a man to *love woman. You are the central figure in all my dreams and plans for the future and I am longing for the time to come when with you, my wife, and <u>always</u> my sweetheart, the dreams come true and the plans are carried out. You are more to me than anything or anybody else on earth and oh, dearest, how I do long for you all the time! It's a mighty long time till December, but if I can only see you every week or so, I guess I can stand it well enough to keep me from going after you and taking you away by force.*

Ridge is still with me, doing nicely, but is going back tomorrow. He and I went to a picnic at McKinney's Mill today and had a good time, though it is so far up there we got tired going and coming. Practice is fairly good, but the people are all scared because of the poor prospects for a good cotton market and, you know, that affects me strongly. If that will clear up, I'll prepare a lot easier.

Vera did not go with you, did she? Don't guess you know yet how long you will be up there, do you? Stay as long as you can, have a good time, but remember that there's a fellow in Canoochee, Georgia that while he is wishing you a most enjoyable visit, would rather see you than anybody living.

Write me just as often as you can, dear, for you know how much your letters mean to me. I'm rather tired and sleepy and while I could write you all night, better judgment tells me I better go to bed.

With Love,
Otis

Author's Note: This was written by Clyde while she was attending a house party in Covington.

Covington, GA
August 20, 1914

Dear Otis,

I came downstairs this morning with the full intention of writing my sweetheart a nice letter, and then did something I seldom ever *do – got two pages written, tore it up and began again. You never would guess what my trouble was, you reckon you would? In spite of my being so <u>good </u>a speller, I spelled several words about like Kathryn would – so I rested a while and am now trying again, hope I'll do better this time.*

Otis, I sure do like this place, guess you think I must by the way I'm staying, but I really do for more reasons than one. There are so many nice people, so many not exactly wealthy people, but people who are in good circumstances, and so many pretty homes, it makes me almost feel covetous. I have just lots to tell you about it when I see you.

Well, how was the election down there? I feel good over Hoke Smith's success but have not heard from the one I was most interested in – Mr. Hughes, guess I will hear today. Don't get me the idea now, that I have been out making stump speeches for any of the candidates, for I haven't but just feel more interest in those two than any of the others.

Otis, I am expecting to leave here either tomorrow or Saturday, but you write me here and it will be forwarded to me for I expect to stop over a day at Greensboro, and probably one day at Union Point on my way to Augusta. Will write you more definitely later, and will write you just as soon as I reach Augusta.

We are having just any quantity of peaches and grapes – some of the prettiest and best I have ever seen. I hope they will do me good if they don't fatten. I enjoy just the same.

Write me as often as you can for your letters are more pleasure to me than anything else. Will write again real soon – have just lots to tell you.

With Love,
Clyde

Author's Note: This letter was written on August 22, 1914, to Clyde who was visiting her friend in Augusta. It is interesting the fear people had of scarlet fever. See the letter from Clyde to Eugene and Hattie Flanders about the death of their daughter, Hattie Lewis.

Canoochee, GA
August 22, 1914
Saturday A.M.

Dear Clyde,

How is visiting? ...I believe you want me to locate in Covington, don't you? From what you say I believe we'd both like it.

Canoochee is quiet enough since the election. This week I have been real busy losing sleep on account of doing night work. One day I was sick, but every time I went to bed I had a call. The other days I'd get a call every time I started a letter to you. Clyde, I have two cases of scarlet fever, they have been ill three days and one of them is in bad shape, though doing fairly well today. You would be afraid for me to go see you – wouldn't you? I'm not delighted at having to attend them.

Well, didn't the election turn out okay though? Most of my men went in, so did the ones you were interested in. Smith [Hoke Smith] as Senator by the greatest majority ever known in Georgia State elections. Then Hughes was elected Congressman over Clements. I was for Clements until the very last day, but after thinking over the matter, I couldn't afford to vote against Hughes. Of Emanuel County Officers, all for whom I voted were elected.

The mail has just come and in it your letter, which I was just delighted to receive. I'm quite sure now that you like Covington and I'm afraid I'll have to go after you to get away from there. But I hope you enjoy your visit to Greensboro, Union Point, Wrens, Wadley, and Augusta, too.

Write me often, for your letters help out wonderfully. They are next best to seeing you so you know how much they must mean. Remember, I love you all that is possible.

Sincerely,
Otis

288

Augusta, GA
August 24, 1914

My Dear,

At last I have reached the city, but am not so terribly tickled over it, for I know this is the hottest place I was ever in. Of course, I like the city all right, but I wouldn't like to live here. I'm afraid I would just naturally "dissolve" in spite of everything.

I had a delightful time at Covington. Met just lots of nice people and saw so many of the girls I was in school with. I stopped over in Greensboro for a day and night and spent yesterday in Union Point, met so many nice people in all those places.

But, sweetheart, I'm beginning to want to see you awfully bad, would give most anything I know if you were here with me this afternoon. I have met just lots of nice boys since I've been up here and they have all tried to rag me about my pin, but nothing will change me, my heart is with you – I'm beginning to feel tired of all this and want to spend the remainder of my days with you, just you and me – we would be so happy. What about the war proposition any way? Are things beginning to take on new life, or prospects any brighter, or will we have to wait and wait on a whole life-time before we can begin our new life – the life that will be worth living.

I certainly do hope that you can come up here and go back home with me, it will be so lonesome for me. When I came up here the other night there was a man on the train who was so much like you I almost jumped when he came in – even to his feet were just like yours – I didn't flirt with him, but I just couldn't keep my eyes from wandering in his direction. I will write you later when I expect to go home – it's according to the way I <u>stand the heat</u>.

Write me at 213 Telfair Street – and do it right away, hear?

With Love,
Clyde

Author's Note: This letter was written August 1914, on Bank of Emanuel stationery. Otis' brother, Arlis Rountree, worked at the bank. The letter was written from Swainsboro, which is about 15 miles from Canoochee.

Swainsboro, GA
August 1914
Monday A.M.

My Dear Clyde,

Had come up here for a few minutes this morning, so while waiting for the one who came with me, will write you a short note. Guess you think I must spend a good part of my time away from my work, judging from where my letters are mailed, but it just happens that way.

When am I going to have the pleasure of seeing you? Honest, sweetheart, seems like you have been away for a whole year. Never in my life have I wanted to see anyone as much as I want to see you right now..., all the time, so far as that goes. I'm loving you with all my heart, Clyde, and longing for you every minute. I know I have the dearest little girl in the world and I am anxious for the time to come when we shall be together for always.

Am looking for a letter from you today from Augusta. At present, I am tied up here at Canoochee with some cases, but I hope to be able to meet you up there. Will see you the first possible minute, anyway. Believe I wrote you of the scarlet fever cases? They are doing nicely. Work is very good right now, but the farmers are up against it with no cotton market, so you can imagine I am feeling a bit uneasy. Here's hoping for the best, though.

Hoping to see you soon.

I Am, Very Sincerely,
Otis

Canoochee, GA
August 27, 1914

Dear Clyde,

I wrote you such a little bit yesterday, I am thinking of you so much and want to see you, so I suppose I had better write you another letter while times are quiet. Fact is, you are constantly in my thoughts I love you so I am always wanting to tell you of it. I am afraid, though, that by the time this reaches Augusta, you will be no more, having "just naturally dissolved" from the heat, as it has not abated any since you wrote.

In 1908, I spent a month up there just at this time, coming home the latter part of September, so I know how to sympathize with you. I spent only two days in Augusta though, the rest of the time being over at Pine Heights in North Augusta. It was just after the flood and the water works were out of commission, which added to the general discomfort.

You evidently have enjoyed your vacation and I am certainly glad that you have. Thanks very much for what you said about the pin and incidentally myself. You are a true and loyal Phi Chi and just as faithful a little sweetheart as ever a fellow had. But I am selfish enough to be glad that it is almost time for you to come home, for it seems like it has been several months since I have a chat with you. I wish I could have about two days off so we could take in the city together, go out to Pine Heights, Akin, and take in the shows...

And you found my double? I'd like mighty well to see the gentleman, feet and all. He was on the same train I wish I could have been on. How we are even. For I once found your double, though she was not as pretty as you, nor was she as good, sweet, attractive, or any of those other complimentary adjectives as you - in short, she just wasn't you. There was a very striking resemblance, however.

You asked about the war proposition, that is, the effects on us people. Well, I'll tell you, the prospect is gloomy, though I am hoping for the best and am not worrying more than I can help. I am afraid I shall not collect 50% of my accounts. There is one thing that will help while I have a big number of names on my books, I haven't over half dozen that will be owing me over $25. So, most of them being small, I can hope for a good part of them. In a month or two I can tell more about it. Cotton prices are way down - about $.07. If I can collect enough to get away from here I am liable to get off in short order.

Write me at once, for you know I'd rather have a letter from you than from anybody.

With Love,
Otis

Author's Note: This letter was written from the Genesta Hotel in Augusta, GA. Again, Otis shows a fear of scarlet fever.

September 1, 1914

Dear Clyde,

I was taken sick Friday and came up here yesterday to see Dr. Houston and possibly take a little vacation in the hospital. I think that perhaps I'll escape the stay in the hospital, but I'm not going back to work for the rest of this week, anyway. If I can get away, I am going to Cobbtown tomorrow – am going down there as soon as I can, anyway. The reason I came up here was that I was afraid I might have scarlet fever, as I was running a temperature right along and I surely didn't want to have a spell of sickness, situated as I was at Canoochee.

I telegraphed you yesterday and then called up Mrs. Devereaux when I got here. She told me of your whereabouts.

Hope your mother is improving and that you got much benefit from your vacation. I am sorry that I didn't get to see you or talk to you before you left, for I'd rather see you than anybody else in the world. Clyde, I love you, dearest, as much as it is possible for one to love another. And hasn't it been a long time since we were together, *though? If I improve as I hope to, I will be in Vidalia Saturday or Sunday. Write me at Cobbtown. Ever your sweetheart.*

Otis

P.S. I have had no letter from you since the first of last week.

September 8, 1914

Dear Clyde,

Well, everything is quiet in Canoochee today, so far as my work is concerned. I have had one office call. These premonitions didn't materialize last night, and I didn't care very much. But I'm glad to get work any time if there is anything to it. You see the commercial side of the thing appeals to me rather strongly, at present, though it is much the weaker side. Cotton is going up, but the people around here are not selling it at all.

Wonder just what you are doing with yourself this afternoon? I want to see you so that I would certainly go down there tonight if I could get away, but I cannot leave some cases I have yet. These people, I hope, will soon get straightened out, for I can't stand to stay right on up here very much longer without seeing my sweetheart. There is talk of driving off two or three trains on the G&F, and if they do, it will not be near so convenient for me to go and come. But it will not be half bad, though, if I am forced to spend the day in Vidalia, will it?

Clyde, have you started back with all of your music classes? You mentioned in one letter about giving up some lessons. Did you tell them when you started that they would have to make other arrangements about December 1st? That you were going to take another pupil who would occupy most of your time? I know they will hate to give you up. And, not only the music pupils, but everybody *in Vidalia will feel the loss of you. And, just think, their loss will be my gain! Well, I guess I am about the luckiest fellow in the world, when it comes to some things.*

Hours later…

Have just been out to see a little malarial fever patient of mine, and his father filled the back of my buggy with sugar cane, which is very fine. I am chewing lots of it, and am getting fat. I had gained only five pounds so far, but I'll be a fat man yet.

Since my return, I have felt fine all the time. The only trouble with me, I guess, was that I wanted a vacation, and, thinking I'd find you in Augusta, I couldn't resist the temptation.

Well, there is not much to write about in the way of local happenings. And you know that I love you more than all else in the world, and long for you all the time, so I'll close for this time. I do wish I could go see you, little sweetheart, it's awful hard staying up here without you. Be a good girl, and write me often as you can.

Sincerely,
Otis

Author's Note: Clyde was in Wrens, Georgia, visiting her relatives. Otis makes his case.

Canoochee, GA
September 9, 1914

Dear Clyde,

Last night I received a letter from you but it was one written at Wrens. Rather slow in getting here, wasn't it? It was a message from the girl I love best, though, and that was the thing I wanted. I believe, Clyde, if I had just gotten this letter in time – before I went to Augusta – I'd have hunted a doctor at Wrens instead of Augusta…

I was real busy Monday and Tuesday, but today has been very quiet. Prospects for work are good; for money not so much, though I am getting some good promises. I'm going to collect what is owing to me if anybody collects anything. I'm going to take anything I can get if there is no money forthcoming -- so I think I can do fairly well. There is a good market for cows, hogs, chickens, eggs, corn, oats, hay, etc., etc., so if I can only get my hands on them I'll be all right. Seriously, I believe I'll be able to collect a good percentage of my accounts. Clyde, do you get tired of my talking stuff like this all the time? You certainly have heard enough of it to tire you, but it means so much for me to come out well this fall, looks like I can't help discussing the matter.

And, Clyde, if I do come out as well as I think I shall -- along about the first of December, don't you think will be a good time to carry out plans? You told me, little sweetheart, that "whenever I wanted you, to let you know." Well, dearest I want you now and want you more than anything in the world. If you had come with me when I first wanted you though, we'd have been here together for a long time. There is a limit to a thing like this and I often feel as if I have reached it and can't stand to be away from you another day. December is the most feasible time, I guess, but I wish that it were tomorrow. Clyde, I believe that my practice will increase at least fifty percent after I am married from that cause alone. Then, I will be so much better satisfied I'll look after what I have with more interest. I honestly believe that it is the best thing for me to do, looking at it from nearly every point of view. Don't you think so too? And sweetheart, you are going to be the happiest little girl in the State, for I know that we truly love each other and we can't help being happy. Anything that is possible for me to do here to make you so I am going to do it.

I have a chance to go to Vidalia Saturday and return in a car which I wish I could take. I have two cases on hand that if I can get through with I'm going to slip in there on that six o'clock G&F train, then come back early next morning in the car. I'm afraid that I can't make it, but you need not be surprised if I do. I'll call you if I do go.

Hope I'll get a letter tonight from you at Vidalia.

With Love,
Otis

September 14, 1914

Dear Clyde,

   My train came last night at 1:30 o'clock and I got in here at 5:00. I slept some in Vidalia and then all the way on the train, getting here [Canoochee] just in time for breakfast. Today I have done a good days work and collected on lone dollar, but I feel more encouraged over the situation (as regards myself) than I have since the war started. Of course I can't tell you, but, sweetheart, I feel lots more hopeful than I did a week ago. I believe that I am going to come out much better than I expected. Don't you hope so?
   Clyde, I've got that great big lonesomeness that I have always when I am away from you, but the memory of the time I spent with you yesterday and the day before make me happy. I never enjoyed anything more than that, for to be with you is happiness supreme for me. Sweetheart, I do hope that the time is near when you come with me for always and I believe that it is. I think that everything will be all O.K. for the time we planned and I'm going to try as I have never tried before to make it all right. I love you so much, dear, that I feel like I can never amount to what I should unless I have you with me. I think we have waited long enough. Five years might be all right for some people, but not for me. I'd be willing to wait ten years for you if there were no other way out, but I think we can arrange better than that, don't you? I'm just as proud of you as can be, Clyde, for I know that your equal is something I have never seen. You have proved to be all that I could ask for and I hope that I can make you always happy and content never regretting for an instant the promise you've made me.
   Well, Clyde, I only have a little time to get this off tonight, so I'll close. Hope I'll hear from you tomorrow. Please excuse haste.

Lovingly,
Otis

   P.S. Hope your mother is improving.

Author's Note: Uncle Willie mentioned in this letter is Willie Wilson, Grandmother Holmes' brother. Grandmother Holmes named Clyde for Willie. Willie was the Great Grandfather of Billy Wilson and Beth Benefield, among others.

Vidalia, GA
September 15, 1914

Dear Otis,

*   ...Otis, I went to another club meeting this afternoon out at Mrs. Bazzell's. It was the literary section of the Women's Club. We had a good program and they have such a lovely house, everything was just fine. We studied France, had several interesting papers on Paris, the rulers of France, the government, etc. Last but not least I played a solo, a selection from La Traviata. We always have some music on these literary programs to break the monotony or brighten things up some.*

*   Uncle Willie was here last week and as usual was teasing me. Something was said about our club and he seemed very much surprised that we did not have a young ladies club and that I belonged to the married ladies club. I would not take anything for being a member of this organization, I get so much real good out of our meetings and programs as well as a great deal of pleasure.*

*   But I will leave the club question for a short while anyway. Don't you think it a good plan? Oh, most everybody here thinks the war will soon close and cotton will go up to about 25 cents and I do hope so, don't you? If it does, maybe we can manage to live and I can get me one new dress and hat anyway...*

It is getting late now so I must tell you good night.

With Lots of Love,
Clyde

Canoochee, GA
September 15, 1914
Tuesday Evening

Dear Clyde,

...Yesterday I had a real nice little stay in Swainsboro, ate dinner with Arlis and was with him most of the afternoon. I had to stop by to see a patient, so I never got home till about eight o'clock. Arlis had lots of questions to ask me, wanted to know about all my affairs and gave me free advice concerning them.

We are planning to go down there in his car Sunday week, but don't know whether I'll be able to get away. I think I ought not to mention that, as we have tried so many times and failed. Here's hoping, though!

Well, dear, I have only a little time in which to write, but I did want to tell you something that perhaps I have mentioned sometime in the past, and that is that I have the dearest, prettiest, sweetest girl anywhere for a sweetheart, that I love her more than all the world. I'd rather have two hours with you tonight than anything. I hope to be down there soon, too.

Sincerely,
Otis

Author's Note: The life of a country doctor was not easy.

Canoochee, GA
September 17, 1914
Thursday Evening

Dear Clyde,

I have taken up the spasmodic style of correspondence, but it is not intentional. You will forgive me when I am really too busy to write, I know I'll give you a little idea of what I've done since I wrote you last. Thursday night I was up with one case till 1:30 a.m., then with another till day. Yesterday I was busy all day, but got a pretty fair night's sleep. This morning I made one call, then stopped in at my uncle's for dinner. After dinner I went to see two patients who live eight miles from each other and I got in at eight o'clock making a ride horseback of 17 miles. I'm rather tired, but can't feel right about it if I don't write you a short letter. It's a bad night and I have a premonition of about two calls in this weather tonight and if they come, I'll not feel like writing tomorrow.

Clyde, your letters help out wonderfully. I enjoy every line of them and read them over and over again. It makes me so glad to think that I have a dear little girl like you who loves me and feels interested in all I do. In spite of hard luck due to the war, inconveniences arising therefrom, I am the most wonderfully blessed fellow in Georgia, for I am to have with me soon the best girl on earth.

Prospects are still good though, that great influx of money has not yet started. Hard times or no hard times, I'm going to have plenty to do and I'll get paid for most of it someday. Following the profession I do, I am much better off than some, for my work is not lessened any, and payday is sure to come after a while. Hope you are right about the war soon closing and cotton going up to 25¢. If cotton would only go up to half that, I'd feel a lot easier...

Sincerely,
Otis

Canoochee, GA
September 23, 1914
Wednesday Evening

Dear Clyde,

...It's raining here tonight, a slow sleepy drizzle – and I hope to get in a full night. Last night, I was out again most of the night. Most of my work for the past two weeks has been at night, though

I have some fairly well in the daytime. But, here's hoping that all these people around here stay in good health tonight.

Are you still working hard? Now, don't go and overdo the thing. Try to leave those poor music teachers over at school a little to do. I hope you collect for your work some better than I have.

Well, dear, about all I have time to say tonight is goodbye, for I have been on the road nearly ever since I woke up this morning, which was pretty late. Even got in too late for supper tonight – with the family. But you may know I love you just the same and long for you all the time. Be good and write me soon.

Sincerely,
Otis

Canoochee, GA
September 27, 1914
Sunday Evening

Dear Clyde,

You need not worry about what I think of you for not writing being so terrible, for I really blame myself and the Canoochee mail service. It was mighty good to get another real letter from you. I certainly enjoyed it. Things are not running in the right channel when I fail to hear from you every day or so.

Arlis came over just as I started to write you and stayed an hour or longer. He went to Camilla Friday night to see Ridge and he and Sam had left from Cobbtown about three hours before I got there. So he spent the day coming back home last night. He called up Papa today and they say Ridge is improving now. I am going down there to see him sometime this week if I can leave here. I guess I can get away for half a day, anyway.

I want to go see you, too, Clyde, at the same time. Looks like my practice is not going to hold up any time soon but I have just got to see you. In the eyes of my patients, it will not be inexcusable to go away and see a sick brother, while leaving to see my girl is a wholly different proposition. Therefore, I will just try to make one trip count for both. I am going to wait a few days, however, and perhaps I can get a better chance that I expect. I am thinking of you Clyde. I am almost sorry I am a doctor for I do hate to know that you will be put to so much inconvenience and will have to undergo so much self-sacrifice. You certainly deserve the best there is in life and I wish I could give you everything you deserve and everything you desire. But there will be a good side to being this doctor's wife, won't there, sweetheart? For the reason that I love you, Clyde, and that you love me. We are bound to be happy, dearest, for, loving each other as we do we will not mind the bad features, for we will be so glad that we have each other, and will enjoy the good things of life so much, it will offset all the other. Don't you think so?

Clyde, if it were only "good times" instead of "hard times" and people were in shape to meet their obligations, I would be doing okay. But you know the old story, I guess you hear it down there . . . the work is pretty good though. I am getting practice for people now that used other doctors entirely until here recently, but I am no nigger doctor. I lost two Negro patients right after I came here and it made me lose out with them. They are better pay for a doctor than white people are, but I do hate to have to work for them.

If you were up here now Clyde, I am afraid I would be sick pretty often at night, for I have had only two nights full sleep since I was down there. I have had more night calls since then than I had all the previous six months. Arlis said tonight "if I were fixed like you are out here and my girl would have me, I would be married in a week". I told him it would be might fine for me, and I asked him what my wife would do at times like the present when I was out part of every night almost. "Oh," he said, "buy you a bulldog and a pistol and with people living all around she would not be scared." What do you think about it?

For yourself, little girl, I am afraid your "old man" will have a mighty bad profession. It will mean many broken plans, disappointments, and hours by yourself.

It is getting bedtime, too, for a countryman, so I will close and mail you your letter early in the morning. I am hoping for a good *nights sleep tonight. Will write you later what I can do about going down there.*

With Love,
Otis

P.S.
Monday A.M.

Meant to mail your letter this morning on the early train but I had a call to a place four miles from here at 3:00 this morning and I never got back in time. My patient, an 18-month-old baby, died about twenty minutes after I got there — a case of just waiting too late. Bad, wasn't it?

Sincerely,
JOR

Vidalia, GA
1914

Dear Otis,

...Otis, you said you had thought of a plan by which I could stay out there, not live in the house with anyone, not take boarders, and yet not have to stay by myself at night, is that it? Well, I don't understand it, I can't see any way out, except to go with you and that would not be always convenient, especially in bad weather. Now tell me what you mean, for I can't figure it out. I think some of those gossipers out there must be equal to some of our Vidalians, the idea of your not coming but one more time to carry me back with you. They seem very much interested in that part of your future, don't they? But then, you find that everywhere — curiosity seekers...

Lovingly,
Clyde

Author's Note: It is from this letter that we obtained the book's title (emphasis added).

Vidalia, GA
1914

My Dear,

   I have just been reading about the war, the War Fund, the Voluntary Army Bill, etc. -- what do you think of it, think you will go? I tell you the thought of war makes you begin to have a feeling of fear and dread in spite of your patriotism, doesn't it?
   Otis, I am not feeling so very fine tonight, in fact I feel rather tired. Have certainly been busy with housecleaning, cooking, and teaching music all day today. But I feel so thankful that this day is over and I can get a good rest pretty soon, I don't know what to do.
   I received your letter this morning and it makes me feel so happy when I read one of your inspiring letters -- it just makes me feel, so glad I'm living and living for you. Without this thought and the hope of someday being happy with you, life would hardly be worth living. I am so happy to know that I am loved by one so noble and manly as you, your love means everything in this world to me. I want to give you a little quotation that I read yesterday and one that expresses my sentiments exactly -- "many there be who call themselves our friends, yet ah, if heaven sends one, only one, so mated to our soul, to make our half a whole, rich beyond price are we." Don't you like that sentiment? I have felt for sometime that you and I were meant for each other or that my life would be incomplete without you.
   Fred has just come from uptown with no letter from you, are you waiting to hear from me or what is the trouble? I certainly do miss your letter when it fails to come. I don't see how I ever stood to wait so long to hear from you before, when you were in school...
   By the way, I had the offer of another music pupil today but don't know that I shall take her. I am afraid I would not feel sure of remuneration for my services...
   Be good and write me every time you can.

Lovingly,
Clyde

Vidalia, GA
1914

Dear Otis,

I have just come in from a joy ride with Vera, just went down the road to Lyons a piece, but it makes you feel a great deal better after such a warm day, doesn't it? Mr. and Mrs. Jenkins are in North Carolina, Mr. Jenkins brother died last Friday, so Vera is this housekeeper, although she doesn't like it at all...

Otis, we had quite an exciting affair Sunday night, as we went to church. Mr. Pat Darby and Mr. Dent were riding in Mr. Darby's buggy when the horse became frightened at something and started running down Church Street. Both the men were thrown from the buggy, and right badly bruised up. The buggy was torn almost to pieces, and the horse had to be cut out of the harness right in front of the church. It created a great deal of excitement for awhile, but I think the men were not hurt so badly as they thought at first...

With Love,
Clyde

Author's Note: This letter is dated 1914 and was written by Otis's younger sister, Mary Lou Crawford. Buster, mentioned in the letter, was George, father of Caroline Rountree Price.

Cobbtown, GA
1914

Dear Otis,

I wrote you a card yesterday and dated it Friday. I did not mean to do it but have been ahead all week. I was sure yesterday was Friday until I asked Papa.

Your letter came this morning and was sure glad to hear from you. I am glad your side is not bothering you so much.

Buster is getting better now. He had some kind of trouble with his head. His nose has been running almost all week. Since it started running, his ... has left him altogether and he can eat all right. Now, we did not give him the arsenic because for two or three days he could not eat or take any medicine at all, so we got Dr. Strickland to come to see him. He is giving him some kind of medicine with a little arsenic in it. I think he will soon be all right now.

Do not know when Sam is coming home. He wrote us yesterday and said that Ridge was doing fine. Now, he wants us to send him some more clothes, so that does not sound much like housecleaning does it?

...Aunt Leta wrote me that she was better and that I could stay with them this fall, but I just know Papa will not let me because he has not the money. If I lose this year it will sure put me back, so I am just in a fever to go. We are not going to have a music teacher worth anything here...

Cobbtown is still dull. I think I have not been downtown since Thursday. I am doing better don't you think?

Let us hear from you again soon.

Lots of Love,
Sister

(Date unclear)
Vidalia, GA

Dear Otis,

...I received your letter this morning and enjoyed it very much as usual, had been feeling rather "down in the mouth" until I got such a nice letter; it made me feel real good all over.

But there is one thing I do not know so much about and that is your solution to our problem, my having a room at some of the neighbors' and staying there. It may be a streak of peculiar disposition in me, but somehow I believe I had rather stay alone. I do that a great deal now and am not foolishly afraid, though I have never been left alone at night; I expect I could hear all kinds of noises there. But I'm going with you when I can, except in bad weather. I

*cannot conceive of your keeping bachelor's quarters out there, how
are you going to manage about breakfast, eat Post-Toasties and raw
eggs? I certainly feel for you, wish I could help you.*

*Guess you did enjoy your trip to Summitt [Twin City], I believe
that uncle of yours [Jot] is especially nice to you. Anyway, am
glad you had chance to hear some good music, too; made you feel
refreshed didn't it?*

It is suppertime, so I must go. Be good and write me often.

With Love,
C –

Author's Note: After having known my great-grandmother, Sophie
Holmes, until I was 19 years old, I can testify that I can sympathize with
Otis' trepidation. She was a great lady but also a very strong character.

Canoochee, GA
October 1914
Sunday P.M.

Dearest,

*Last night I received your letter written Friday morning and it
was wholly satisfactory if it was short. If there are only a few lines
it always is much better than no letter at all, but I'm looking for the
long one you were going to write yesterday.*

*Ridge and I drove down to Garfield this morning and that is the
only event of any importance to us to date. We got some magazines
and a Sunday paper, so we have spent the day so far in reading.
There was preaching near here by your fellow townsman – Mr.
Williamson, and there is Sunday school this afternoon, but I didn't
feel inclined to attend either, thought I would rather write you than
to go to Sunday school. I wish I were at your home today, for time
spent with you would be the happiest way I could spend it. I'm
going down there soon and spend a whole Sunday there with you.
But that visit will be when our announcement is published for I
believe you said you didn't want to "face the music" alone. It <u>will</u>*

be a rather trying experience; and then there is another experience that I have coming to me before then that I dread somewhat. And the latter I want to get through with some time this week. When I think of it, it makes me feel like I would prefer taking an ice cold plunge on January morning. But at that, I'll be glad to do it for it is essential to my gaining my greatest prize in the world for me – the dearest, truest little girl anywhere.

Have you said anything to Mrs. Holmes yet about the matter? I really want to discuss it with her, but I don't know how I'm going to come out with my plea. I may be so scared I can't open my mouth. Clyde, if you can think of any plan to help me out, for goodness sake, let me have it. You can tell me this at least, do you think I had better talk to her before seeing you, wait a bit later that same evening, or wait still later and come back next morning? I don't believe in putting things off much so if you think best, we'll get it over with first thing.

Won't you be glad when it is all over with and we are together, living with and for each other? I want you so, dear, I can hardly wait and when this day comes, our day of all days, I'll be one happy man. I want you when I can be with you every day and show you in a thousand ways my love for and appreciation of you. Often I think of the things you will be giving up by leaving your home and coming to a place like this, and I wonder if I'm doing you right. Of course, you are not ignorant of these facts, you are fully aware of them and because of your love for me you are willing to make the sacrifice. It is because of that, that I think I am not doing the right thing but, my little sweetheart, I love you so I just can't stay away from you any longer and you are going to be happy, for all I can do to make you so will be done.

I wish I could take you to ride this afternoon behind "Black Bess". She is mighty pretty now and the best driving horse you ever rode behind. When you do come up here, we'll have to make up for all of those drives with me, you haven't been getting. I enjoy getting out in the woods now, the trees are so pretty with their full colors on and it is such pleasant weather, too. If I only had my little girl with me, that would be enjoyment supreme.

My work has been rather slim for the last few days, but looks like there is always enough to keep me hanging around. Ridge and I are having an easy time at present riding around to see the few *patients I have and reading when at the house. We are to take dinner at my uncle's tomorrow, [probably Uncle Jot] an event Ridge is looking forward to with much pleasure, as all he seems to care very much about at present is eating. As soon as I can get away, I'll let you know posthaste (or even hastier) and will go down to see you.*

With Love,
Otis

Author's Note: When Otis speaks of "through sorrow as well as sunshine," like Clyde, he is being quite prophetic. It is also interesting to note that his landlord is a Methodist preacher and a "persistent law-breaker".

Otis is suffering from extreme fear and trepidation when he thinks of asking Mrs. Holmes for Clyde's hand.

Canoochee, GA
October 1914
Wednesday P.M.

Dear Clyde,

...It hurts me now to think that I haven't more of this world's goods to start out with, for I have often wondered how a man could be so satisfied as to marry a girl when he could not give her what she was accustomed to before marriage. But, sweetheart, there is no way to remedy that except by long, long wait, during which we could see each other no more often than once a month. If we get married now we'll get along someway (and alright, too) and we'll get so much more, out of life by being with each other and our time of prosperity will be no longer if as long, in coming. I hate to ask so much of you, but I love you a 1,012 times more for your being so willing to share my lot through sorrow as well as sunshine. You deserve everything good there is on earth, you are such a dear, good, faithful little girl and all that is in my power to make you happy will be done.

For nearly ten years I have not had the blessed privilege of staying for more than a month at the time at home. To think that at last I am to have a home of my own and someone to share that home with me, I am to have the girl whom I love beyond all else, it makes me feel like jumping up and shouting for pure joy because I am so fortunate. We'll have a home that is worthy of the name, one that means all the word implies...

The old man with whom we board is a very religious old fellow, a Methodist, by the way and was a preacher for 12 years. But every day that comes, he goes bird hunting and kills a mess of birds nearly every day. He is such a persistent lawbreaker, we are beginning to doubt the sincerity of his religion, but the birds certainly taste good. We have just come back from a good bird supper tonight.

Have you summoned that courage needed to speak to Mrs. Holmes yet? Mine is growing stronger all the while, but I fear I'm going to lose most of it as soon as I get to your house again. Don't you fail to talk it over with her for I want to get things more definitely arranged next time I am there, for the next time after that will be getting near December. By then we must know all about our plans. Don't forget to meet me at the door, for I might get scared speechless if you didn't. Be sure to write me about everything before I go, write so I can get it by Saturday night, anyway.

Sincerely Yours,
Otis

Author's Note: Apparently, Otis has talked Clyde into talking to her mother and paving the way for him to ask for her hand.

Canoochee, GA
October 1914
Sunday A.M.

Sweetheart,

I received your note in regard to conditions at your house today and on that account, I think it best that my trip down there be postponed for a day or two. Anyway, I could not have gone had all been favorable because of some work on hand. But you can just bet that I want to see you a little of the worst. I'd like to be with you at church, the singing convention, anywhere just so I was with you, but I'd rather wait till about Tuesday when you have no visitors and when we can do more at arranging our affairs.

How are you by now? Have you mustered courage enough to have the little talk with "mother"? Don't fail to do that before Tuesday, hear? Hope it will not scare you as much as it will me...

Sincerely,
Otis

Canoochee, GA
November 2, 1914
Monday Evening

My Own Little Sweetheart,

...Clyde, I'd give anything I have if you were only here with me tonight, sitting before this oak fire, and me with nothing to do but make love to you and glory in the fact that the dearest girl on earth is mine for all time to come. I miss you, dear, every moment and long for you more than words can tell. In our little home here, we're going to be just as happy as any two people can be, even if we do have to start with considerably less than some people have. We're not going to be always poor, though, for the depression of business will not last very long and then, too, I'll be working all the time and what I do will be paid for – most of it – whenever times do get better. For your sake, little sweetheart, I wish that I were rich as could be, for I do hate to have so little for you when you deserve so much. When I think of your willingness to share my lot with me at the time when I can promise you the least, knowing that you do so because of your love, for me, it makes me – oh, so proud of you and so happy. After all, Clyde, love is what counts most isn't it? With a foundation of genuine, true love a couple can overcome any difficulties, most that may arise, so we have little need to sorrow

about coming out okay in the long run, have we?

...You know we are to eat Christmas dinner with <u>our</u> people at Cobbtown? I'll go down there one afternoon the last of this week or the first of next, just for the night, and we'll talk that over.

And you can just bet that I'll feel lots easier with next trip than I did part of the time I was there last. No wonder I was pale that night, for I was about as scared as ever I have been. I'm glad that it is all over and that we have Mrs. Holmes' consent, for that was a hard job.

Write me often as you have time, dear, for your letters help me wonderfully. Just remember that I love you more than all else.

Sincerely,
Otis

Author's Note: Otis went to Cobbtown to tell his parents of his engagement to Clyde.

Canoochee, GA
November 7, 1914
Saturday A.M.

Dear Clyde,

I got back here last night after being at home Thursday night and yesterday morning. My trip down there was an unexpected one, but I was mighty glad to see Papa and Mama and to have a talk with them. The reason I went was that Ridge was sick when I got back from Vidalia and I thought it best to take him home. He was much better yesterday morning and I think he'll go to his work by tomorrow. Well, I told Mama of our plans and she said that while it looked like a bad time to start out she thought it would be the best thing in the world for me if I had the right girl. I told her just how right you were, that you were the most practical, sensible little lady I ever met, and then a few hundred other things about you, most of which I had told her before. She laughed and said that all men thought that about the girl they love, "but", she added, "this <u>must</u> be

311

a mighty fine girl, I have heard so much that is good about her from everyone who has ever mentioned her to me." She also said, "I hope you have not kept anything hidden from her, have told her about your financial condition and all." I assured her she need have no fear on that score. We discussed the plans for a while and Papa came in, and I told him. He said that he thought a man never amounted to much till he got married and to the right girl. He said that it seemed like I had taken the worst time a fellow could ever take to get married, though perhaps the profession I followed would make it different. Well, we talked a good while on the subject and I know they both are really glad of it. And I know, too, that they are going to love you, dear, as much as any of the children, for to know you is to love you.

We have not had a mail since I came back from Vidalia on account of a big wreck below Garfield. And then there is no prospect of having any before tomorrow. That is the reason you have not heard from me before. If I can get away, I am going to Garfield this afternoon or tomorrow morning, for I don't want you to think I'm hiding out.

I tell you, little sweetheart, it is lonesome up here without you. I'd give almost anything to see you and talk to you for two or three hours this morning. I love you, Clyde, as I could never possibly love anyone else and you know, dear, it is awfully hard to stay away from one whom you care so much for. It will be a great day for us when we are joined together for all time to come, when you become mine to love, to care for, to work for life. We're going to have a happy little home, for, as you once said in one of your letters, love shall reign supreme therein.

What have you decided about announcing our engagement? Do just as you like about that, anytime you wish or not at all. If it is to be tomorrow a week, I'll make arrangements to be right there.

I'm going to close for this time and try to get this off to Garfield. If there are any big mistakes, charge them to one Bob Mixon, a young man about 9 years old who has been standing by me looking on nearly the whole time I was working. He never read any of it though. I'll do better tomorrow. Loving you more than all the world, I remain.

Sincerely,
Otis

Vidalia, GA
November 8, 1914

Dear Otis,

Have been on the go today as usual, went to church this morning and have just gotten home from Sunday school this afternoon. Our church looks about ninety-nine percent better since it has been cleaned up. I think it would really be a dandy place for our wedding, don't you? I'm so glad it has been done, let's imagine it was especially for our benefit, hear?

I received your letter this afternoon and I'm so glad you have been home and discussed our plans with your people. Am glad, too, that they did not disapprove of our plans, they are just fine anyway though, and I know it.

Mama and I are planning to go to Macon on Tuesday to get my suit, and some dresses. Don't you want to go and help me select them? That reminds me of our trip to Macon last year, though I don't expect to take in the fair this time. Am glad our relationship is not exactly the same this year as last, however, aren't you?

Otis, this is what I call "writing under difficulties" for I am sitting in the hall with Pierce blowing his clarinet right at my elbow and Kathryn in the parlor at the piano. So you'll have to charge mistakes to the family I guess, don't know how to express it any better.

I must get ready for church now, be good and write me often. Remember I'm still loving you with all my heart and am wishing for you all the time. Hope I can do a better job on letter writing next time.

As Ever,
Clyde

313

Canoochee, GA
November 21, 1914

Well, Sweetheart,

    The bears haven't got me yet, but Jack Frost is right in behind me, started last night. I had to go three long miles out in the country and that storm was in full blast by the time I started back. It was so dark, I couldn't see Bess's head and it was raining and sleeting, the wind was blowing trees down all around us. I made the horse gallop as much as I dared, but she soon scared me out of that, for she took a short cut that I sometimes take in the day time-a mere path-and got in a ditch, and look like she'd never get out of it. She made it all right though, without hurting her <u>or</u> myself, and then I took it quietly until we got to the clay road, when I gave her free reign. I got in bed around 11:30 and went to sleep then around 4:00 this morning. Was up and the wind was about to blow me out of bed, and cold. My! My! Today I have stayed by a big fire most of the time. I did make two calls and the rest of the time I cut wood. I wished that you were up here with me so that I could be telling you things instead of writing them. Wouldn't it be happy, though, if that dearest of all girls-your only darling self-were here with me tonight, sitting before a big oak fire in our home-yours and mine! And you would be happy too, my sweetheart, for where our home is, there love will always be...
    Must go now to see a sick baby, so will stop in time to get this off. Will do my best to get down there Tuesday, but if there are many sick ones, may not can make it. Will write tomorrow anyway.

Lovingly,
Otis

314

Author's Note: Otis' Thanksgiving message.

Canoochee, GA
November 26, 1914
Thursday Evening

Dear Clyde,

I wonder what you have been doing this pretty Thanksgiving Day, hope you enjoyed every moment of it. You didn't have to work all day because I delayed you so much yesterday, did you? Anyway, we have lots to be thankful for, haven't we? As for myself, I think I must have more to be thankful for than anybody. When I think of the fact that I have my professional education, that I have regained my health, and, the best of all, that I soon to have with me as my life companion the dearest, best little girl on earth, I feel that I am the most fortunate fellow living. It is true that business is bad everywhere, but it can't stay that way long. My debts worry me very much indeed, but I'll have them all offhand before so very long when business conditions become normal. What hundreds of other fellows have done I know I can do, so I'm going to stop worrying over anything I am not forced to and I enjoy all the good things with which I am blessed.

Today I went to a church about a mile from here where the Sunday schools had a program and the people had more dinner on the grounds than was needed for a crowd twice the size of the one there. I didn't get there in time for the program but was there at dinner with a big appetite. It seems kind o' like dinner was all I went for, doesn't it?

Well, Clyde, little sweetheart, I did enjoy being with you yesterday and day before. It was mighty hard to come off and leave you, but I am so happy I feel like telling everyone I meet of my rare good fortune in winning the heart of a girl like you. Only a little over three weeks! I can hardly realize it, can you? I wish I could see you every day now, but if I could we surely would have to postpone our wedding because of the short time, wouldn't we? I may make it down there Sunday, but it is somewhat doubtful. I wish I could be with you to meet the people that day, for I'd love to hear what these people have to say when they first hear the news, mainly, though, just because I want to be with you. Did you find out whether Bill Jones got it off in time?

...and I want you to send me the ring measurements too, and also tell me what to have engraved inside it. I forgot all that the other day as I often forget things when I'm talking to you.

While I was gone I had only one call and I made that last night. I didn't get here till four o'clock and I got three calls before supper time. I have collected a huge amount of $3 and several promises since my return, too. For the next 2-3 weeks though, I will collect more than I have all previously, for I have been promised by some men whom I know to be good.

Well, it's about time, so I'll ring off. I'm thinking of you all the time, sweetheart, planning for our future. Last night I dreamed of you all night – I even dreamed of the wedding.

Loving you with all my heart, I remain.

Sincerely,
Otis

Author's Note: This letter was written by Dr. Sauls, who was Otis's good friend and fraternity brother. The Miss J. mentioned is Vera Jenkins. She married Joe Jackson. Otis and Clyde originally planned their wedding for December 22, 1914, but, as you will see in the next several letters, they had to postpone it until December 31, 1914.

November 28, 1914

Dear Buck.

...Buck, I was glad to hear that you and Clyde had actually named the day. I think that should be the ambition of every man to win the hand of one good woman, and I truly think you have succeeded along that line. I don't know anyone in my brief acquaintance that would make you as good and true a help mate as Miss Holmes, you are to be congratulated, and you may never have one minutes regret for the step you are going to make. Buck, write me what kind of affair you are going to have, your attendants, etc., of course Miss J. and those

damn Jackson boys will be there with bells on, won't they?

...I can't get away for both so close together, but as you and Clyde are coming to Atlanta you must take Christmas dinner with me, I am going to plan for it and expect it so make your plans accordingly.

Fraternally Yours,
Jake

Author's Note: This letter was sent special delivery. Mr. Jones, editor of the Vidalia Advance, got the date wrong. He said early Spring instead of December.

December 1, 1914
Tuesday, A.M.

Dear Clyde,

I received your letter last night and was mighty glad to get it. I am sorry that you have an occasion to be out of sorts – can't blame you a bit though. I didn't tell you that it made me mad, too, but I was pretty sore. The first thing I thought was that perhaps you had

Jake Sauls and Otis Rountree.

got to thinking the matter over and decided you could not <u>possibly</u> get ready by the date decided upon and had called Mr. Jones and had him change it. I soon dismissed that idea, though, for I remembered that you wrote me he lost the notice I carried down there, so then I knew that he just forgot the date. It is a mess, but we will just have to disregard that and feel good as we can over it.

Clyde, please don't lets put it off until after Christmas if there is any reasonable way out. Now, if you just cannot get ready by the 22nd without working until you are all nervous and tired out, of course I am willing to wait. You know dear, I would wait a year, or five years, for you if I had to, though I would hate to have to wait even a day or two longer than the 22nd, unless it were necessary for your wellbeing. As we are going to have only a few days to spare, we could not select a better time than we have selected – during the Christmas holidays. Even if you have to omit a thing or two that will be better than to have to wait through Christmas. I know you are having a good deal of preparation to make, but couldn't you leave off some of them? There is a limit to all things and the limit to my doing without you and staying off where I see you only occasionally has just about come. I don't see, little sweetheart, how I can do without you much longer. If I didn't have a critical case on my hands I expect I would go down there and have a talk with you, but I am sure I can't get away before Sunday. Then I don't want to take up so much of your "work day" time anyway now unless I could help you more than I do. You won't even let me help you cook, so I guess I would be in the way, for I am even a poorer dressmaker than I am a cook.

Last night I had a very nice letter from Jake [Sauls]. He says he can't come to the wedding, but will try to get down here a little later. He gives us a very urgent invitation to take Christmas dinner with him. I am going to write him that instead of being his guest Christmas Day he must dine with us Christmas Eve. I will show you his letter when I see you. He writes that Shanks is at Grady Hospital now.

I am mighty anxious to see you, had rather have three hours with you than anything I know. Yes, I will make it about Sunday, will do my best anyway. It already seems like a month since I was down there.

Now, Clyde, try your best to get ready by December 22nd, hear? I wish I could talk with you about it but can't so I am writing you just how I stand on the matter. Tell Mr. J.P. Stevens to engrave on *those invitations and put in "high noon" December 22, 1914, and to hurry up about it. Don't forget – I love you.*

Otis

Canoochee, GA
December 8, 1914

Dear Clyde,

It seems that I am falling down on promises about writing also, but this time – for a change – I have failed to write because I was actually too busy making calls. There hasn't been much to do for some time, but practice is picking up right along now.

Yesterday I had to make some calls between here and Swainsboro, so I drove on over there. Arlis says that he and Lillian will go to Vidalia on the twenty-second. There are several people over there who say they are going, among them Mr & Mrs. Penton Wilson, Mrs. Bell, Mr. & Mrs. Bill Rountree, and Lucile Rountree.

Have your invitations come yet? I haven't finished my list, but will do so and take it down Friday. I hope those people will not delay about getting them out for we have just two weeks today.

Is it cold weather in Vidalia today? The ink is freezing on my pen, I believe, it is so cold. I had a man bring me a big load of wood, already cut yesterday, just in a good time, but I'm not at the house by a big fire, am down at the depot writing with my overcoat on. I want to get this off via Summit today, as I didn't get a chance to write yesterday.

I want to see you, Clyde, very, very much. Between times now seems mighty long, I don't believe I could stand to do without you longer for more than the two weeks under any conditions. I'm going to be a mighty happy man, Clyde, for I know I've got the best, sweetest, prettiest little lady in all the land for my sweetheart. I love you, dear, as I could never love anyone else, for you are more than all the world to me. You are going to be happy, too, sweetheart, for I am going to do all that is possible to make life a pleasure for you.

It's time for me to close, so I'll write you more later. I'll call

*you up tomorrow or Thursday and let you know when I am going
down there.*

Sincere
Otis

Canoochee, GA
December 1914

Dear Clyde,

Will a letter with a penny lead pencil do just as well as one with
pen and ink? You see, it's mighty cold weather this morning and I
want to sit close to the fire while I write, and it's hard to manage pen
and ink on your knees.

When I got in Monday, it was past supper time, the train was
so slow. Mrs. Dr. Thompson was on the train and I talked to her for
about two hours of the trip, about the lives doctors lead, things they
have to contend with, especially Dr. Thompson, and of weddings
soon to take place, etc. She tried to find out our plans, but I didn't
tell her a thing.

I didn't have a call while I was away, but got one about three
miles out about bedtime – a baby with the croup. So, I got to bed
about the same time I did this night before and my sleepiness last
night was the cause of my not writing. But, I'll go to Garfield this
PM and mail my letter, so you will get it just as soon.

Clyde, sweetheart, I am so glad that you are soon to be with me
up here, for I want you so much. You are all the time in my thoughts
and I love you so that I am not content one minute I am away from
you. I know that you are the dearest, best, most true-hearted little
girl anywhere, or you would never have consented to come with me
just at this time. But, you are going to be happy, Clyde, for I will do
all possible to make you so. While we will not belong <u>exactly</u> in the
"rich folks" class, we will have a fairly good home and a good living,
even if the war does keep going on, so we can get along alright on
that for a year or two, knowing that there is better to come. And, if
I had to be away from you another year as I have been this one, I
wouldn't amount to a thing, for I'd be going down to Vidalia twice

320

a week and would never do any work. Thank goodness, though, that doesn't have to be. This year, 1915, will be the first of the most important years of my life, for, with the girl I love more than all else, I can accomplish something that is worthwhile. Any man would be inspired by the love of a girl like you.

...There seems to be little sickness around here now, but this cold spell will soon be telling. By the week after Christmas, I'll be getting more than I can do, I expect. I am having plenty of time to do collecting now, though it amounts to mighty little.

Let me hear from you just as often as you have time to write for you know how I want your letters. I'll try to write you again tomorrow.

Sincerely,
Otis

Canoochee, GA
December 11, 1914
Friday Evening

Sweetheart,

Don't you think me an awful fellow for waiting so long to write? Well I was really busy till yesterday afternoon and I found out I couldn't get off any mail because our postmaster was drunk, so I waited till this morning to write one to mail in Fairfield. I had to make a call, though, so I went down there and called you up. That was better than a letter anyway, wasn't it? It certainly did me a world of good to talk to you, I have felt 100% better ever since.

I'm getting along fine, too, Clyde. Seems like I am in lots better condition than I was before I got sick and you may know I'm being more careful. Really, yesterday and today I feel better than I have felt since the war started.

That was a mighty good little letter I had tonight, too. You can't imagine, sweetheart, how I want to see you. Each time I am with you it makes it harder for me to stay away from you. Yes! But I'm glad we have only a little over two weeks to wait till we commence our new life, when we shall each have the one whose companionship we desire and whose love we value above those of all others with us for all our time on earth. I am lonesome for you as can be now, little girl, but two and one-half weeks is not a long time, is it?

Had a letter from Ridge tonight saying he would be on hand. I'm going to see Arlis tomorrow.

Ridge says that he will be without a job about Christmas time, as they are cutting out that work on account of the financial stringency over the country. He wants to farm and asked me about coming up here. If we stay in Canoochee. I'm going to try to get him up here to run a truck farm. As we are on a direct line to Savannah and have good freight rates I know it would pay – better than cotton, anyway. The main reason he wants to be here is that he knows it will be easier for him to keep in the "straight and narrow way." If he had stayed up here this year all the time I'd have been better off. He has been doing well, though, since he left here and I believe he is going to come out all o.k.

Clyde, I'm going to see you one night the latter part of next week, for I haven't found out exactly yet just what we are going to need in the way of flowers and such. I have ordered the ring and if it has come by then I'll take it to you for inspection. My suit has come and it looks good. Shall I take it down for your inspection also? You never did show me yours.

Well, dear, it's getting late for a countryman, so I'll not write you very much tonight. I wish you were here with me. You picture's presence brightens the room wonderfully for me, but it doesn't fill the place that you would. That picture has helped me out many a time this year when I was feeling blue and down in the dumps. I had only to take a look at the likeness of that lovely, and lovable, face of yours and think, "As long as <u>she</u> loves me, why need worry?" It was a sure cure, too. And when you yourself come with me, Clyde, I can overcome all obstacles and gain that success we all wish for

With Love,
Otis

P.S. Will write again Sunday.
J.O.R. –

Canoochee, GA
December 12, 1914

Dearest Little Girl,

I have just read your letter of yesterday and you may know I was glad to get it. Last night I expected one, but was disappointed. It seems like two weeks or longer since I was down there, so I am sorely tempted to go back tomorrow. I love you so, little sweetheart, I can hardly stay up here without you, but guess I'll have to stick around and get things in readiness if you come, won't I?

Since my return I have not had a great amount of work to do, though I have collected about $35.00, nearly all in real cash, too. Besides that I got a $12.00 hog on account from a very doubtful party today, which transaction tickled me much. I'll soon be a farmer right- more farmer than doctor I fear. It's a settled fact that I am going to have more farm produce than some of the farmers themselves, better that than nothing, though. Perhaps I can sell the stuff next year.

I'm glad Mr. Jones got our announcement in early enough for the Sunday papers. In the morning I'll meet the train and buy me an armful of papers, for I'm anxious to see how it looks in print. I'm sure it will look much better that way than it did in writing. And only three weeks from Tuesday! Aren't you glad? Clyde, this is the happiest time of my life – these days when I am planning for your coming with me and for our home – that is, the happiest of my life so far. The part of our lives that is going to mean the most is yet to come.

Are you having very much work to do? Don't tire yourself down, for it will not pay you. I don't want my little girl to work so hard she becomes ill for I certainly do not want her to become a patient of _any_ doctor, even myself.

I'm not going to write you much this time, sweetheart, but will try to give you a real good letter tomorrow or next day. Guess you'll get this tomorrow if I can get over to Garfield.

With Love.
Otis

Author's Note: This letter was written in December of 1914, a few days before the wedding.

Canoochee, GA
December 1914
Tuesday A.M.

My Dear Girl,

Will write you only a short note this morning, so you'll get it today. Meant to write you last night, but went for Ridge to Summitt and never got back in time.

Ridge told me how he filled my place Sunday night, and you may know I envy his good fortune - in being with you, I mean. He seems to be the original hard luck story, doesn't he? Hope he'll dodge that luck on the thirty-first. Don't you?

Clyde, I am awfully lonesome for you. Seems like I have nothing at all to keep me here, for I want you so. You are everything to me, dear, and I am the happiest fellow you ever saw because of my sweetheart. I certainly enjoyed being with you down there, every minute of the time, and to know that you soon are to be with me for all time makes me glad beyond measure. You are the dearest little girl on earth, and I love you with all my heart, with a love that will last as long as life. I am counting the hours now until our time comes, for that will be the greatest day of my life. I will write you again tonight, sweetheart, if I am here and I will try to write a bit more. It is mail time now.

Sincerely,
Otis

Author's Note: Eight days before the wedding.

Stulb & Vorhauer, Props,
Hotel Genesta
Augusta, GA
December 23, 1914

Dear Clyde,

Before retiring will scribble you a few lines, for I'm thinking of you and want to see you. I wish you were right here with me, for I think we'd enjoy seeing the Christmas displays and doing our shopping together. I have just finished my shopping, but there were some of the stores closed that I wanted to get in. My shopping was not so very heavy, so I suppose I can get along with what I have done. I did not buy the flowers here – will get them from Atlanta; I found most of the other things that I wanted though.

Had you thought that one week from tonight we have our reception? And then a week from tomorrow - , time is passing swiftly enough now, isn't it? It is passing none too swiftly, however, for seems like, little girl, we have waited for each for years and years. I am mighty glad, Clyde, that this coming new year we are to start together on the chapter of our lives that is the most important and the happiest of all. I shall be proud indeed of you as my wife, for you are the dearest little woman of them all. I love you as I can never think of loving anyone else, with all my heart, soul and body, and so I shall love you as long – as I live.

Have you decided you had rather live in Canoochee than anywhere else? Well, even if we do not go to Vienna, I hardly think we shall be at Canoochee another year, for I have fully decided to make a change if it be possible. Above all else I want you to have a place where you will like to live and I fear you will not have that there.

Will do my best to see you Xmas and that means I'll come mighty near doing it.

Sincerely,
Otis

1915-1920

Otis and Clyde were married in December of 1914. For the next five years, they were occupied with starting their family, as well as a successful medical practice. James Otis Rountree, Jr. was born October of 1915, and Virginia was born in 1917. Otis was a very popular doctor in Canoochee. He encouraged the improvement of sanitation, as well as the digging of deep wells, in order to prevent disease.

Sarah Underwood said that her mother, Hattie, loved Otis. She related how Otis would go to the medicine cabinet and take a large dose of bicarbonate of soda for his stomach. Hattie's reaction would be to tell Otis that such large doses would kill him.

In 1918, Otis and Clyde moved to Vidalia. They purchased a home on Durden Street.

In a 2000 letter to Johnny Anderson expressing sympathy for Christine's death, Bill Warthen, a local historian, tells a story about Otis' Vidalia practice. "My father was a druggist, and he often told me of a conversation held in the prescription room of his store, just weeks after

Spring 1916 - Clyde with James, taken in Canoochee.

326

the 1918 flu epidemic had passed. It just happened that the three or four doctors in Vidalia were there (one had died from flu) and they were talking about the number of patients they lost during the three month's epidemic and what they had prescribed. Dr. Rountree was able to tell the others that he had not lost a single patient. This surprised them, and they wanted to know what he had been prescribing. It seems Dr. Rountree had been insisting his patients take three aspirin every four hours. This startled the others, as aspirin was a prescription drug considered quite dangerous to prescribe. The medicine greatly reduced fever, and the group realized the high fever caused by the flu virus so weakened the patients that pneumonia followed, and many did not survive. Until the editor of our paper called last week to get Dr. Rountree's name, I had not realized how young he was at the time of his death. He had not practiced in Vidalia but a short time."

Our letters begin as Otis is traveling to Rochester, Minnesota, in order to have his stomach problem treated. He is being accompanied by Vidalia physician Dr. Thompson. Please remember that, as these events transpire, Clyde is eight months pregnant with Christine.

Author's Note: The following is an excerpt from a letter Clyde wrote the parents of Sarah Underwood after the death of Sarah's sister, Hattie Lewis. Sarah went to the county fair and caught scarlet fever. She was sick for several days. Sarah survived, but Hattie Lewis died four days later, after having caught this illness from her sister. It is rather instructive as to what Clyde said about losing her husband which happened nine months later.

Eugene and Hattie Flanders were Otis Rountree's aunt and uncle.

Vidalia, GA
January 12, 1920

My Dear Aunt and Uncle,

...I know what it is to lose a loved one, I lost my father when I was about 15 years old and I know how it hurts. Now I don't know of anything that would hurt me like the loss of one of my little ones or my husband. But after all, God just lends them to us and we can thank him for the time that we do have them with us.

But dear little Lewis is happy with Jesus, she is an angel up in Heaven. She is not in this world of sin, sorrow and suffering – some

L to R - Virginia, Dorothy, and James Rountree.

day you will meet her and then how happy you will all be.

I am in the very best of health now, weigh more than I have before in my life. Am so fat Otis teases me all the time. Think it really worries him, but I feel good so I don't let it worry me. The children are fine, have grown so much you would not know them. The little baby [Dorothy] will be ten months old Thursday and looks very much like Virginia did at that age.... Again I want to *express to you all my heart-felt sympathy for I love you people, and you were so kind and sweet to us when we were there in Canoochee away from all our people.*

Write me when you feel like it and can.

Sincerely,
Clyde R.

Vidalia, GA
September 21, 1920
Tuesday Evening

Dear Otis,

I have been receiving all this afternoon, have had company all the time from about 3:00 on. Miss Lizzy Coleman, Mrs. Lemon, Mrs. Bowen, Mrs. Timmerman, Mrs. Godby, Mrs. Thomas and Annie Laurie all came. All interested in inquiring about you. Pete Davis called up tonight and asked if Miss Rountree would mind telling him how Dr. Rountree was. They tell me they are trying so hard to keep well until you get back, they just don't know what they would do if they should get sick until you get out of town. They help my feelings a whole lot by saying those things.

I went up town this morning, to your office for awhile and then did a little shopping. There were a few things I wanted to see about in the office. I brought your charge book home for I need it occasionally. Do you know anything about C.H. Fowler's account, he called up to find out about it and I can't find it at all.

I am so tired out tonight I can't write long so will tell you good night. Remember my thoughts are of you all the time, I miss you so I can hardly wait for you to come home. I want your letters just as soon as you are able to write.

Love,
Clyde

Author's Note: This letter was written by Otis on his way to Rochester, Minnesota.

October 7, 1920
Thursday P.M.

We made our train all right and are all present getting tired. I am having no trouble, feeling well and I ate a hearty dinner. We passed through Chattanooga at 1:00 p.m. and will reach Nashville when I shall mail this at 5:55.

You must write me <u>at once</u> the condition of yourself and the children. Mail to Rochester, Minnesota. I will get it at general delivery. I'm hoping for the best. If Virginia should get worse, telegraph me and I will come home. This is very pretty mountainous country all the way from Atlanta to Nashville. I wish you were with me.

Love,
Otis

Rochester, MN
October 9, 1920
Saturday Noon

Dear Clyde,

Your telegram has eased my mind considerably. Be careful with Dorothy's diet and don't let Virginia run around much for a week.

We had a stop of 1½ hours in Atlanta. We made no change till we got to Chicago, but had a 25 minute wait in Nashville, where we stretched our legs a little. All day Thursday we were through a mountainous country, passed through Marietta, Dalton, Chattanooga and Nashville, very beautiful mountain scenery, but homes were very poor, few and far apart. We reached the Kentucky line about night, Evansville, Indiana, about 10:40, and in Chicago, 7:45 next morning. I woke about 6:00 a.m. and instead of the rough rugged country of the day before, the land was level and greatly rolling, no trees except what has been planted, mostly poplar and oak for shade purposes only. All the land from there to seventy-five miles past Chicago was of that nature, ninety percent or more of it under cultivation. Corn, such as we never see, alfalfa and other hay crops, grasses, and small grains, some up and growing and some being planted, are the things they plant. The plowing is done by riding plows drawn by 3-5 big Percheron horses or by tractors. Every farm house is a large, painted, nice looking affair, with several barns, from one to three of them bigger than the dwelling and all buildings are painted, the barns invariably red. These houses are close together and the farms will average between 100-200 acres, all that area in use. Most of these farms in the country I am writing of have a bunch of dairy cattle and throughout Wisconsin, <u>everyone</u> has a herd of Holstein from the size of Hart's bunch on up. They all have from 1-3 silos, a mountain of oat and wheat straw and some land cut off for grazing purposes. Yesterday through Wisconsin, the farms were pretty much the same as to what they raised in that they all had a big bunch of dairy cattle but the land is rolling and is mountainous in sections. We passed through several tunnels both days. It looks funny to see all the streams without any trees around them, some of the rivers larger than the Altamaha. I didn't see the Mississippi or any of the Iowa country, as we passed it during the night.

The trip was pleasant enough most of the way. There was sleet on the cars coming in Atlanta on Thursday A.M., but Thursday P.M. and Friday it was very hot in the train except at night. I wished for the B.V.D.'s all day yesterday. Outside of that and worry over Virginia and Dorothy, the trip was an enjoyable one. In Chicago, we had to make a transfer of a mile and made our train only by the skin of our teeth. We reached here at 9:00 p.m. I have been at the clinic awaiting my time and then be examined all the morning. They will probably get me to the operating table by the middle of the week. I'll write you later of all that.

My stomach has been doing unusually well.

I am delighted that you are well, I feel lots better. Must go now. Will write tomorrow.

Love – Lots of It,
Otis

331

Vidalia, GA

Dear Otis,

Received your card and telegram this morning. Am so glad you made the trip without any trouble. Hope you are still feeling fine. I will be anxious to hear what happens every day now. The suspense is awful.

Virginia had been doing fine, that anti-toxin must be wonderful medicine. I could hardly keep her in bed the next day after you left and yesterday. I did not even try to keep her in the house. Dr. Mercer came around twice Thursday, said her throat looked right bad that morning, but he would wait until tonight about giving her any more. By night, she had no fever and her throat was about entirely clear. I never dreamed it would get well so quickly.

Dorothy is still improving but stays very cross. I am beginning to increase her feed just a little, am trying to be very careful though. Still giving her protein milk, scraped steak, oatmeal gruel and zwiebac.

I am feeling very well and trying to sew some, but am sleeping some better than I did for a while. I am so yellow and brown, I expect I need some Calomel, don't you? Maybe I would get better of that cough and what goes with it, that you think is all put-on.

People have not quit calling for you yet. Someone out in the country called yesterday and the day before, Mr. Allnioud called yesterday for you, too.

People have been very thoughtful and considerate of me, just numbers and numbers of people have called to inquire about you and hope you will soon get back home.

I want to go uptown this morning for a few minutes, so I must close this up. Will write you again tomorrow. Let me hear from you every day. Next to seeing you and hearing you talk is getting a letter from you.

Lots of Love,
Clyde

Vidalia, GA
October 10, 1920
Sunday Evening

Dear Otis,

I have been so lonesome and blue without you today. I could hardly stand it, have thought of you and wondered about you all day. I am so anxious to know how you are and what you are doing and what they are doing with you. You must let me know just as soon as you know anything definite. The children were all so anxious to get out this afternoon, so I called Tommie and he went with me. We went to Lyons and out to Mr. Giles' place. I drove nearly all the way, got along fine, think I can manage the car very well now. I do not expect to use it much, but there are times when I really need it and need to know how to drive myself...

I received a letter from Alex today, he says he is coming home for the holidays and will make plans to come back to America to stay. Says he will leave there in about six weeks...

Some of your bills are being paid, so George and Tom tell me. But everything is so blue, cotton has been eighteen and twenty cents.

I want to get this off tonight, so we'll close.

Love,
Clyde

Author's Note: Notice the cultural differences between the North and South.

October 10, 1920
Sunday P.M.

Dear Clyde,

I'm still free. They took my history yesterday, gave me a superficial examination, examined my blood and made x-ray pictures of my teeth. The clinic is closed on Sunday and they do no surgery except emergency work, so I am just resting today. Tomorrow they make pictures and tests of my stomach and by Tuesday, they will probably pass sentence. Then Wednesday or Thursday I get the knife.

Thompson and I have been spending the time by going over the clinic and to the hospital. The clinic building covers a block and is seven stories high. There they start the patients off, making all examinations, x-rays, blood tests, urinalysis, and finally assign them to the hospital. There are three or four large hospitals beside the clinic building, all owned by the Mayos and Dr. Judd, except St. Mary's, which is a Catholic institution. The Mayos do practically all the surgery at St. Mary's, although they are not Catholics themselves. The sisters built the hospital for them about 30 years ago, when they had little money, and they appreciated it so much that they do their personal work there while owning the other newer and more modern hospitals themselves. The whole business – clinic and hospitals – are run by the Mayos, although under their personal supervision. They have here about 225 men M.D.'s – working for them and these men are surely busy.

Rochester is a town of 15,000 with very pretty wide paved streets, all lined with large trees. It is made by the Mayos, though. Everything in it is dependent on the hospitals and people who come here. They have very nice stores, some picture shows, and numbers of hotels – several new ones. The Mayos' corporation owns drug stores, hotels, and other town property. They are now building another hotel about 8 or 9 stories of it up, which is to cost a million. The Carlton, at which we are stopping, has been open only 3 weeks.

We went to church this morning and to the picture show this afternoon. While the hospital staff seems to observe the Sabbath more than is the rule, the people generally don't regard it as we do. Sunday is the great holiday here. They go fishing and hunting and the season is so much shorter than ours, the farmer works all day, same as in the week. I have seen wagons passing today with loads of Timothy hay, others with Irish potatoes. It really is time for cold weather and these fellows are behind. They say that one year ago yesterday, there fell four or five inches of snow. It is very pleasant yet, though.

I hope you and the children are well, I'd give most anything to *see you. I wish you could every one be here with me. My health and appetite remains good, so I think I shall be in good condition for the operation.*

Don't worry about me any, little sweetheart, for this is the thing I need. They have done thousands of operations like I am to have, and they seem to always get good results. I'm coming back home with all the bad cut out, even to my disposition. I'm sorry I have to be away now, but I'll be back before you absolutely need me.

With Love,
Otis

Author's Note: The term "getting sick" meant to have a baby.

Vidalia, GA
October 11, 1920
Monday Evening

Dear Otis,

I am pretty well tired out tonight but am going to write you a short note anyway. I was so disappointed that I did not hear from you tonight. Mama went to the office after the MD&S Train but found no letter from you. I am beginning to want a letter real badly.

Mama finished up your pajamas tonight. They are ready to be mailed to you but I don't know whether to send them to the hospital or not. Hope you will like these alright. Don't think the sleeves will be too large and bulging like those others.

Mr. and Mrs. Gay and Mr. and Mrs. Isaac Rountree went to Cobbtown to the sing yesterday. They said your people were all well and were anxious about you, had not heard anything until I sent them word you had arrived safely.

People call up and ask about you every day and tell me how they miss you. Mrs. Jones, as unconcerned as she always is, says she doesn't know what to do, she expects to be sick the last of this month and she doesn't know who to call. Says she would rather have Dr. Thompson, but is afraid he will not take the case unless she goes to the hospital and she doesn't want to do that on account of leaving the children...

Lots of Love,
Clyde

Rochester, MN
October 11, 1920
Monday P.M.

Dear Clyde,

I'm having quite a busy day. Last night I took a test meal, two more this morning, have had my stomach washed and re-washed, and am to go to the x-ray room for x-ray of the stomach in a little while. Then I'm to have another stomach washing and then probably I'll get a real meal. I've had no trouble with my stomach till last night and that was caused by not taking soda so that the test could be correct. It was a bad night, but I'm alright today. X-ray pictures of the teeth show two bad teeth, one lower and one upper – both of them come out. They are both front teeth and I guess I'll come home without any in their places, unless I have more time than it seems like I shall. The operation is still in the future – it may be the last of the week.

You should have started writing me the day I left, for I haven't had a line yet.

I hope Mrs. Holmes is better. Unless you are feeling well I want you to get eight ounces of I.Q.'s with Arsenic and take a teaspoon full on a half glass of water after meals.

It's almost time for the x-ray so we'll close. Tell Jim and Virginia that I want them to be good and do all that you tell them to do. Are they still improving?

Love,
Otis

October 12, 1920
Tuesday P.M.

Dear Clyde,

...They finished examinations today and made a diagnosis of acute bleeding ulcer of the stomach along the line of suture of the former operation. I should have gotten my operation tomorrow, but the hospital to which I was assigned was full. I will probably get it Thursday or Friday.

How are you and the others? I hope you are all doing well. You must take good care of yourself. If Lucille quits, you get another cook. As to my getting back in time, I will probably be back by the fifth of November if I get my operation this week, possibly earlier. So, you see, I will make it all right.

I do wish you could be here with me. The weather has been delightful, just cool enough for you to feel good and have a good appetite, the kind that you like so well. If you were only here with Dorothy, she would get well in a hurry.

Wish you would mail the Vidalia Advance and the Swainsboro paper to me each week till I leave.

I met my surgeon and saw him operate this morning. They say he is the best in the world. He is a smooth, swift operator. They do several operations daily like mine and nearly always get good results.

I am going to write George a short letter, then I am ready for supper. Wish you could eat with me.

Be brave and cheerful, little sweetheart, all this is for a good purpose. I will be able to do a man's share of work when I get back, and I will do for my little girl things I have never been able to do before.

With love to all of you, I remain,

Your "Old Man,"
Otis

Vidalia, GA
October 13, 1920
Wednesday P.M.

My Dear,

Just one week ago tonight you left me and it seems like one month at least. I received a letter from you yesterday and one today. I appreciated every bit of both of them, can hardly wait to hear again, I have grown so anxious and I need you about me today. Do have Dr. Thompson write me as soon as the operation is over. I will be nearly crazy until the suspense is over.

Dorothy is improving rapidly now, is not near as cross as she was when you left either. Virginia is as well as ever as far as I can tell. James is looking better and doing better than when you left. I am feeling better, too, have been sleeping more and better since Dorothy is so much better.

Mama thinks I had better get rid of Lucille as there is not much for her to do, but I haven't done it. I don't think I had better get rid of her until Dorothy gets to be less trouble because there will be so much for Maddie to do and I will have the entire care of her and I know I can't hold up at it...

Lots of Love,
Clyde

October 14, 1920
Thursday Evening

Dear Otis,

I wonder what kind of tests you have had today and how you are feeling tonight. I think of you all the time and miss you more than I can begin to tell you. The children talk about Daddy and when Daddy comes home every day. James says he is taking your place. Has been sleeping with me until last night. I thought it best for him not to sleep with Virginia.

I have grown to be a real good driver since you left. I drove the car out to Horris Wardlaws Tuesday afternoon. They had just finished grinding cane, and he gave me a half gallon of new syrup. It is real good. The only thing is there is not enough of it...

You must let me hear from you as often as you can, I am so anxious about you.

Love,
Clyde

Author's Note: Three times Otis writes he will be home by the first of October. Three times we think these letters are written during October. I cannot see an explanation. I think he meant the first of November.

Probably October 14, 1920
Thursday Evening

My Dear Clyde,

Have heard only once from you. I am worried about it a little, although I am laying it to the mail service. You must write me, little girl, for I want to see you so, and can not, so the most satisfying thing possible are your letters.

Well, I am suppose to go to St. Mary's Hospital tomorrow and get my operation done Saturday A.M. Rooms have all been filled and they have had me on a diet, anyway together with stomach washing. You will probably get a telegram from Dr. Thompson stating my condition, for I shall have him send one after the operation, before you get my letter. Every one I see who has had the operation I am to get here seems to have had good results. The usual length of time in a hospital is from ten days to two weeks. Sounds good, doesn't it? But I'm going to have my tooth work done here, for I want that done right. That will occasion a delay of one to two days. I expect to get home during the first part of October.

Clyde, there is a Dr. Rowntree here, who has been on the medical staff at the University of Minn. and has recently been given a place

L to R - Lucille, Virginia, Dorothy, James, and Unidentified.

on the Staff of Consultants here. He has been very nice to me. Says we came from the same origin in England. He is worse on tracing family trees than I am. Guess we are about thirty-fifth cousins: is that close enough to claim?

Thompson is having a great time. He seems to be well liked by the men and also especially by the ladies. One of the interns says he is a "regular pump handle", he does so much hand-shaking. He says he will go home so as to be back by the first of Oct. I asked him to see after you till I get back and he said he would be glad to.

Still warm weather here and today it has been raining all day. Guess it will change when the rain is over. Write me if you have sent any package. If you have not done so, I can get along alright without any of those things, for I'll have to buy some anyway before I could get your package.

I do want to see you, dear, and wish you could be here with me. I love you, sweetheart, with a love that never dies, you and the children. Things are going to be better in our home when I regain my health. It will be a happy home with all of us in good health and with me able to do all the work I can get. Don't you worry about me, little girl, three weeks is a short time. More tomorrow.

Otis

Author's Note: This is apparently the last letter Otis wrote before his operation which took place on October 16, 1920.

October 15, 1920
Friday P.M.

Dear Clyde,

Have just been out to St. Mary's Hospital, was assigned a room and then told that I could go to town till 4:30, so I came back to the hotel and found the letters written by you Sunday and Monday. They send them all to Dr. L. G. Rowntree. Send all of the rest of my mail to St. Mary's Hospital. I am to be operated upon sometime in the morning. Thompson will telegraph you. I am glad you are driving the car. Try to get out often. Better have the timing gears "dope," also see that there is air enough in the tires. Silas will do that for you.

I have not paid Darby for some time, probably since July. Look after that. Tell George to add to his list J. I. Dixon $18, Oliver Simpson $13.50, W.G. Simpson $8 and Elder Wilkers $10 and Hackel $3. I may have them on there, but I do not think I have. I am sorry cotton is down, and I am afraid there will be lots of unpaid bills.

Tell Mrs. Jones that I will probably get back in time to see after her. There is a possibility of my being back by the first. It will not be much later than that. I have not written George yet but will just as soon as I am able to write after the operation.

It is raining a little today but still warm. I am looking for cold before I get away, though.

I 'm glad Alex is coming home. Has Pierce gone to Athens yet? You give him the difference between what he owed me and the $100, for I am going to use the $100.

This will be the last letter for a few days, but I will let you hear daily.

Love – Lots of It,
Otis

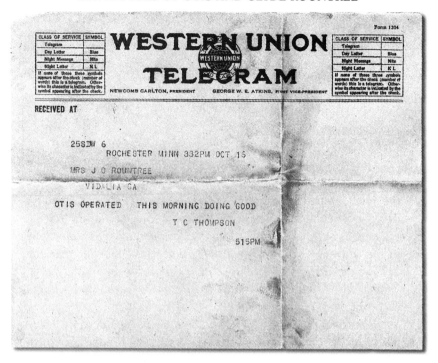

October 16, 1920
Saturday Evening

My Dear Otis,

Was so glad to get the telegram from Dr. Thompson this afternoon stating that you had been operated on and were doing well. I have been in dreadful suspense these last few days. I realized that the danger and suffering is not over by any means, but I do feel somewhat relieved that the real operation is over. I hope Dr. Thompson will keep me posted until you are able to be writing again yourself. I don't allow myself to think very much at night because I could not sleep a bit if I did, but I have really been sleeping very well considering everything...

Dorothy is playing out here in the hall in her nightie like she used to play with you. She seems to feel real well, but is not very strong yet. Does not try to walk very much yet. She falls over doorsills and the like so she is afraid. I don't think she would be quite so cross to you now if she could walk, though she is shaking *her fist at me now.*

Maydee [Aunt Maydee, George Rountree's wife] carried the children to the circus this afternoon and they enjoyed it so much. Virginia keeps telling what the elephant and the clowns did and James tells about the pretty horses. Says he wants all those horses, would feed them on some of the cows hay...

Will send you some papers next week.

Lots of Love,
Clyde

Vidalia, GA
October 17, 1920
Sunday Evening

My Sweetheart,

Your letters are very encouraging. I hope everything will be as bright in the end as you think it will. The greatest desire of my heart is that you will be a well man, able to eat anything you want. That would make me happier than anything in the world. If you could be perfectly well, some other things would be so different, in fact life in our home would be so very different.

Dr. Thompson sent me a telegram yesterday that you had been operated on and were doing good. I hope to hear again today, but did not, so I guess you must be doing all right. I am so glad he stayed until the operation was over, it is so good for you to have someone whom you know with you.

I certainly hope you are getting some of my letters by now, for I have written you regularly. I mailed your packages on Tuesday afternoon. You should have gotten it by Friday anyway, sent it in care of Mayo Clinic though so I do not know whether you got it or not. Hope you did before you bought any more pajamas. Mama took special pains to try to make them nice...

Your uncle Ike has been inquiring about you quite often. He came around this afternoon and sat a good long time. Was very interesting, you know. I took the children to ride this afternoon, we went up the Mount Vernon Road nearly to Ailey and back. I think I am driving real well now, do not jerk and bounce very much…

Mr. Pierce is back with Leon now, and he says he is going to get rid of all the others. He is going to start a strictly cash business, and he and Lloyd Pierce can run it alone. How do you suppose he will manage without "Reddick talking" to answer the phone?

The Darkies had an association at Uvalda today, and Lucile went to that so I had to cook dinner, and am tired out tonight. Driving the car tires some, too, though I do not drive under such a strain as I did.

Sweetheart, I want you to get home just as early as you can, I miss you so, but do stay there until you are strong and well enough to come home. I do not want you to have any of this to do over.

Love,
Clyde

Author's Note: The letter below is from Wash Rountree. You can tell by his letter that he was very worried.

Cobbtown, GA
October 17, 1920
Sunday

Dear Otis,

Four letters received last Thursday. Glad you were able at least to enjoy the scenery. Clyde sent us word of you each week, but we have heard nothing since Friday. There is not anything here that would interest you. Our health is very good, and we are having perfect weather, though with this, farmers were never so blue. Conditions are certainly ongoing a change, and I think people will soon be made willing to work or do worse. I did not attend our Association last week on account of being here to hear what I could from you. I have been intending, Providence permitting, to leave next Thursday *for Boston to be with Joe a few days, but I can't get any satisfactory news from you, will hardly get off if nothing else prevents. Ike sent me word he would go with me, and if I go, we'll first go to Vidalia to carry Clyde some more work your Ma did for her, and to hear the latest from you. We are all very anxious about you and impatient to hear. We tried to pray for your restoration to health, and truly hope it may prove very beneficial, if not a permanent cure. I can only commend you to the mercies of an all wise and loving Savior, who is the greatest physician ever consulted or trusted. We watch every mail, will carry the children some green cane. Remember, if I don't get some definite news from you before Thursday noon, will not get off until I do. Hoping for the best results and to hear through some source soon.*

Your Anxious Pa

October 18, 1920
Monday Evening

My Dear,

    I wonder how you are feeling tonight, if you are having to do without water and food yet, if you are in much pain example, etc. I do wish it was not quite so far and that I could go to see how you are. Mrs. Glover says you must hurry and get back, Edna is sick now and she needs you. I hear something like that every day, often several times each day...
    Write me as soon as you are able. Have appreciated and enjoyed your letters so much. Will miss them while you can't write.

Love,
Clyde

Vidalia, GA
October 20, 1920
Wednesday Evening

My Dear,

I am trying to write you tonight when I am in no mood for writing but I want to let you know I am thinking of you. The baby [Dorothy] is not doing so well today, her eyes are real bad, her little stomach is distended all the time and she seems to have a lot of gas on her bowels... I hope she will be alright tomorrow. I am up against it with you gone. I think the main trouble is giving her cane but I hate to act so butt headed and all these older heads around here say give it to her. It will do her good. But I won't listen anymore.

Your uncle Ike [Ike Rountree] has been here tonight and bored me to death. I was waiting to write to you and he would not go. He is so interested in you and your condition now. I guess I ought to appreciate that anyway. He and Mr. Murchison are planning a fishing trip for tomorrow but he said he would come back tomorrow night to see if I had heard anymore. I'm expecting your father tomorrow afternoon. He wrote me Monday that he would be here if your condition permitted, I think he is on his way to Boston [Georgia] and intends coming by to hear from you before he goes. He wrote that he was going to bring the children some cane [sugar cane] which was cut during October and November.

I had a letter from Mary Lou [Mary Lou Rountree was Otis' sister] this morning. She was anxious to hear directly from you, said she had written you but did not know whether you got it or not.

Do have your nurse or Dr. Thompson to write me till you are able to write yourself. I feel like I can't stand it if I don't hear from you real soon. I appreciate him sending those telegrams but I want more now. Have you gotten any of my letters or the package of pajamas?

I feel so blue and lonesome for you tonight. If I could see you and talk to you for a little while I would feel better. Take good care of yourself so you can soon come home.

Lots of Love,
Clyde

October 22, 1920
Friday Evening

My Dear Otis,

I am sending you this letter special delivery so you will be sure to get at least one from me . . .
You must not exert yourself too much, but write me as often as you can.
Otis, the baby [Dorothy] is not well yet...She is perfectly miserable after each meal, she is puffed up so tight. Dr. Williams told me to use limewater in her milk and I have done that today. I think I will give her oil tonight and keep her on buttermilk for several days. Am giving her scrape steak and strained oatmeal and toast.
Ruth French entertained the club this afternoon, came over and insisted on my going, but I did not feel equal to it. I took the children to Lyons, got James a hat and Virginia a sweater. Am driving very well now, learn a little more about it each time I drive. The roads are so dusty it isn't much pleasure to ride now though.
James tells me something to tell you every day, it is usually something else that he wants you to bring him though. He says too to tell you that he still has his wagon not torn up. He and Virginia are both doing fine, are fat and rosy as can be...
Take good care of yourself sweetheart, I want to see you more than anyone thing I know, but I want to see you well and in good shape. Life without you would not be worth living for me.

Clyde

Author's Note: This is a post card. Again the mystery about October 5th . This card was dated fifteen days later.

Rochester, MN
October 21, 1920

Dear Clyde,

Your letter received today. I wrote him yesterday. The package came Tuesday. All okay, but heavy for the climate. The only bed covering I sleep under is one sheet, some nights without it. Wouldn't have thought it, would you?

Doing well today. Just had instructions to get out of bed Saturday and will leave the hospital about Tuesday. What do you think of that?

Thompson has not been out since Monday, but I hear that his throat is doing alright. Looking for him this p.m.

Keep Lucille, hear? You and Mrs. Holmes need her.

Expect I'll stay here at least a week after getting out for recuperation and dentistry. I want everything done to me necessary. Look about October fifth.

J.O.R.

Cobbtown, GA
October 22, 1920
Friday Night

Dear Otis,

Your card came today. I was so glad to get a hearing from you. Clyde is very thoughtful to let us know as soon as she heard anything from you. Had a note from her today saying they were all well, but she hadn't heard anything since Monday. I am all alone tonight, except Joshua and he is asleep. Emma and Buster are going with Mrs. Hicks and her children to a cane grinding.

Papa left yesterday morning for Boston to spend a week or two with your Uncle Joe and to fish. He is bad as a little boy about fishing. Hope he has a good time. I think your Uncle Ike was going with him. I expect he'd just as soon he didn't go though. I didn't hear him express himself. Joshua is going to school. He seems to do all right, but I am afraid he is not going to learn very easy. He reads right along without looking in his book (very much better than he does to look at it). That kind is hard to do anything with. The others seem to be getting on fine. Another year, and you will begin to realize what it is to have children in school. We are having beautiful weather, except dry. Hasn't rained since I was at your house. Had a letter from Sam today. They seem to be well, but look as broke as usual. He sent us a dozen Japanese persimmons. They are very large and beautiful to look at. I like them real well. Says he is going to send us a crate. I don't think we need so many at a time. I don't know how to preserve them. I had a letter from Amanda today. They are always in a stew. I don't see what it is become of them. Will send you Amanda's letter. The children have come. Will quit and go to bed. So hope you will soon be feeling fine and receive much good from the treatment.

With a Heart Full of Love,
Mamma

October 24, 1920
Sunday Evening

My Dear,

I am so lonesome for you tonight. I want to see you so bad. I wish you were ready to come home now, took the children to ride this afternoon, I could not enjoy the ride except for their sakes. They enjoyed it, and I tried to carry them where they wanted to go. Dorothy began begging for something to eat before we could get home though and spoiled part of the ride anyway.

She has seemed better today, so I gave her another irrigation tonight. The distension has been bad, though not as bad yesterday. I gave her buttermilk, oatmeal cream of wheat with some chicken juice on it, and toast, is that a good diet? She has seemed better but begs for something to eat all the time. I gave her some orange juice this morning, too.

We are having our last service in the old church tonight, not having a sermon just talks by different ones. Wish I could have gone, but I guess my church going is over for a while anyway.

Write me what they do to you where they operated. Are you going to have to keep on taking soda? Will it take so long for your stomach to empty itself? And tell me all about it...

You must write me as often as you can. Your letters mean so much to me since I can't see you.

Love,
Clyde

Rochester, MN
October 24, 1920
Sunday P.M.

My Dear Clyde,

I received your letters of Tuesday and Wednesday this morning. Sorry to hear of Dorothy's set back, but it is not likely to amount to much. You will have to be careful with her for some time. You never mentioned your own condition, except that you are tired. I hope you are keeping yourself in good shape. I told Dr. Thompson to see you as soon as he gets home, which will be Tuesday.

He had his tonsils removed and was to have a Submucous Resection (the operation we had in Augusta) but he gets cold feet. He had a right bad case of homesickness, aggravated by worry over the financial outlook at home, so he had all he could stand. If there is another person from Georgia besides myself in Rochester I haven't heard from him, so I may soon get the same complaint. I am walking around the hospital and will leave about middle of the week. I will have to stay downtown then for awhile. They say it is generally about three weeks from the time of the operation until the patient is dismissed from the clinic. I still believe I will get home about the fifth of November. I will have to lose two, possibly four – one upper and three lower front teeth. Don't say anything about that, though, for I hope to get them replaced before leaving here.

It is just about as cold here now as our winter, but today is so pretty, fair a day as you ever saw. If I just had my sweetheart and the kids, together with the car and some help up here, we will soon be on the road to Georgia. We have lots of good times coming to us on Georgia roads, though I would love to be home and riding with you this afternoon, but I have reconciled myself to the fact that I am in Rochester for improved health and I will stay until I have all the good there is for me.

All the same I love my little family and I know I am blessed with one of the very best of wives. More tomorrow.

Love,
Otis

Author's Note: This is another letter from Wash Rountree to Otis. Apparently, he has gone to see his brother in Boston, Georgia.

US Post Office
J.B. Rountree Postmaster
Boston, Ga.

Boston, GA
October 24, 1920
Sunday

Dear Otis,

Came here on Thursday night, and before leaving, for some days and since I have been here, have had no suitable chance to write you. I ran over to Vidalia Thursday morning, and carried Clyde some work and cane for the children. Then caught the westbound Seaboard and got in here by bedtime. Yesterday, I got a letter from Emma with a card from you and a letter from Sam. This p.m. I am expecting another letter from home, and I hope more news from you. Clyde had written them since I left, so I heard from nearly all. We rejoice to know you are doing so well, and hope to see you home soon. Have just read our family history as published in our County paper years ago. Your Uncle Joe has kept it. It is more than I can write now, but will say all Rountrees, however, spelled now came from one child found abandoned under a Rowan tree in Shropshire, England. Will get you a copy of the history when I have time. Don't know just when I will leave from home, though tomorrow or Tuesday. My health is good. Will have to close here to get this off on present mail. Also hope you may improve rapidly and soon be home. Have been very anxious about you.

Best wishes for your welfare.

Your Pa

Appling, GA
October 24, 1920
Sunday Night

My Dear Otis,

Just got your card today. You don't know how glad I am that you are improving. I sure have thought about you often since you have been away, but could hear nothing only what Clyde wrote me a time or two...

I sure do feel like I am a long ways from home sometimes, but in spite of that I am happy for Gus is as good as can be to me.

Gus's brother gave us a chest of silver for a wedding present. It hasn't come yet, and I am just crazy to see it. Folks sure have been good to us. We have three of the prettiest hounds you ever saw. I hated them when they first came, but I am worse than Gus about them now. He hunts all the morning while I teach. We have all the rabbit to eat we care about and then some.

My health is almost perfect now. I seldom ever have indigestion. That is due to the fact that we have nothing to eat but just good wholesome things. We can't afford fancies for money is a scarce article.

Let me hear from you as often as you can.

Heart Full of Love,
Mary Lou

Author's Note: I don't understand this deal about Miss Willie. Do you?

Vidalia, GA
October 26, 1920

My Dear,

Your card brought me good news today. I'm so glad you are doing so well. I feel like it won't be very long before you will be at home again. Don't be in too big a hurry though and come before you're able. I am so anxious to see you and want you at home so bad, but I want you to be well after this.

I am glad Dr. Thompson is doing nicely since his operation, guess he will soon be at home again. Tom Willet's little girl, Jeanette, has pneumonia and is real sick, I think.

Mrs. Jones' baby is real sick, too, they say one of her lungs is affected. One of the girls dropped her yesterday and she fainted. Then Mrs. Jones fainted, too. I have not been down to see them but feel anxious about them, it is time for her to be sick tomorrow. They had Dr. Mercer with the baby.

Miss Willie Walker and Mr. Jim Glaze married Sunday. Aunt Kate says Mr. Walker came over today and talked to her about it. He cried and she cried. She was grieving because she had picked out

Miss Willie for the husband when she cracked...

Mr. Lee Lailor phoned me to get my syrup bottles ready and he would send for them this week and fill them. I had Lucille wash them today and get them all ready. Guess I will let him fill them all. Write me as often as you can.

Lots of Love,
Clyde

Rochester, MN
October 26, 1920
Tuesday A.M.

Dear Clyde,

I never wrote you yesterday, so will do so this morning. There's nothing of interest to you here except my condition, for I've certainly gotten out of our world.

How is my sweetheart doing this morning? I hope you are feeling good and fit for anything. I'd rather see you than anyone on earth this morning, for I'm getting a bit homesick now. If you and the children could only come and see me every day I should not get impatient. But probably I'll be back in another week or two. That's not a long time, is it? And so then I hope we'll all be well and happy. They wanted to get me out of the hospital today, but I shall have to stay here in Rochester another week or two anyway. So I shan't leave right now. I've just had a dose of Castor oil prescribed.

Hope you're getting lots of pleasure from the car. Get out as often as you can. Tell Mrs. Holmes to use it anytime she wants to and can get a driver. I guess she's afraid of it, isn't she?

Tell the children to be good and I'll stop over in Chicago on my way home and see if I can't find them some things. If you have anything to suggest that you'd like me to get for them or yourself or Mrs. Holmes, write me.

Tell Charlie Fowler that he'll have to wait till I get home. I don't *see how I missed his account it is not posted, so I know you could not get it up. If he wants to pay anything on it, though, you haven't forgotten how to receive it. His account could total $50, at least and is more I think. Tell George to add to his list Mrs. Flossie Hightower $11, Louise Blocker $12.50, AL Van $5, Charlie Dire $2.*

The mail has just come and your letter of Thursday and Friday, one from Mr. Mather and one from mama came. That helps after receiving none since Saturday.

Perhaps you're giving Dorothy too much food at the time. What you are giving her is alright. Those cases always improve slowly, but I hope she'll soon get better. If you should hear of Mulheirn anywhere around have him come to see her. If you are in condition I'd suggest your taking her up there.

I think I wrote you that I received the package and have gotten most of your letters. Write often.

Otis

Author's Note: When reading this letter, it should be remembered that Clyde was quite far along in her pregnancy. Dr. Thompson had been with Otis and accompanied him to Rochester, and was in attendance at the operation.

October 27, 1920
Wednesday A.M.

My Dear Otis,

I was delighted yesterday morning when Dr. Thompson came in to see me. I felt like I was getting direct news from you. I surely did ask him a lot of questions too. He says you are doing fine but they will probably keep you up there for about two weeks longer for observation. I want you to stay as long as is necessary but I certainly am getting impatient and anxious about you.

Dr. Thompson asked me all about myself and advised me to

take salts and cream of tartar every morning. Said he would fix me a tonic too, but I told him I didn't think that was necessary. I feel perfectly well. The only thing, my ankles have been swelling some but I have to do some machine sewing everyday. I have done so little. I guess the salts will relieve that...

Mr. Rountree [Wash] came through yesterday on his way back from Boston [Georgia], has been attending an Association down there [Primitive Baptist]. I took him over to see Mrs. Stubbs yesterday afternoon. He seemed to enjoy talking to her and Mrs. Gay. I went on and carried the clothes and cane back by for him. He was certainly anxious to get home but Everett Aldmore said he would charge him six dollars to take him so he decided to wait for the train.

Dorothy seems much better this morning, is in such a good humor, her eyes better and her stomach better...

Sweetheart, do write me as often as you can, and feel like it. I miss you so much, I try to be bright and cheerful but it is so hard when I am really so lonesome for you. Mr. McBride is coming so I will have to close.

Lots of love,
Clyde

Rochester, MN
October 27, 1920
Wednesday P.M.

Dear Clyde,

The letter you wrote Saturday a.m. came this morning. Mail service seems to be very poor. I wonder if you have been getting my letters?

I thought I'd get out to the hospital tonight but they put me off for at least another day. They have me on a diet and some more stomach washing scheduled for tomorrow. It will not be long, though *for they have promised to rush me through.*

I'm feeling good and doing as well as I could, but I want to get it all over with and on my way back home. I'm impatient at any delay.

Everyone here is talking of the fine weather. Today there was a thunderstorm and heavy rain. These people say they expected it to end in a heavy sleet and snow, but it faired off warm.

I'm mighty glad Virginia did so well and I hope that you and Dorothy are improving. <u>Don't forget to take care of yourself,</u> if you have to get still another nigger.

Have you driven the car? Take the children out everyday. It'll do you good.

Will let you know more about things tomorrow.

Lovingly,
Otis

Vidalia, GA
October 30, 1920
Saturday A.M.

My Dear,

I did not write you yesterday, was busy in the morning and went to Mount Vernon with Aunt Kate yesterday afternoon…

I received your letter written Tuesday last night and am so glad you are doing so nicely. I am getting very impatient for you to get home, though I want you to stay as long s they think necessary. I miss you so and want to see you so bad I can hardly stand it sometimes. The nearer the time for your return it seems so much harder for me to wait. I realize more and more every day that I love you and the children with my whole life.

Dorothy is doing much better and have not had any trouble with her for the last few days. She is not herself exactly yet, but not near as cross as she has been. She is not as fat as she was before she got sick, but is gaining real fast. Mrs. Rattry, Mrs. Youngblood, Mrs. Brinson, and Mrs. Spurgeon Meadows all have new babies. I think all of them are girls. Mrs. Jones is still up though I think she has been expecting to be sick [have her baby] all this week. Dr. Thompson told me to send a specimen of my urine up there to him. I don't think it is necessary, but I guess I had better do it, don't you? I don't like this idea of being without my doctor a bit. I don't care about your getting us anything in Chicago. I would rather have you home than anything else. Virginia needs some shoes. She wears an 8. Mattie needs a hat, a black felt sailor would suit better than anything else. Socks or fay stockings for all of them would be nice. Would like to have some wholeproof hose for myself. These are things they will have to have and they would appreciate them as much as anything.

Write me when you can.

Lots of Love,
Clyde

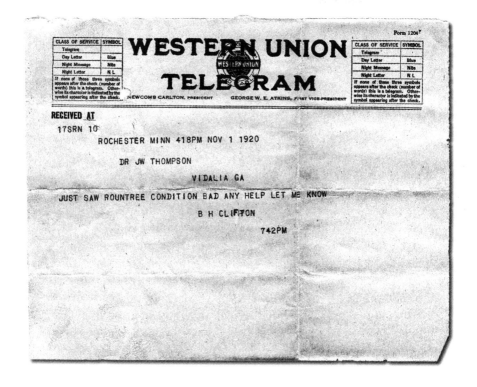

358

Author's Note: This letter was obviously written to Otis the night before he died. It was mailed on November the first, the day he died.

Vidalia, GA
October 31, 1920
Sunday Evening

My Dearest,

I am nearly crazy tonight. I am so worried about you, and you are so far away. I can't go to see you. I do not feel like I can even get a message that is satisfactory, a telegram is not very explicit, and a letter is old by the time it gets here. I wish I could hear directly from you tonight, do have them to keep me posted if you are not able yourself.

We are all well. The baby is doing better and looking lots better. The only thing troubling now is your absence. Otis, do take care of yourself and be careful of your diet, you know better than they do what you can eat. I want you to hurry and be back home if you do have to stay on a diet.

The Methodists went into the new church today and had quite a crowd. Mr. Ike Rountree [Otis' uncle] was here tonight on his way to church, carried his wife to the Primitive [Primitive Baptist Church], but said he was a Methodist as long as brother Malther was here. Chester Shuman and Mrs. Morris were married in the new church tonight, about 6:30, and left on the MD&S train for Macon, Jacksonville, and other points south. There was a returned soldier buried out here at the cemetery this afternoon, a man named Booth. They had a military service, had several of the town boys here who were in the Army in their uniforms and with their guns.

Mrs. Fanning, Aunt Kate, and Miss Susie Mae and Ben have all been in to ask about you and interrupted my letter. Will write more next time.

Lots of Love,
Clyde

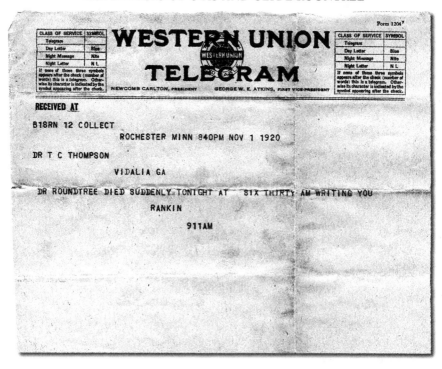

WESTERN UNION TELEGRAM

NEWCOMB CARLTON, PRESIDENT   GEORGE W. E. ATKINS, FIRST VICE-PRESIDENT

RECEIVED AT

B1SRN 12 COLLECT

ROCHESTER MINN 840PM NOV 1 1920

DR T C THOMPSON

VIDALIA GA

DR ROUNDTREE DIED SUDDENLY TONIGHT AT SIX THIRTY AM WRITING YOU

RANKIN

911AM

Author's Note: A letter from Amanda Rountree, who was Ridge Rountree's widow.

November 1, 1920

Dear Clyde,

Clyde! What can I say? Nothing but that I know every inch of the ground over which you are now traveling. My heart has bled! Every anxiety, every prayer! Ah, my blessed girl, I know, I know, and I would give anything if I could just be with you tonight and tomorrow and the next day! You will not miss me though, as there will be so many. But I shall be there, too, in spirit! I simply have not the money or I would stop this week and go, but things are terribly hard up at home and the last few dollars I have in George's [George Rountree, Vidalia Banker] bank account I expect to use for bread this winter. Nothing but dire necessity can keep me away from you and Otis and mother tonight. I had a message from George this

THE FIRST NATIONAL BANK OF VIDALIA

CAPITAL $ 35.000.00
9879

W.O.DONOVAN, PRESIDENT.
J. W. SHARPE, VICE-PRESIDENT.
J. B. MANRY, VICE-PRESIDENT.
GEO. S. ROUNTREE, CASHIER.
T. W. WILLETS, JR., ASST. CASHIER.

VIDALIA, GA.,

MAYO CLINIC
ROCHESTER, MINN.

Dr E.Starr Judd

Nov.3.1920.

Dr T.C.Thompson,
~~First~~ Vidalia, Ga.

Dear Dr. Thompson;-

Dr Rankin wired you regarding Dr Rountree, who died suddenly on Monday night.

As you will recall, when you left, his convalescence had been normal in every way. It continued this way until the 9th. day without the slightest indication of any deviation from a normal convalescence. On that day he was dismissed and was ready to leave the hospital when he complained of nausea and vomited. We kept him in the hospital on this account and from then on his condition was intermittently improved, until Sunday evening, when he suddenly developed the Cheyne Stokes type of respiration and this continued until his death. At no time was there any increa se in his pulse rate or any temperature. His abdomen was never tender or ballooned, and stomach washing resorted to regularly every 6 hours never showed more than 6 oz. except the first washing on the 9th. day which was about 16 oz.

We could not locate any condition complicating his convalescence and were confident that his stomach was without infection, and felt that vomiting was due to one of those cydes which sometimes occur following gastroenterostomy and which at times it is impossible to explain. At autopsy his abdomen to be absolutely free from infection and his gastroenterostomy was loose and patent. The stomach which had not been washed in 12 hours contained a few ounces of gastric contents. The ~~jejunum~~ jejunum was bound down by a few old adhesions which you saw at operation, but there was no evidence of stasis. Examination of chest showed a slight bronchial pneumonia, which no doubt was a terminal affair.

You readily understand that we are at a loss to explain th exact cause of his death. We had several medical and surgical men see him in consultation and acted upon their suggestions, but nothing seemed to have any effect upon his condition, and we regret very much indeed that the case terminated as it did.

Yours truly, E.S.Judd.

COPY .

361

Form 1204

WESTERN UNION TELEGRAM

CLASS OF SERVICE	SYMBOL
Telegram	
Day Letter	Blue
Night Message	Nite
Night Letter	N L

If none of these three symbols appears after the check (number of words) this is a telegram. Otherwise its character is indicated by the symbol appearing after the check.

NEWCOMB CARLTON, PRESIDENT   GEORGE W. E. ATKINS, FIRST VICE-PRESIDENT

CLASS OF SERVICE	SYMBOL
Telegram	
Day Letter	Blue
Night Message	Nite
Night Letter	N L

If none of these three symbols appears after the check (number of words) this is a telegram. Otherwise its character is indicated by the symbol appearing after the check.

RECEIVED AT

B12SRN 9

BOSTON MA 220PM NOV 2 1920

MRS CLYDE ROUNTREE

VIDALIA GA

YOU HAVE OUR DEEPEST SYMPATHY   IN THIS DARK HOUR

J B ROUNTREE

237PM

afternoon at 2:30, so glad he knew to wire me when I know his hands were so full. It seems that it is unbearable and no ordinary human can stand it, but Clyde, we can't be ordinary under these conditions. You had him five years and five months (less three days) longer than I had Ridge! So God was good! I know you have been in the past the bravest thing in the world. Now when the time has come to make the ultimate sacrifice, you will not be found wanting, for his sake. I have tried to figure out how I could go, but it would not work out all right. So here I just sit thinking and praying that you are strong.

God Bless You,
Amanda

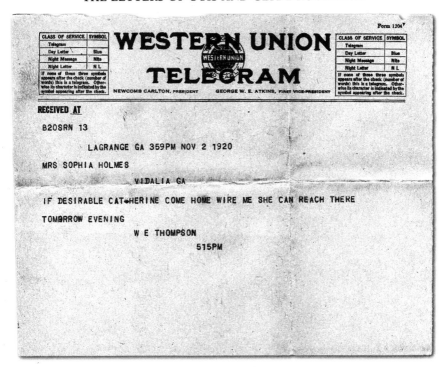

November 1920

My Dear Clyde,

I am too grieved to try to write you a letter, but I must say my whole heart goes out to you in this sad hour. The only thing I can think to say that might be of value is to remember him who said, "Come onto me all ye that are heavy laden and I will give you rest" and to his Disciples "be not afraid it is I."

I cannot understand why you are called upon to suffer this great affliction just now, but some day it will be white light of eternity it may be revealed. I have just written to George to keep me posted as to when the body arrives and when the funeral will be. I will be with you at that time. God bless you and your darlings.

Very Sincerely,
Jot Flanders

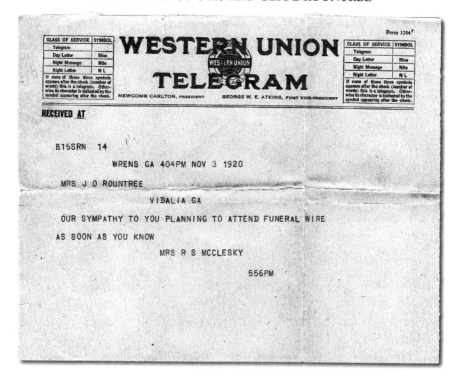

Author's Note: Below is a letter from a patient in Canoochee. You will remember Otis practiced in Canoochee before he and Clyde moved to Vidalia.

Canoochee, GA
November 4, 1920

Dear Clyde,

We are made to feel so sad when we received the sad news that Dr. Rountree was dead. We certainly sympathize with you in your trouble but we hope that our loss was His gain. But we certainly hate to give him up. We sure loved him as a man and also as a doctor. He was so good to us when John was sick. We were talking of him one night last week and I told John if he ever got sick I would have Dr. Rountree. I didn't know he was sick but the Lord never puts more on us than we can bear. I hope he will be with you and the

*children and help and strengthen you in this sad trouble. Would love
so much to come and see him one more time. You have my prayers
and sympathy.*

Love to Each,
Mrs. J.J. Willoughby

Author's Note: Uncle Jot was cashier of the People's Bank in what was
then Summitt, Georgia. Summitt is now part of Twin City.
Jot Flanders was Zannie's brother and had no children.

Summitt, GA
November 7, 1920

My Dear Clyde,

*We are loving you and sympathizing with you with our whole
heart. I just wish I could do something that would be cheerful and
helpful to you. I know that you are a dandy sweet girl, brave, and
true to God and while you are troubled at this particular dispensation
of his providence, you will still be sweet and submissive. I was so
glad and heavy hearted all the time I was with you, I felt like I was
a burden instead of a pleasure, but I did love Otis so much, I was
heartbroken.*

*I want to love and be lots of comfort and help to you and your
dear babies. I wish I was where I could see after you often. I want
you to let me have Jim and Virginia some along. If you will let them
come visit me some I will be so glad.*

*Clyde, we are planning next week to go to conference [Methodist
conference] to be back home two weeks from today. Then we want
to come stay a week or so with you. You may feel like you can't, but
you can, and now please do. I just want you with us some. I feel like
we can be of some comfort and cheer to you but we cannot much
this far from you. I know you feel like now you never will get over
your trouble, but you must begin to feel another way and look to
God for light. He will surely give it. He is light himself and we trust*

Mr. and Mrs. Jot Flanders. Jot was a great friend to Otis, before and after his death.

him and follow him. We will not stumble or fall. It will be awful hard for you to find the first step in the light but when you find the first one you can find the second. That way we have to go on . . .

I was pleased with the way people looked after you and the beautiful floral offerings. I was overcome, and just went about the house all the time choked with emotion. It was such a satisfaction to see how people loved him and how they love and sympathize with you and the children.

If you need me for anything that you might have an idea I can do for you, I just beg you to call on me and let me know what little I can. If you were to need me and I didn't know it, I could not help you. But if I did know, then I could have a place to discharge a duty I cherish . . .

God bless you and keep you all is my prayer. Give my regards to your mother. We love her like our mother – almost.

Very Sincerely,
Uncle Jot

Author's Note: The note below is from Madeline and Ivy Rountree. Otis lived with Ivy some while they were in elementary school. Otis and Ivy were first cousins. Ivy was the father of Bill Rountree of Swainsboro.

Dearest Clyde,

Our hearts go out to you in deepest sympathy. At a time like this, there is so little of comfort that can be shared.

May the Great Comforter be very near to you and give you strength with a heart full of love.

Madeline and Ivy Rountree

Author's Note: For several years I have been an agent with New York Life. It was quite a pleasant surprise to find this letter written by a New York Life Agent. The letter expresses sympathy and is written on New York Life stationery. I wrote the company to research whether or not Otis and Clyde had insurance with our company.

Mr. Steve Nelson, who was head of the southeastern zone service center, was kind enough to research this and informed me that Otis had apparently tried to get insurance with the company but because of his stomach condition was uninsurable.

Clyde, however, had a policy with New York Life written by George Rountree, who was a long-time agent with our company. Below is the letter of sympathy, written by Agent, Murphy Norris. I have this letter framed hanging in my office. It was given to me by Becky Grist Waldron.

James Otis Rountree, Jr., a good-looking young man.

New York Life
Darwin P. Kingsley, President

Wade, GA
November 8, 1920

Dear Clyde:

In this hour of your grief I want to tell you that my heart goes out to you and your children, over the loss of Otis.
Someday we will be able to understand the workings of a Divine Being and I know your knowledge of Him will be a wonderful consolation to you now...
In love to you and the children.

Believe Me, Your Friend,
Murphy Norris

Author's Note: Dr. Meadows was a very good friend of Dr. Rountree. Dr. Meadows died at a young age shortly before Dr. Rountree. Mrs. Meadows remained a good friend of the Rountree family.

My Dear, Dear Clyde,

A letter from Vidalia has just brought me the news of Dr. Rountree's death, and oh, little girl, how I do sympathize with you! How I long to do the impossible and say one thing that would make your anguish less, but too well I know that while you are so grateful for the kindly words and deeds of loved ones, no pen, no tongue, no deed can lift the crushing load of grief from your stricken soul. And though time may take off the edge of our suffering, the unutterable loneliness remains.
I have never known of two cases so nearly parallel as ours, and when I think of the children, his children, I know you must have something to live for still. They are such little darlings. I do

not know any children who have appealed to me more or have a warmer place in my heart. As great as the responsibility of raising them, life without them would be intolerable. Then, too, you have, as I have, a wonderful mother to help you. We cannot understand it. So many times I have thought that from a human standpoint it would have been much better for me to have been taken than Dr. Jim (Dr. Jim Meadows), when I served in such a limited spear and he, in so much wider one...

The children are like mine, too small to realize their loss, but isn't it wonderful to think that when they have grown older no one will be able to tell them anything that is not good and noble of their father.

I cannot write – my own grief comes back so fresh upon my soul that I hardly know whether I sorrow for it or for your own, but I just wanted you to know that my sympathy and my prayers are yours. Mama joins me in this, and we pray that you may be able to know that.

Sincerely Your Friend,
Carolyn Harris Meadows

Author's Note: Below is part of a letter from Mrs. Moye, wife of Dr. Moye, a close friend of Otis. Mrs. Moye lived in Atlanta.

...I feel that in the death of Dr. Rountree, Vidalia and the profession have had a distinct loss. Because of my love for you and the high esteem in which Dr. Moye held Dr. Rountree, I feel a personal loss. It seems hard for one with such a brilliant future to have to lay down his work so early, but we must try to realize that God knows best. How my heart aches for you and those dear little ones. I wish I could do or say something to help you.

Sincerely Your Friend,
Kittie Moye

Author's Note: This is part of a letter written to Sophie Holmes from Lizzie Parrish, Sophie's aunt. The first part of the letter expresses concern for Clyde and the children and also says how glad she is that Clyde is living with Sophie. An interesting take on the post WWI economy.
Take up the letter in the middle:

Sister Sophie, I do hope money matters are easier and business not so congested in your town as they are in ours. Have never seen the equal before. Cotton crop was short and prices far below the cost of production, and people are in bad shape. Merchants are overloaded, can't sell or collect either, so they are as blue as the farmers. We are fine, almost nothing. Wear what we had last winter, and eat what we have raised. As to money I believe it is harder to get than I have ever known before. We have held cotton so far, but prices decrease instead of getting better. People who have seemed before to have been in good financial shape are now pressed also. . .

December 9, 1920

Dear Clyde,

My heartiest congratulations to you on the arrival of another sweet little daughter.

Hope you are both doing fine now. So sorry to hear of your recent illness.

Hope you may speedily recover your strength and health again, that you may be prepared to fill the grandest calling on earth -- mother. God in his love has given you such sweet children to cheer and comfort you, and for such blessings we should thank and praise God. Your task continues, and it may seem greater than you consider your ability, yet God promises to help those who ask him and tells us that all things work for good to those who love the Lord, and I am sure you and the family all love Him. So, doubtless your heart still bleeds. It could not be otherwise, yet we must try to be reconciled to God's will. Dearest, I know you will experience many lonely hours to follow your sad loss, but remember you have our sympathy as sincere as it is possible to sympathize and our prayers also.

Dearest, it should afford you much joy and comfort to think of your departed loved one as an ideal man. A universal benefactor, so faithful to his home and of life's duties. So many friends in his daily devotion as a Christian...

It is getting real cloudy. Think it should rain and turn cold. Then hog killing time is on the program for us. We have eaten some small shoats, but have had none to make sausage yet. ...

Well, Christmas is almost here but I can't rejoice as the kiddies do, for we have sold no cotton yet and money matters are tight. Hoping you and yours a happy, pleasant time. Will Katherine come home for the holidays? I do want to see her, in fact, all of you so much. Hope Katherine will have a pleasant, successful year at school. How is Sister Sophie getting along collecting her rents? Times are hard here.

I am so glad you and Sister Sophie can live together and be helpful to one another and so much company to each other.

Well, I must close. Give my love to Sister Sophie and love and fond kisses to your sweet children. May Jesus the Great Comforter bless you and sympathy to each of you.

Love,
Lizzie [Parrish]

Author's Note: This is a letter from Mr. Everhart. Clyde sent Otis's medical instruments to him in order to have them sold. As you can see, she did not do very well on the sale.

Dear Mrs. Rountree:

In reply to yours of the twenty-first, beg you say that I have sold $13.25 worth of Dr. Rountree's instruments, and after deducting his bill of $11.67, leaves a net amount of $1.50 due you, check for which I have enclosed herein ...

Yours Very Truly,
Laurence Everhart

AFTER OTIS' DEATH

This picture was taken less than a year after Otis' death. L to R - Sophie Holmes holding Christine, Clyde Rountree holding Dorothy, Clyde's sister Katherine, James Otis Rountree, Jr.

Sixteen days after Otis' death, Clyde was faced not only with the ongoing tragedy of her great loss, but the conflicting joyous emotion of Christine's birth. Experts say that it takes months to begin to sort out such a traumatic occurrence. As a part of dealing with such a death, persons have difficulty with even life's most mundane tasks. However, Clyde did not have the luxury of such a personal mourning period. Christine was born and there were three other young children to care for.

The death of Otis brought Clyde not only huge personal tragedy but significant financial challenges. She was left with sorting out the loss of income, disposing of Otis' practice, collecting unpaid fees, and trying to figure out how she could raise and educate four young children. Clyde was fortunate to have received a good education, enabling her to pursue a career in teaching. Clyde sold the house on Durden Street and moved in with her mother, Sophie Holmes. Sophie was also a widow, having lost her husband, Robert, when Clyde was 15 years old.

Right after Otis' death, Clyde taught music and took care of her very young children. In 1923, she received a teaching certificate and began a 39-year career in public education. Clyde's first assignment was in a one-teacher schoolhouse. She then moved to a three-teacher schoolhouse and also served as principal.

Clyde taught in several rural communities – Center for six years, Mt. Vernon for three years, and Alston for eight years. In 1944, Clyde was appointed teacher of history and civics at Vidalia High School. In 1947, she became the Vidalia High School Librarian.

In 1912, Clyde had received a certificate in music from LaGrange College. So, in order to further her education, she began taking her children to Athens, Georgia, each summer in order to receive a Bachelor's of Science in Education. The University of Georgia had programs for the students' children that Dorothy still remembers fondly. Mrs. Rountree also earned a

The Vidalia High School football team about 1930. James is second row, third from the right. James played center.

Even in 1925, mischievous little boys stressed little girls. Front L to R - Virginia, Dorothy, and Christine Rountree. Back - William Wilson.

Back row, L to R - William Wilson, Virginia Rountree, and James Rountree. Front row, L to R - Christine and Dorothy Rountree.

Master's degree in Library Science from Peabody College. When Christine was born, Uncle Jot Flanders offered to raise her in his home. Mr. and Mrs. Flanders were childless and Uncle Jot and Otis were very close. However, Clyde would not hear of it. Uncle El Flanders, a prosperous banker and widowed brother of Jot, wanted to court Clyde, but she was not interested. She devoted the remainder of her life to her children and her profession.

Clyde was also active in the First Methodist Church, as well as the Daughters of the American Revolution. She also served as Regent of the D.A.R. In 1962, Clyde retired from teaching and became librarian at Brewton Parker College.

A few years after Clyde retired, Dorothy Budd accompanied her back to Alston to look for the old schoolhouse. After stopping for directions, Clyde asked a man if she had taught him. "Yes, ma'am, Miss Rountree. I'm Toodle. You teeched me, but you didn't larn me nothin' – but you wuz nice."

Dorothy said that many times, Clyde and the children would eat Sunday dinner with a student's family. After church, they would get in the Ford and travel to the country. Mother said that the host's table would groan with so many gastronomic delicacies. Fried chicken, country ham, cornbread made with buttermilk, fried okra, home-grown tomatoes, snap beans cooked with fatback, creamed corn, butter beans, turnip greens, biscuits made with lard, sweet potato pie, pecan pie, and a bottle of cane syrup for soppin'.

When the schools were closed in these small communities, Clyde recognized this as a great mistake. She always said that the center of the community was the school and the church, and that the closing of these schools would decimate the community. History proved her to be correct.

Clyde with her four children. L to R - Christine, Virginia, Dorothy, and James Otis, Jr.

L to R - Clyde, James, and Sophie, taken about 1937.

The following is an excerpt of a letter from Bill Warthen, who grew up with Christine and Dorothy Rountree in Vidalia:

"My Dad was aware of the serious problems your Grandmother [Clyde] had raising four children, the oldest only 6, with Agricultural Depression beginning in 1921, continuing through the 20's, and getting much worse when banks began to fail in the early 30's, Clyde had to teach and principal the rural school at Center. Her pay during this time was no more than $70.00 a month, for five to seven months, and much of that time there would be months in which the county could not pay, and script would be issued and the teacher had to find a property owner

Two loving sisters - Dorothy (left) and Christine Rountree.

Two close sisters - Christine Rountree Anderson (left) and Dorothy Rountree Budd.

who would pay her cash, and then the property owner would pay his taxes with the script, obtained at eighty to ninety cents on the dollar. My Aunt taught with Mrs. Rountree, and she too was having a very difficult time. Knowing the family well, Daddy always told me Clyde's brothers had to be helping her out. This situation was prevalent everywhere in America, but the burden of four small children was extreme, but they had a wonderful home, a very supportive and popular Grand Mother, a great many friends, and the entire Family was very important to their Methodist Church."

Dorothy, with tears in her eyes, would relate that the most pleasant sound she could remember was that of Clyde's car coming home. When Dorothy was in her second year at Wesleyan College, Clyde lost her job. Dorothy offered to come home, but Clyde said they would "stay the course." She was a truly remarkable lady.

Author's Note: Dr. Rountree first practiced in Emanuel County. Apparently this debt was collected from a bill before he moved to Vidalia. Jot was good at collecting a debt.

AFTER OTIS' DEATH

Swainsboro, GA
March 2, 1921

My Dear Clyde,

I am of the opinion you will be surprised at this letter. I am myself. I collected from a fellow for you this morning $10.

Otis did some work for [name withheld], and drew a draft on him and left it here a long time ago. He always put me off with a little excuse, but enough to get away. Today I made an appeal to him to help you and them dear little children, and he paid me $10 and told me he would pay you the other $10 next fall. I told him thank you, we were delighted to wait on him until fall. I am so proud to get this if we never get the other. It is better than the others have done.

God bless you and yours. I think of you so often. Hurry and get ready to come see us. We want you a long time, you know.

Sincerely,
Uncle Jot

Dedication

Because she has given of herself: her time, her abilities and her love, to make high school life more enjoyable for so many, it is with great pleasure that we, the Senior Class and the Hobachee Staff of 1962, dedicate this issue of our yearbook to Mrs. Clyde Rountree.

Mrs. Rountree is always ready to help each student in the library with any problems. She has also served as advisor for the annual since 1948—so long that Hobachee and Rountree have become almost synonymous.

For all her services to each of us and to our school, we thank her.

MRS. CLYDE ROUNTREE

Mrs. Rountree is retiring this year after 39 years of service.

381

The Children of Otis and Clyde Rountree

James Otis Rountree, Jr.   Dorothy Rountree (Budd)
Virginia Rountree (Grist)   Christine Rountree (Anderson)

JAMES OTIS ROUNTREE, JR.

By Dr. James Otis Rountree, III

Early life without a father means no one to teach a young man how to fish, how to be honorable, how to focus on the task at hand, or how to be a gentleman. These things Bubba had to learn for himself and learn he did. Fathers know, usually, how and when to tighten the leash on adolescent boys and even though Bubba had no father during his formative years, he would remember fondly that grandmamma, Sophie Holmes, would supply any strict discipline that may have been necessary. However, from many talks from my father, I believe Bubba had so much love and respect for M'Dear and felt so much responsibility for her and the rest of the family that he would have never intentionally done anything to cause them any embarrassment or worry. This difficult life helped him learn to be straightforward and honorable in business as well as his personal life to the point where he could not tolerate dishonor in anyone.

Following graduation from high school, Bubba went for a brief time to Seattle where he worked with his Uncle Alex Holmes and learned the fur trade. Even later in life this knowledge stayed with him for when we might find ourselves in various department stores he would often be found perusing the ladies fur coats "just to see how prices have changed."

Even though Bubba enjoyed Seattle, he returned after six months. Kelsey Messink (Uncle Kelsey) was working for the RJ Reynolds Tobacco Company and may have been instrumental in Bubba obtaining a job with that company. It was then in the mid-1930's when Bubba left Vidalia for Middle Tennessee.

Bubba's bride was from Dickson, Tennessee, his family was raised there but there was always South Georgia sand under his fingernails. He always referred to Vidalia as home and we went there as often as we could.

When we visited Vidalia we had to see Tommy Q. Vann at the hardware store, the Blands down the road from the Methodist Church, Dr. Mercer, who was a dominate male figure in Bubba's upbringing, and of course Katherine and Kelsey Messink. Other people would come by and visit but these garnered the most attention.

The Kelsey and Kathryn Messink family. L to R - Unidentified, Kay, Kelsey, and Kathryn.

Bubba met his future wife, Ann Sugg, on the tennis court in Dickson, Tennessee. They played tennis with and against each other and were friends before they began to see each other socially.

Their wedding announcement came out in the paper on December 7, 1941, and in spite of the outbreak of World War II, they were married later that month. Shortly afterward the newly weds returned from their honeymoon, Bubba joined the US Army Air Force.

Basic training was at Fort Oglethorpe, Georgia and even today I occasionally see a man named Maynard Corlew who left Dickson with Bubba to serve and I think we both enjoy each other because of my father. Maynard enjoys telling of sharing Bubba's gifts from home when boxes of pecans were sent but he laughs when telling that Bubba wouldn't share if he received a box of boiled peanuts. Bubba served as an armoruer in the Air Force and was stationed in London. The service to him was something

The Family of James Otis Rountree, Jr.

that had to be done but he longed for home. His feeling was summed up in one of his favorite stories. While traveling Bubba picked up a young man in uniform who was hitchhiking. During his conversation with the young soldier, the young man confessed he had recently been discharged. Bubba innocently asked, "Did you re-enter?" Young man was silent, and then said, "Sir, I don't mean to give you any short answer but hell no!"

The sole bright spot in his service experience was meeting up with Virginia Rountree who was in London with the Red Cross. Bubba never knew which of them was more homesick.

After the war Bubba began life. His first post war occupation was as a car salesman. Along with three others he helped run the Ford Dealership in Dixon. His share was purchased by one of the partners and Bubba had landed a job with Bell Knap Hardware Company in Lewisville, Kentucky. The first opening for him as a salesman was in Clarksdale, Mississippi so with wife and newborn son in tow, Bubba moved to Mississippi where he worked for almost a year traveling to small town hardware stores for the parent company. When an opening came in Dixon, still with Bell Knapp, we moved back.

Dixon had good quail hunting and good fishing and hardly a weekend would past without enjoying these sports. Quail hunting was good but Bubba always compared it to the hunting in and around Vidalia.

In 1952, Bubba's second child, a daughter, was born and his life was complete.

We children always knew where we stood with daddy. If we missed behaved punishment would follow. Honor was the primary virtue in his life-his word was of primary importance and expected us to act the same.

I remember seeing him on his knees in prayer every night before bed, I remember his affinity for Georgia Tech football, and I remember him having a profound love for small children.

I regret that he didn't live to see any of his grandchildren but he knew that eldest was coming and called his sisters with the happy news. Today he would have six beautiful grandchildren and one great grandson who would be the apple of his eye.

My father and I, aside from the love that father and son have for one another, really liked each other and enjoyed doing things together. Even though I have missed him very much, there's not a day that passes that I don't hear advice he gave me. When I don't hear that advice, I find life more difficult.

So, here's to Bubba—I just hope I can be half the father he was.

VIRGINIA ROUNTREE GRIST

By Rebecca Grist Waldron

Virginia Rountree

To write of my mother's life is not an easy task. She touched so many lives in such a special way. Not only was she kind and gentle, but she looked right at you and listened to every word you had to say. When she walked into a room she could give you her big, beautiful smile, and it would warm your heart. She was intelligent, curious, and hard headed. I know that I should sum up her full life in a few pages. It is not possible! Another memory gets triggered by a photograph or another clipping, and I want to add more to what I have written. So many friends and family were not mentioned because I must finish this for Warren's book.

Born January 4, 1917, in Canoochee, Georgia, Virginia was the eldest daughter of Clyde and Otis. She first attended South Georgia Teacher's College in Statesboro. In 1934, Virginia enrolled at LaGrange College as a freshman. She was interested in good sportsmanship and fair play, so she became Vice President of the Athletic Association. She participated in tennis, soccer, and horseshoes. As a sophomore at LaGrange, she was in the art club and was the advertising manager for the production of Little Women. In 1936, as a junior at LaGrange she joined the glee club and the yearbook staff. She remained active with the Athletic Association playing soccer and baseball. During the summer of 1936 Virginia worked at Camp Juliet Lowe, a Girl Scout retreat in Cloudland, Georgia. Ms. Lutie Neese, director of the camp was someone that Mama admired. We would visit her often when she was older and lived in a nursing home not far from Albany. Below is an excerpt from an article written for the Vidalia Advance by Virginia:

> "Vidalia's scout troop was one of the oldest in America. And did you know that when Ms. Lowe, Girl Scout founder, died in 1927 and the English girl guides sent a letter of sympathy to the American Girl Scouts, National headquarters asked the Vidalia troop to answer? That troop was under the leadership of Ms. Lutie Neese who is now director of Camp Juliet Lowe."

In 1940 and 1941 I had found a letter from a third grade pupil in Waycross. This child liked her teacher, Ms. Rountree because she "gave me spelling that i could spell. I have made better in spelling." I believe that Virginia began teaching in Albany in 1942, because of several photographs that I have.

On June 6, 1944, Virginia began training with the American Red Cross in Washington, D.C. She served in Europe from July 1944 to November 1945. She was assigned to Braintree, England and Beauvois, France in 1944. In May 1945 she returned to duty in Auxerre, France. Then she went to Berchtesgaden, Germany in the Bavarian Alps. This was famous as Hitler's mountain retreat. Later she served in Seno, France. After her return home, Virginia lived in Savannah and worked for WCCP Broadcasting.

Virginia met Bill through a blind date set up by a friend, Frances Harrel. On December 8, 1946, William James Grist and Virginia Lucille Rountree married at the First Methodist Church in Vidalia. Virginia's brother-in-law, Reverend Candler Budd, performed the ceremony. Virginia's sister, Dorothy played the organ.

Bill and Virginia had their first child, Billy, on June 2, 1948. Bobby was born on February 9, 1950. Becky was born on December 14, 1955.

As early as 1954, eight years into their marriage, Bill's health began to fail. He underwent extensive testing at Emory University Hospital in 1954 and 1955. A decade later in 1964, he suffered a massive stroke. At that time, he was confined to a wheelchair. The whole family was saddened by his illness. Yet the devotion and love shown by our family was inspirational to others. It made us bond together even closer.

On July 24, 1967, William Grist died. He had been severely handicapped for more than three years. His funeral took place in Albany. Sadly, during that same summer, Virginia lost her beloved mother, M'dear, as well.

Virginia realized that she needed to get back in the workforce to help our family meet its needs. She held a secretarial job and pursued getting her master's degree. Through night classes at a local community college and summer school at the university of Georgia, she earned her master's degree in library science. She began working at Mary Aker's Junior High as a media specialist.

Virginia raised her three children, worked at Mary Aker's, and stayed active in her community. She was proud of her connection with Porterfield Methodist Church where she attended. The American Red Cross remained dear to her as she continued to volunteer for them during their blood drives. She also gave her time to the Albany Art Museum. Virginia's knowledge of plants and love for gardening inspired all who were fortunate enough to share in her beautiful arrangements – maybe something as simple as a walk around the house admiring the green thumb and listening to the Latin or scientific name for everything that grows.

Mama genuinely loved young people and enjoyed talking with all ages. Through their connection with students at school, she touched a lot of lives in a very positive way. When I was a teenager, kids would arrive at my backdoor and there would be a student wanting to talk with Virginia. They weren't coming to see my brothers or me, just Virginia.

After my father's death Virginia had many social invitations and a few dates with different gentlemen. One night when I was "helping" her get ready to go out she told me that there would never be another man for her to marry. Bill was her one and only love and that was the way it would always be. She was true to him always.

Billy married his college sweetheart, Marilyn Terhune Frailey, on August 21, 1971, in Winter Park, Florida. We were all very proud of them and their beautiful wedding. Seven years later they blessed Virginia with her first grandchild, Megan Frailey Grist. She was born February 6, 1978, in Massachusetts, during the snowstorm of the century. Megan's brother, David, Virginia's first grandson, was born on December 14, 1981.

Becky married Michael Waldron on August 18, 1984, in Albany at Porterfield Methodist Church. One month before the wedding Virginia suffered a stroke and had to be hospitalized. She fought a tough battle to be able to walk down the aisle for the wedding only a few weeks later.

Virginia's son Bobby was the third child to get married. He married Sarah Williams of Maxeys, Georgia. Their beautiful ceremony took place at the University of Georgia Botanical Conservatory in Athens.

Virginia was blessed with the birth of another granddaughter Lindsay Grist Waldron on April 30, 1988. She came to Florida for several weeks to help me get used to having a baby. What a loving grandmother and devoted mother. William Michael Waldron was born on November 24, 1989. Virginia patiently stayed with me for several weeks awaiting Michael's birth. James Rountree Waldron, Virginia's youngest grandchild was born on January 19, 1992. He was named after Dr. James Otis Rountree, Virginia's father.

There is nothing that Virginia valued more than family. I can remember her telling me that if we ever had a fire or hurricane (which we have had many times) and had to leave our home the two things that needed to be packed were the family photographs and the silver. To this day that is the rule I follow. Family is the most precious treasure we have. Aren't we lucky that our family heritage is strong and that we are proud to be a part of it all? I hope that my children will embody the spirit of their grandmother, Virginia. She has left us with lofty goals to strive for.

Mama died in Atlanta on April 7, 1994.

Author's Note: Below is a letter written by Virginia Rountree to her mother, Clyde, on D-Day. Virginia was 26 years old and was attached to the Red Cross.

June 6, 1944

My Dearest,

> *I wish I could have been with you this day. It really is a day to be remembered for always. Our classes surely took on a serious aspect because of it. There were no sirens here. All was very quiet. I bought a*

paper right after breakfast, and it took me some time to realize that the headlines meant D-Day was actually here. Not having a radio, I feel as if I had really missed some of the important news. All I know is it started and I guess that accounts for the fact that no one has had any mail from England in so long a time.

All during the day I was so glad in my heart that I could be here actually preparing to do something useful and exciting. We've had some of the most wonderful speakers – most attractive people. We've had them steadily from 9:30 this A.M. until 6 o'clock this P.M. except for an hour for lunch and 15 minutes at church.

There are about 400 people at this American Methodist University training for the RC Service. There are some very interesting people in the class. We went at 2 o'clock to the little Methodist Church just off the campus for prayer. It was a beautiful little church and the seriousness of the occasion made that whole crowd of 400 as quiet, serious and reverent as any group I had ever seen.

We were so happy about our set-up here at the Roger Smith, until tonight we got notices (about 10 girls in the hotel) to report to some club. I think it will be boarding houses. I hate to go, because we are right in the midst of things here. As one girl said, you can sit on the Johnny and look down Pennsylvania Avenue.

The cafeteria at the college closed today and the staff out there had the problem of feeding 400 with no facilities. They called for volunteer workers from Washington who came out and made sandwiches for us all.

I am sure that I'll be here until Saturday, June 17. Then I'll probably go to someplace in the U.S. for extension training. Then after a few weeks I think I'll be called back to Washington, to be sent out. I'll not know where I'm going until I am on board the ship, so be expecting that, but don't worry about me. As they told us today, we are under protection of the U.S. Army and Navy. Things should have quieted down considerably by that time.

Honestly, I am so thrilled and enthusiastic about the job. I wish you could be here to catch some of the enthusiasm. It's going to be a wonderful experience. I'll have tall tales to tell for a long time.

We are allowed to take with us much more baggage than I thought. We can have a dinner dress, two afternoon dresses, a suit, a coat – all civilian clothes – but I don't think I'll do that. I might want that black jumper and blouse if you can get it finished by the first of next week. I'll let you know.

I tried to call George Rountree, but didn't get him. Will try again.

Please write to me soon. I need mail from you. I hope you'll realize how thrilled I am over this job and will begin to feel some of the same enthusiasm for it that I do. I've been thinking of you all.

With Lots of Love,
Virginia

The Family of Virginia Rountree Grist

DOROTHY ROUNTREE BUDD

By W. Candler Budd, III

Candler and Dorothy Budd (1950). The occasion is the dedication of the new parsonage at Hapeville Methodist Church.

Dorothy Rountree Budd has had a profound impact on my life. I love and admire her. She's hilarious! Just ask her where she's from, "I'm from Vidalia, Georgia, and I was there before the onions were." Through the years, my friends have enjoyed hearing countless stories of my grandmother.

Why do I love her? Well, she's just so darn cute! You couldn't help but love her. She is always interested in what her grandchildren are up to. Now I know that most grandparents are that way; but she is truly excited to be actively a part of my life and the lives of the other grandchildren, and now, great-grandchildren. I can always count on her to give me an update on all the cousins. She has a lovely way of bragging to one grandchild about another grandchild that wasn't there at the time. My cousin George would often tell me what Grandmother had said about me. I would think, "Man, I didn't know I did all that!"

She has a beautiful sense of humor. It's wonderful having a grandmother that's such a good sport. She has no problem laughing at herself and never takes herself too seriously.

We were once leaving a restaurant, and Grandmother Budd has been known to take more than two after dinner mints from the basket by the exit. More than three, more than four, more than ten, you get the idea. As she grabbed for the mints, my brother Bryant yelled, "Mints beware! Mints beware!" She laughed louder than all of us put together.

My father and I sat down with her at Wesley Woods for an interview in January of 2005 for the purpose of this book. Although it was emotional at times, her joyous laughter and outlook on life was better than ever. She told us stories of her mother, Clyde Rountree, saying what a pretty woman she was. My father responded, "Well, you were a good-looking woman then, too." "*Then*? What about *now*?" she said with an adorable grin.

Why do I admire her? For one, she's an amazing musician. I will always treasure the times when she would play several Christmas carols and hymns on the piano, completely by memory. She is extremely dedicated to her music and to her students. Through the years, her teaching has been in such demand she had to have a waiting list. Thirty-five students a week was a good manageable number for her. Now, at 86, she has ten students. Be sure and ask her, "How's the teaching going?" rather than, "Are you *still* teaching?" She doesn't like that question, and I don't blame her one bit.

It is amazing to me how she can transpose a difficult piece of music on sight. For those of you who can play an instrument, you know how arduous a task that can be. One Christmas Eve service, she had to play *Pie Jesu* by memory when the sheet music was lost at the last minute.

She began studying the piano in the 7th grade. In high school, the Presbyterian Church of Vidalia asked her to play at their services. They offered to pay her, but she felt guilty, saying, "I can't get paid for playing in church!" The preacher insisted because they would be taking her out of her own church. They paid her fifty cents a week. Getting that check for two dollars every month "felt like all the money in the world," she said with a laugh.

Dorothy went on to study music after high school. She auditioned in a piano competition for the radio scholarship. She first learned the results when her name was announced on the radio as one of the winners. She won a full tuition scholarship to Wesleyan Conservatory in Macon. The scholarship was for one year, her first year. After that, she thought, "What will I do now?" about paying for the second year. Her piano teacher, Mrs. Jelks, suggested that she audition for an organ scholarship, which she won for her second year. She explained, "Well, I was doubling up. I wasn't going to summer school. I was taking extra courses. You know, taking as heavy a load as I could. So I finished college in three years without summer school. For my senior (third) year, I got a job playing for Cherokee Heights Methodist and I got a teacher's discount with my mother being a teacher."

She graduated valedictorian and continued her education at Wesleyan Conservatory as a postgraduate, receiving two scholarships. After graduation, she went to Byron, Georgia, for a teaching job. Months later, the Georgia State College for Women in Milledgeville hired her on as a faculty member.

Dorothy was born in 1919 and grew up in Vidalia without the pleasure of knowing her father, Otis Rountree, who died before she was two. Her grandmother, Sophie Holmes, and her mother, Clyde Rountree (M'dear), reared her to be an outstanding wife, mother, musician, and teacher.

M'dear taught English to Jewish immigrants before Dorothy, her two sisters, and brother were all old enough to be in school. The job kept M'dear at home. When all the children were in school, M'dear started teaching in another town. Dorothy recalled how excited she was every afternoon to hear her mother coming home from work. "Hearing that Ford pulling into the driveway was the sweetest sound I ever heard," she said while wiping away a tear. It was easy to see that Grandmother Budd and her mother had a very special bond.

As a kid from the eighties, it is hard for me to imagine raising four children as a single parent during the Depression. Dorothy's family didn't have much money, but they were rich with happiness.

"M'dear was such a happy person, even though she had so much on her. She had the most beautiful disposition and was always happy. She would...one of the things that (tearing up)...I'm sorry...I haven't (still choking up)...when we'd go out on dates, she'd stay up and see us when we came in. I'd tell her stories and we'd sit there on the bed and laugh so hard tears would come. There was never anything but just fun! You think about this...five of us lived in one room. My brother's room was the "trunk room" we used to call it. You know, it was that tiny little room between our room and the bathroom (she laughs). Grandmother saved the front bedroom for people that came in. So we just all stayed in one room."

Dorothy's grandmother lived with the family, or rather, they moved in with her when Otis died.

"She was a wonderful person, wonderful to us, and never, *never* once mentioned that that house belonged to her. It was *ours*. She was so good to us. She raised all sorts of vegetables. It was so good. And peas, we'd sit on the back steps shelling peas. She'd go out and gather them all. She was an industrious person. She'd walk around through the house and she'd say, 'If I don't do this, I'll get to where I can't walk.' And she lived to be ninety-five."

Dorothy also told us humorous stories of when her grandmother would drive her crazy.

"On rainy days, in pouring rain, Grandmother Holmes, very embarrassing to me, she'd stand out there on the porch. A car would go out and she'd do like this (she waves her arms in dramatic fashion), you know, wave them to try to make them stop and take us [to school]. We were standing there. Nobody had a school bus. We were going to have to walk in heavy rain to school and she'd just do this (waving again in even more dramatic fashion) until she got somebody."

She then mentioned a well-known man in town who was less than accommodating. "He had a big car, a wife, and no children. And he'd drive *right by* and never look our way with that back seat empty. He would not pick anybody up. Nooo!" She laughs.

It seemed that the industrious Grandmother Holmes was good at finding work for the children, much to their dismay. "When Grandmother Holmes would think up a job, I'd climb up the china berry tree and read a book. She couldn't find me, I guess."

During young Dorothy's free time, when she wasn't hiding from Grandmother Holmes, she would play with her pet chicken named Cutie. The chicken was quite talented and could be considered Dorothy's first music student. "If I just held her, she'd sing, 'Cah, cah, cah, cah, cah!' and I'd say, 'Hush, Cutie,' and then I'd squeeze her and she'd hush. That was it.

Grandmother [Holmes], all practicality, [later] cooked her and served her there on the table, and I wouldn't eat her." She then joked about other pet chickens she had as a child, finally saying, "The chickens were my friends, and they had more sense than people gave them credit for."

I asked Dorothy how much traveling they did, if any, when they were growing up. "When I graduated from high school, I had never been out of the state of Georgia. But when I was twelve years old, my mother took us to Atlanta. This was a big trip from Vidalia. The only time I ever went to Atlanta [as a child]. We just took a big sack of oranges. We ate oranges all the way. Everybody said they could have followed us with the orange peels thrown out along the way."

Dorothy later lived in Atlanta with her husband, the late Dr. Candler Budd. He was a Methodist minister and ten years her senior. They were married for fifty-five years, until his death in 1996. They have four children, thirteen grandchildren, and five great grandchildren. He was the love of her life.

Candler's sister, Lillian, introduced them back in Macon when Dorothy was still at Wesleyan Conservatory. On their first date, they went out to dinner. Candler had a little more to eat than she did. Apparently, Dorothy, trying to be considerate during a time when money was tight, ordered the cheapest thing on the menu. Candler, assuming that was what she wanted, ordered what he wanted. Dorothy was stuck with a small chicken salad sandwich, while Candler enjoyed a feast – a steak with several vegetables and other delicious side dishes. Dorothy stared at his plate with great envy.

The courtship lasted a few years before they were married in 1941. Dorothy, very admirably, wanted to get out of debt before she tied the knot. Candler offered to pay it for her, but she refused. Someone later asked Dorothy if she paid her debt off first because she didn't want her husband to "hold it over her." The thought of Candler Budd being anything less than benevolent was strange to Dorothy, and she replied, "You never met my husband."

Candler Budd was a very successful minister. Everything he did was for others. His story could be another book entirely. On many occasions, my grandfather told me how he respected Dorothy's advice. The marriage was a fantastic partnership.

Dorothy was revered as a preacher's wife, a full time job in itself. She was extremely active in the church. You could always count on her to play a beautiful melody or bake a delicious treat.

My father, uncle, and aunts had a fantastic childhood growing up

The Family of Dorothy Rountree Budd

under Dorothy's roof. There is a rumor that in the winter of 1941, Dorothy made a big pot of soup for the family. At the end of the day, she put the soup in the refrigerator. The next day, she reheated the pot and served it. She would do this for several days, adding vegetables and meat to it when necessary. When springtime rolled around, she moved it to the back of the freezer, not to be seen again until 1942. She would pull that large pot of soup out and start the whole process again. She had the same pot of soup from 1941 to 1996. Now, I don't know if this story is true or not. Maybe it's just an old family joke. But I bet there is *some* truth to it. Where there's smoke, there's fire, and where there's fire, maybe there's a fifty-five year old pot of soup.

Grandmother Budd, if you are reading this, I love you. Thank you for always being there for us, for the happy memories, and for being such and inspiration.

BRIEF HISTORY OF
CHRISTINE HOLMES ROUNTREE
ANDERSON'S FAMILY

By Jean Estelle Anderson and Christine Holmes Anderson Williams

John Anderson and Christine Rountree on their wedding day

In 1943, Christine Holmes Rountree lived in Milledgeville, Georgia, teaching piano at Georgia State College for Women. There she met John Martin Anderson, Jr., who was completing his residency in psychiatry at Milledgeville State Hospital. John had chosen Milledgeville in order to be able to care for his mother in nearby Barnesville. Soon after his mother passed away, he met Christine. The couple married after three months'

401

courtship on August 27, 1943, in Vidalia, with brother-in-law Candler Budd officiating and sister Dorothy providing the music.

Soon the Andersons moved to Lexington, Kentucky, where John practiced medicine through the U.S. Public Health Service. Their first child, Jean Estelle, was born in 1946. The family moved to Topeka, Kansas, while Jean was an infant, after John accepted a fellowship with the Menninger School of Psychiatry. After he became Superintendent of Topeka State Hospital, he and his colleagues began a movement that revolutionized residential psychiatric care.

Christine Holmes was born in 1949 in Topeka, followed by John Martin, III, in 1952. Soon after Johnny's birth, the family returned to Georgia, and John began the private practice of psychiatry in Atlanta. The family stayed with the Budds until they found a place to live, and the two families always remained close.

In 1957, a fourth child was born: Earl Rountree. The Andersons moved from their house on St. Charles Avenue to a larger one on Club Drive, where they enjoyed many happy years and made lifelong friendships.

As her own children grew, Christine touched the lives of countless other children through her piano teaching. She maintained an active studio throughout the rest of her life, achieving National Certification in 1977, and continuing to perform, study, and teach until days before her death in 2000. Christine came home from the hospital, having bravely endured a course of chemotherapy that ultimately failed. When she could not sit through an entire lesson, her daughter Chrissy helped out. Through their grief, students were comforted only by knowing that Mrs. Anderson was listening from the other room.

Jeanie, Chrissy, Johnny, and Earl all have fond memories of life at home. In the evenings, John played violin or sang while Christine accompanied him on piano and sang along. They had their favorites, a fairly large repertoire, and the children often went to sleep to the sound of their parents' music from downstairs.

Music was the medium of communication at the Anderson home at least as much as words were. If Christine was not teaching, one of the children was usually practicing, or (just as likely) "fooling around" at the piano, singing, playing, or sightreading. Jeanie continues to enjoy piano and violin. Johnny's main instrument is French horn. Earl loved the double bass from an early age and has played professionally as an adult. Chrissy, like her mother, is a piano teacher and performing artist.

During the 1950's and 1960's, John often recorded on tape the

The Family of Christine Rountree Anderson

activities at home. The children discovered years later what a treasure these tape recordings were. The tapes captured mealtime conversations, music performances, impromptu interviews, Christmas mornings, visits with relatives, children behaving well and not so well – in short, a real time capsule of the life of this family.

In 1976, John became ill with cancer and soon closed his practice. After a year of treatment, he died at home with his family caring for him. Christine continued to live in the house for a few years, then moved to a smaller house that she had been eyeing in the same neighborhood. She had always pictured her piano in the bay window of that house, which was exactly where she moved it. She had a serious struggle with cancer but miraculously survived it and had some wonderful years in her new house. In march of 2000, however, she was diagnosed with leukemia, and despite superb medical treatment and her own heroic efforts once again with chemotherapy, she died at home on May 5th, 2000, in the care of her devoted children, children-in-law, and grandchildren.

The children as adults have remained close even though they live apart. Jean Estelle, a behavioral psychologist, lives in Oxford, Mississippi, and is married to Alan Michael Gross, also a psychologist. She has three children, Ryan Christopher Rasheed, Elijah Walter Gross, and Hannah Elizabeth Gross. Christine Anderson Williams, a pianist, lives in Raphine, Virginia, and is married to Edgar Warren Williams, a composer and conductor. She has two children: Ann Anderson Williams Duncan and Joel Edgar Williams. Ann is married to Daniel Edward Duncan and has one son, Noah Williams Duncan. John Martin Anderson, III, a teacher and school administrator, lives in Marietta, Georgia, and is married to Jo Ewing Anderson, organist and harpist. He has one child, Luke David Anderson. Earl Rountree Anderson is also a teacher, lives in Winston-Salem, North Carolina, and is married to Anita Clark-Anderson, an artist. He has one child, Sophie Christine Anderson.

GREAT RICHES IN THEIR HUMAN RELATIONS

MY REMARKS AT THE MEMORIAL SERVICE AT
PEACHTREE PRESBYTERIAN

By Johnny Anderson

When Mama was sitting on her screen porch a few days ago, the last time she ever sat in that pleasant spot, she lifted her hand, pointed outside to the one lone wild rose stem, and said, "I love that red flower." Just as she saw beyond the surrounding weeds, which have flourished during her illness, to the beautiful flower, our mother, Christine Rountree Anderson, saw beyond human flaws and affirmed the beauty and goodness that she could always find in practically everyone she met. She knew the weeds or flaws were there, but her way was always to nurture our better qualities so that they would predominate and prevail. Mama and Daddy's attitude of looking for, expecting, and encouraging the best in all individuals was their method of discipline in raising their children. Jeanie, Chrissy, Earl, and I wanted so much to please them, which was easy to do since they thought we were just great, and we so dreaded the thought of disappointing them that we stayed under control, most of the time. If we went too far, all it took was Mama's stern expression with nostrils flared for us to shape up fast.

My brother Earl mentioned to the Rev. Dr. Huntley that no matter how small his accomplishments as a child – balancing on one foot or doing a trick on his bike – she made him feel special. My sister Chrissy has emulated Mama in so many ways, most notably by carrying on her tradition of piano performance and teaching. My sister Jeanie has referred to Mama as her "rock." Mama accepted, upheld, encouraged, and loved us every second of every day.

The strength and power of her love was not limited to her family. On family vacations, I was often impatient when she and Daddy laughed and made friends with weary waitresses and tollbooth operators, and everyone else we'd encounter. In the hospital last month, Mama won over the most detached clerks, nurses, and doctors with her candor and kindness. She always, even throughout this horrible illness, put people at ease so that they could drop their guard and be their most noble and natural selves. So many of you have told us that our mother taught you so much more than piano.

One of Christine Anderson's gifts was her innate ability to perceive what needed to be done. And once she perceived it, she took action. It was mostly small things like giving a child an orange or providing a friend a place to rest or inviting a neighbor in for supper or playing the piano for Sunday School. She ministered to those of us in need.

In March, her oncologist, Dr. Lesesne, described to her her two grim alternatives: chemotherapy, which would be devastating, or doing nothing, which would mean a gradual fading away. Mama's practical, fighting spirit compelled her to choose the chemo. She questioned Dr. Lesesne's lack of enthusiasm about her decision, and he said, "Mrs. Anderson, you just seem so frail." At that instant, she changed visibly, looked him in the eye, and responded, "Yes, I'm frail, but I'm strong." This contradiction puzzled me until I realized that to Mama, the physical self was separate from and inferior to the spiritual self.

My good friend Corner Yates, who recently visited Mama, told me yesterday with a time of awe that, in spite of her physical condition, my mother's spirit was still so strong, almost palpable. Her spirit almost seemed disassociated from the physical as a separate entity, undaunted, undeniable, and now, today and forever, freed from the physical shell to live on, stronger than ever, with God and through us in this room.

As a child in the 1920's and 30's, on the front porch of their Vidalia home, Mama played, talked, and sat around with her sisters Dorothy and Virginia, her brother Bubba, her mother M'dear, and her grandmother. Her daddy had died before she was even born. The Rountrees didn't have a lot of things, but they had great riches in their human relationships, both within their family and among their neighbors, who strolled up and down the sidewalk to keep cool and stop and visit in the evenings. From those precious days, I believe, her immense love of humanity was thoroughly and deeply ingrained. This wonderful heritage of love she brought with her wherever she went. What happened over many years at my mother's house in Brookhaven was not so different from those simpler days in Vidalia. As we in this room came to her house for piano lessons, for bridge, for tennis, for meals, for rest, or just for visits, we came in and out of those unlocked, open doors in a continuous circulation of human love. Mama said to me recently, "I don't mind dying. I'm not afraid. It's just that I'll miss you all as much."

So many of you have asked us, "What can I do?" and you have all done so much with the food, cards, prayers, and support. We thank you. And we particularly want to thank Dr. Huntley of Peachtree Presbyterian whose friendship to my mother over the years and whole ministerial gifts during this time have brought God's strength closer to us all. Finally, for our mother, Christine Rountree Anderson, we ask you to do one more thing: continue her legacy of love and kindness through your human relationships.

MUSIC ACROSS THE
GENERATIONS

Clyde Rountree

A trait would be a talent or occupation that is particular to one family, spanning the generations, which in our case would be a love of music. My mother's grandparents on both sides of her family encouraged their children in the pursuit of music. In the letters of Otis and Clyde you will notice Clyde commenting on how three of the Holmes offspring, Clyde, Kathryn, and Pierce, were all practicing a different instrument and a different tune at the same time. Since Clyde's children were not burdened with television, they would spend the evenings playing musical games on the piano. This activity prepared them well for music theory classes.

Subsequent generations saw Dorothy Budd and Christine Anderson, both well known in Atlanta music circles, as profoundly successful music teachers. Chrissy Williams has carried on this tradition by teaching music. Earl Anderson has played the contra-bass professionally and still pursues the instrument. Dotty Murray obtained her master's degree in music at Northwestern and has taught voice at Georgia College and Gordon College. Dotty is also very generous to give of her talent in churches.

In the next generation, Courtenay "Becky" Budd Caramico is a nationally known opera singer, having performed at Carnegie Hall several times. This year she sang in Japan with the New York City Opera. She is a featured performer at Spaletto, Central City, Colorado, New York City Opera, and several other well-known opera companies. Becky's brother, Candler, has a great voice and has performed professionally in several musicals. Their brother, Wesley, performs with a band and has made a commercially successful CD. Wesley performs acoustic rock by playing the guitar and also writes his own music. Ryan Rasheed, son of Jeanie Anderson, is a well-known expert on hip-hop and uses a synthesizer to practice his craft. Ryan's sister, Hannah, is an accomplished musician as well.

It is very interesting how traits pass down through the generations.

FAMILY PHOTO ALBUM

Dorothy Rountree and W. Candler Budd on their wedding day

Lillian Budd and Jim Rountree at the wedding of Ann Ross. Lillian remembers her feet hurting because her shoes were too tight!

Virginia – classic Virginia, sporting activities and her Chesterfield

The Candler Budd Family. Front row, L to R – Candler, Dotty, Lillian, Dorothy, and David. Standing – Warren.

Kay Messink, daughter of Kelsey and Kathryn Messink. Kay spent part of her childhood living with Sophie Holmes and her family.

Story time at the Anderson home

Dotty Budd, Chrissy Anderson, Jeanie Anderson, and Lillian Budd.

Virginia and Becky Grist – loving mother and daughter.

Dorothy, Candler, Bryant, and Becky Budd with baby Wesley.

This picture was taken at our home four months and five days before we lost Bryant. At our Christmas Eve party, December 24, 1998, Courtenay felt led to take a picture of our children. I would never have had the presence of mind to do such a thing. Bryant was missing for two and one-half years, then we received the terrible news – we had lost him. During that very difficult time, several people told us that we would get closure when we found out what had happened. You never get closure. Not a day goes by that we do not think about him and, on most days, six years later, the tears come. But that's all right. We don't want to forget Andrew Bryant Budd – he was a very unique individual. He was smart, handsome, funny, musically talented, caring, and a terrific baseball player, also. We would certainly rather have been blessed with Bryant for 21 years than not at all. Since Bryant's death, Dorothy and Becky have each had a son, both of whom share Bryant's name. Life goes on, but sometimes, it can be very tough.

Dorothy Rountree Budd with her grandson, Wesley. Dorothy has always been very close to her grandchildren, always interested in their various pursuits.

L to R – Becky Grist Waldron, Chrissy Anderson Williams, Dorothy Rountree Budd, Dotty Budd Murray, Jeanie Anderson, at Ann Williams' wedding, September 2000.

Five generations of John R. Flanders, Jr.,'s descendants. Front row, L to R – Sarah Underwood holding her great-great-granddaughter Emma North, and John Underwood, son of Sarah. Back row, L to R – Great-granddaughter Sarah North and granddaughter Jill Barrett, daughter of Jeanie Underwood. Jeanie was Sarah's daughter. She died in 1996.

Megan Grist is very special to the Budds. For three years, Megan and our son Bryant were high school classmates. They were soul mates as well. When Bryant went missing, Megan suffered along with us. Megan has chosen to spend her life helping others. Presently, she is in her last year of graduate school at the University of New England, Portland, Maine. She is working on a master's degree in Social Work with the goal of teaching learning disabled adolescents.

413

Three Candlers. L to R – W. Candler Budd III, Warren Candler Budd, Jr., and Candler Rich. All are named for W. Candler Budd, Sr. Candler Budd, Sr. was a man of unusual talent, drive, and intelligence. During his life, he accomplished great things, but much more important was the fact that he was a wonderful Daddy and Granddaddy. He was compassionate, generous, and loved his family. His relationship with my mother was a romance from beginning to end. He was very supportive of all our activities. One time, he was almost thrown out of a wrestling meet for supporting me too loudly. Even at the end of his life, after suffering from a stroke, Daddy was looking out for others. We miss him.

Sophie Christine Anderson, daughter of Earl and Anita Clark Anderson, born March 19, 2000. The Rountree descendants are beautiful children!

Front row, L to R – Kathryn Price, Caroline Long, Carolyn Rountree Odom holding Peri Price, Buff Rountree Price, Melissa Price, and Chuck Price. Back row, L to R – Jason Motes, Carol Buff Price Motes, Tony Price, and Jordan Price. Buff Price is the daughter of George Rountree, brother of Otis.

dly 4, 1976

1. Tim Ross
2. Dorothy Rountree Budd
3. Christy Darden
4. Todd Ross
5. Becky Rountree
6. Virginia Rountree Grist
7. Kathryn Holmes Messink
8. W. Candler Budd
9. Dorothy Rountree Budd
10. Becky Budd
11. Dotty Budd
12. Matt Rountree
13. Ann Rountree
14. Jim Rountree
15. Candler Budd
16. Courtenay Budd
17. Ann Messink Ross
18. Warren Budd
19. Jeanie Anderson
20. Wayne Underwood
21. Ann Rountree
    Underwood

22. Gayla Rountree
23. Christine Rountree Anderson
24. John M. Anderson, Jr.
25. Travis Ross
26. Earl Anderson
27. Dick Ross
28. Kay Messink
29. John Anderson

EPILOGUE

It is April 19, 2005. I am sitting in the Intensive Care Unit of Northside Hospital in Atlanta. My mother, Dorothy Rountree Budd, is asleep after having endured a six-hour operation. Four weeks ago she broke her arm in two places. She also dislocated her shoulder. For some unknown reason the emergency room doctor did not set the arm. Thanks to my sister Dotty we finally consulted our friend, Dr. Chip Pendleton, who performed the delicate operation from which she is now recovering. He told us that he did not know how mother had endured four weeks of such intense pain. I cannot believe that we did not know to take action earlier. But when Dotty and I walked her hospital room, even in this stressful situation, mother was upbeat. But that is not unusual. She has been that way since her childhood.

I believe that this attitude came from her mother and grandmother as well as the community of friends and relatives that surrounded her in Vidalia, Georgia.

An example of this strong support is an instance that occurred when Dorothy was eight. While in class, she pinched another girl, who let out a bloodcurdling scream. When asked if she was the guilty party, Dorothy denied pinching her classmate. That night at supper Dorothy asked her mother Clyde if a liar would go to Heaven. Clyde instantly asked, "What did you do?" Dorothy then related the incident. Clyde took immediate action. She called the teacher and asked her to come over. When the teacher arrived, Dorothy tearfully confessed to her indiscretion. The teacher allayed Dorothy's fears and assured her that she would go to Heaven. Dorothy was crying, the teacher was crying, and Clyde was crying. It does take a village, but a village of friends and family, not a government.

Throughout our childhood, my siblings and I witnessed Dorothy's continued resilience as well as her profound optimism. Once, when we were going on a family vacation, things were not going well in the Budd family Hudson. Daddy had already mashed his hand in the trunk, we were lost, and Dotty and David, my younger siblings, were acting up in the backseat. Mother considered the situation and then turning around to the backseat said in a forceful manner, "We are going to have a good time!"

Another typical instance occurred when I was a senior in high school and was upset because I had not done as well as on my Scholastic Aptitude Test as I thought I should. Mother said, "Well, it is more important for you to be happy."

We have seen by the stories in this book that this mental toughness and optimism is a trait that has transcended the generations. My Uncle Bubba and Aunt Christine also manifested this quality when they battled cancer, as did Aunt Virginia when she lost her husband at a young age.

I wonder if my children and those who follow will display the many fine qualities of those who went before. Will they show the strong faith, devotion to family, and amazing recuperative powers that were exhibited by Clyde Rountree, Sophie Holmes, Nancy Jordan Flanders, and John R. Flanders, Jr.? My prayer is that they will. Certainly if they do, they will be *Rich Beyond Price.*

"Will the circle be unbroken?
By and by Lord, by and by,
There's a better home a-waitin'
In the sky Lord, in the sky."

BIBLIOGRAPHY

Anonymous. (1898, August 4). "D.Q. Morrison..." Montgomery County *Monitor*.

Anonymous. (1909, April 3). "Mrs. Emma..." Swainsboro *Forrest Blade*.

Anonymous. (1915, June 3). "Ordinary..." Swainsboro *Forrest Blade*.

Anonymous. (1915, June 5). "John..." Swainsboro *Forrest Blade*.

Beitzell, E.W. (n.d.). *Point Lookout Prison Camp for Confederates*. Edwin W. Beitzell.

Bryan, T.C. (1953). *Confederate Georgia*. Athens, GA: University of Georgia Press.

Caldwell, W.W. (2001). *The Courthouse and the Depot*. Macon, GA: Mercer University Press.

Davis, R.S. (1992). *History of Montgomery County Georgia to 1918*. Roswell, GA: W.H. Wolfe Associates.

Dorsey, J.E. & Derden, J.K. (1983). *Montgomery County Georgia: A Source Book of Genealogy and History*. Spartanburg, SC: The Reprint Company.

Dorsey, J.E. (1989). *Footprints Along the Hoopee: A History of Emanuel County*
1900-1900.   Gainesville, GA: Magnolia Press.

Dorsey, J.E. (1991). *Montgomery County, Georgia Genealogical Source Material*. Gainesville, GA: Magnolia Press.

Douglas, S.C. (1995). *The Fighting Boys of Wiregrass*. Athens, GA: Southern Regional Publishing.

Douglas, J. (1995). *Notes on Development of Phelps, Dodge, and Co.'s Copper and Railroad Interests*. Bisbue, AZ: Frontera House Press.

Drake, R.E. (1980). *Descendants of Exum Drake, Volume V*. (1977). American Lithographers.

Engstrom, R.T., Kirkman, L.K., and Mitchell, R.J. (2001). The natural history of the fire forest. Georgia Wildlife Federation. Natural Georgia Services, Volume 8/2. The Fire Forest: Longleaf Pine-Wiregrass Ecosystem.

Evans, T. (1992). "The Battle of Breakfast Branch." Savannah, GA.

BIBLIOGRAPHY

Fischer, D.H. (1989). *Albion's Seed*. New York, NY: Oxford University Press.

Folsom, J.M. (1864). *Heroes and Martyrs of Georgia*. Macon, GA: Burke Boykin and Company.

Freeman, D.S. (1948) *George Washington, Volume 2: Young George Washington*. New York, NY: Charles Scribner's Sons.

Furgurson, E.B. (2000). *Not War But Murder*. New York, NY: Vintage Books.

Gillis, M.B. (2000). *Gillis and Other Pioneer Families* (2nd ed.). St. Simons Island, GA: Marvin B. Gillis.

Henderson, L. (1964). *Roster of Confederate Soldiers of Georgia 1861-1865*. College Park, GA: Longino and Porter.

Hofe, M.W. *That There Be No Stain Upon My Stones*. Gettysburg, PA: Thomas Publications.

Hudgins, F.L. (1918). "With the 38th Georgia." *Confederate Veteran*. Chamblee, GA.

Huxford, F. (1951). *Pioneers of Wiregrass Georgia, Volume 1*. Ann Arbor, MI: Edwards Brothers, Inc.

Johnson, A.S. (1993). *Longpondium*. Decatur, GA.

Johnson, B. (1972). *This Is Your Georgia*. Montgomery, AL: Viewpoint Publications, Inc.

Johnson, P.D., ed. *Under the Southern Cross: Soldier Life With Gordon Bradwell and the 31st Georgia*. Macon, GA: Mercer University Press.

Martin, S.W. (1987). *Epworth: A Mission by the Sea*. St. Simons Island, GA: Parthenon Press.

McWhiney, G. (1989). *Cracker Culture*. Tuscaloosa, AL: University of Alabama Press.

Metcalf, C.G. (1984). *Scots and Their Kin, Volume 1*. Enterprise, AL: Clayton G. Metcalf.

Morrison, C.A. (2003). *Running the River*. St. Simons Island, GA: Saltmarsh Press.

Morrison, S. (n.d.). "Big Oak on Former Troop Plantation."

Murray, A.J. (1976). *South Georgia Rebels*. St. Mary's, GA.

O'Reilly, F.A. (1993). *Stonewall Jackson at Fredericksburg*. Lynchburg, VA: H.E. Howard, Inc.

Patton, W. "Floridians at Cold Harbor."

Ray, J. (1999). *The Ecology of a Cracker Childhood*. Minneapolis, MN: Milkweed Editions.

Rhea, G.C. (2000). *To the North Anna River*. Baton Rouge, LA: LSU Press.

Rhea, G.C. (2002). *Cold Harbor*. Baton Rouge, LA: LSU Press.

Rogers, G. (2005, September 7). Satilla River Keepers.

Rogers, W.C. (1976). *Emanuel County Memories*. Swainsboro, GA: Swainsboro Forest-Blade Publishing.

Rountree, E.D. (1993). *Tenacity in Adversity: A History of the Rountree Family 1550-1993*. Savannah, GA: Edward Donald Rountree.

Scaife, W.R. (1988). *The Georgia Brigade*. Atlanta, GA: William R. Scaife.

Smedlund, W.S. (1990). *Campfires of Georgia's Troops, 1861-1865*. Kennesaw, GA: Kennesaw Mountain Press.

Smith, D.G. (2003). *Ways Baptist Church Minutes/History, 1817-1900*. Martinez, GA: Doris G. Smith.

Trimble, S.W. (1975). *Present and Prospective Technology for Predicting Sediment Yields and Sources*. U.S. Department of Agriculture – Agriculture Research Service Publication S-40, pp. 142.

Walters, K.B. (1995). *Oconee River: Tales to Tell*. Spartanburg, SC: The Reprint Company.

Webb, J. (2004). *Born Fighting – How the Scots-Irish Shaped America*. New York, NY: Broadway Books.

Wetherington, M.V. (2005). *Plain Folk's Fight: The Civil War and Reconstruction In Piney Woods Georgia*. Chapel Hill, NC: UNC Press.

Zwemer, J. (1999). *For Home and the Southland*. Baltimore, MD: Butternut and Blue.